# Homosexuality

Other books in the Current Controversies series:

The Abortion Controversy
Alcoholism
Assisted Suicide
Biodiversity
Capital Punishment
Censorship
Child Abuse
Civil Liberties
Computers and Society
Conserving the Environment
Crime
Developing Nations
The Disabled
Drug Abuse
Drug Legalization
Drug Trafficking
Ethics
Europe
Family Violence
Free Speech
Garbage and Waste
Gay Rights
Genetic Engineering
Guns and Violence
Hate Crimes
Hunger
Illegal Drugs
Illegal Immigration
The Information Age

Interventionism
Iraq
Marriage and Divorce
Medical Ethics
Mental Health
Minorities
Nationalism and Ethnic
   Conflict
Native American Rights
Police Brutality
Politicians and Ethics
Pollution
Prisons
Racism
Reproductive Technologies
The Rights of Animals
Sexual Harassment
Sexually Transmitted Diseases
Smoking
Suicide
Teen Addiction
Teen Pregnancy and Parenting
Teens and Alcohol
The Terrorist Attack on
   America
Urban Terrorism
Violence Against Women
Violence in the Media
Women in the Military

# Homosexuality

**Helen Cothran**, *Book Editor*

**Daniel Leone**, *President*
**Bonnie Szumski**, *Publisher*
**Scott Barbour**, *Managing Editor*

CURRENT CONTROVERSIES

GREENHAVEN
PRESS®

THOMSON
™
GALE

San Diego • Detroit • New York • San Francisco • Cleveland
New Haven, Conn. • Waterville, Maine • London • Munich

LIBRARY OF CONGRESS CATALOGING-IN-PUBLICATION DATA

Homosexuality / Helen Cothran, book editor.
   p. cm. — (Current controversies)
Includes bibliographical references and index.
ISBN 0-7377-1182-5 (lib. bdg. : alk. paper) —
ISBN 0-7377-1181-7 (pbk. : alk. paper)
   1. Homosexuality. I. Cothran, Helen. II. Series.
HQ76.25 .H6739 2003
306.76'6—dc21
                               2002066819

# Contents

United States, homosexuality should be viewed as a spiritual and moral illness. Moreover, homosexuals can—and should—change into heterosexuals.

# Chapter 2: Do Homosexuals Face Serious Discrimination?

## Yes: Homosexuals Face Serious Discrimination

## No: Homosexuals Do Not Face Serious Discrimination

# Chapter 3: Should Society Encourage Increased Acceptance of Homosexuality?

## Yes: Society Should Encourage Increased Acceptance of Homosexuality

uals. Moreover, such discrimination violates the organization's own code of conduct, which stresses acceptance of all people.

## No: Society Should Not Encourage Increased Acceptance of Homosexuality

# Chapter 4: Should Society Sanction Gay and Lesbian Families?

## Yes: Society Should Sanction Gay and Lesbian Families

# Foreword

By definition, controversies are "discussions of questions in which opposing opinions clash" (Webster's Twentieth Century Dictionary Unabridged). Few would deny that controversies are a pervasive part of the human condition and exist on virtually every level of human enterprise. Controversies transpire between individuals and among groups, within nations and between nations. Controversies supply the grist necessary for progress by providing challenges and challengers to the status quo. They also create atmospheres where strife and warfare can flourish. A world without controversies would be a peaceful world; but it also would be, by and large, static and prosaic.

## The Series' Purpose

The purpose of the Current Controversies series is to explore many of the social, political, and economic controversies dominating the national and international scenes today. Titles selected for inclusion in the series are highly focused and specific. For example, from the larger category of criminal justice, Current Controversies deals with specific topics such as police brutality, gun control, white collar crime, and others. The debates in Current Controversies also are presented in a useful, timeless fashion. Articles and book excerpts included in each title are selected if they contribute valuable, long-range ideas to the overall debate. And wherever possible, current information is enhanced with historical documents and other relevant materials. Thus, while individual titles are current in focus, every effort is made to ensure that they will not become quickly outdated. Books in the Current Controversies series will remain important resources for librarians, teachers, and students for many years.

In addition to keeping the titles focused and specific, great care is taken in the editorial format of each book in the series. Book introductions and chapter prefaces are offered to provide background material for readers. Chapters are organized around several key questions that are answered with diverse opinions representing all points on the political spectrum. Materials in each chapter include opinions in which authors clearly disagree as well as alternative opinions in which authors may agree on a broader issue but disagree on the possible solutions. In this way, the content of each volume in Current Controversies mirrors the mosaic of opinions encountered in society. Readers will quickly realize that there are many viable answers to these complex issues. By questioning each author's conclusions, students and casual readers can begin to develop the critical thinking skills so important to evaluating opinionated material.

Current Controversies is also ideal for controlled research. Each anthology in the series is composed of primary sources taken from a wide gamut of informational categories including periodicals, newspapers, books, United States and foreign government documents, and the publications of private and public organizations. Readers will find factual support for reports, debates, and research papers covering all areas of important issues. In addition, an annotated table of contents, an index, a book and periodical bibliography, and a list of organizations to contact are included in each book to expedite further research.

Perhaps more than ever before in history, people are confronted with diverse and contradictory information. During the Persian Gulf War, for example, the public was not only treated to minute-to-minute coverage of the war, it was also inundated with critiques of the coverage and countless analyses of the factors motivating U.S. involvement. Being able to sort through the plethora of opinions accompanying today's major issues, and to draw one's own conclusions, can be a complicated and frustrating struggle. It is the editors' hope that Current Controversies will help readers with this struggle.

Greenhaven Press anthologies primarily consist of previously published material taken from a variety of sources, including periodicals, books, scholarly journals, newspapers, government documents, and position papers from private and public organizations. These original sources are often edited for length and to ensure their accessibility for a young adult audience. The anthology editors also change the original titles of these works in order to clearly present the main thesis of each viewpoint and to explicitly indicate the opinion presented in the viewpoint. These alterations are made in consideration of both the reading and comprehension levels of a young adult audience. Every effort is made to ensure that Greenhaven Press accurately reflects the original intent of the authors included in this anthology.

*"On the one hand, parents do not want schools espousing beliefs about homosexuality that they do not share. On the other hand, schools are in a unique position to educate students about homosexuality and possibly help stop discrimination and hate crimes."*

# Introduction

When Jamie Nabozny entered the restroom at his high school one morning, two boys assaulted him. "One pushed his knee into the back of mine," says Nabozny. "I fell into the urinal, and another kid started peeing on me. I just remember sitting there waiting for it to get over with." Unfortunately, the incident in the restroom was just one of many that Nabozny suffered at school because he is gay.

According to many experts, America's schools are bastions of homophobia. Gay youth get shoved, spit on, and physically assaulted. In 1997, a Des Moines, Iowa, student group called Concerned Students recorded hallway and classroom conversations at five high schools. The group reports that the average high school student hears about twenty-five anti-gay remarks each day. Professors of education Jonatha Vare and Terry L. Norton note: "Mocked, rejected, and misunderstood by parents, educators, and classmates, gay and lesbian youth grow up in a society that condemns and devalues their identity."

Indeed, schools are a microcosm of society—campus homophobia merely reflects America's general disapproval of homosexuality. Matt Foreman, who directs Empire State Pride Agenda, a gay political organization in New York, observes, "There are a lot of people preaching anti-racism and anti-Semitism. But it is still very much O.K. to make anti-gay jokes, to express anti-gay sentiments." Although acceptance of gays and lesbians has been steadily increasing over the last twenty years, the General Social Survey found that as of 1998, 56 percent of Americans still thought homosexuality was morally wrong.

Despite viewing homosexuality as wrong, decreasing numbers of Americans are willing to withhold basic civil rights from gays and lesbians, however. In 1998, 65 percent of Americans reported that they would not restrict any civil liberties for gays and lesbians. Many analysts believe this phenomenon is part of a trend that began in the 1960s toward embracing civil rights for all people. As a result of more support for all minorities, more gays and lesbians—including politicians, actors, and sports figures— have chosen to openly embrace their sexual identities.

Ironically, while the increased visibility of gays and lesbians has helped many homosexuals come to terms with their sexuality, it has also caused a backlash among a minority of Americans. These people feel threatened by what they call the "gay agenda" and have lent support to conservative and religious groups who work to prohibit civil rights gains for gays and lesbians. This backlash has been acutely felt on America's campuses. As more gay adolescents come out of the closet, there have been increasing incidents of harassment against homosexual students.

As Jamie Nabozny discovered, being identified as gay can make adolescence more difficult than it usually is. Professors Vare and Norton note, "For gay and lesbian youth, adolescence is a time of 'double jeopardy' in which they are highly likely to face harassment, violence, and suicide." Vare and Norton claim that "socially and emotionally, gay and lesbian young adults may end up as fearful, withdrawn, chronically depressed, and full of despair that life will be no better than it is."

Some gay and lesbian teens become so fearful and depressed that they drop out of school, run away from home, or begin abusing drugs and alcohol. Many experts claim that gay youth are also at high risk for attempting and committing suicide. Some commentators argue that gay and lesbian teens are two to six times more likely than other teens to attempt suicide and claim that homosexual youth account for 30 percent of all completed suicides among young adults. Vare and Norton conclude, "This group of teens can be described as the most alienated, rejected, and isolated youth in American schools."

Those concerned about discrimination on campus readily concede that most gay teens learn to cope with homophobia and grow into healthy adults. Nevertheless, activists believe that discrimination against gay students deserves more attention from America's public schools. A 1998 study by the Gay, Lesbian and Straight Education Network found that 76 percent of the nation's forty-two largest school districts did not train teachers on issues facing gay students, and 42 percent lacked policies to protect students from discrimination based on sexual orientation.

Activists working to change school policies claim that the problem is difficult to address because homophobia occurs at all levels of the campus hierarchy. Gay and lesbian students report that they get little support from teachers to combat homophobia in the classroom or from school officials to stop serious incidents such as beatings on school grounds. One gay student claimed that when he went to his principal to report harassment against him, the principal told him that "he wouldn't have me acting like a faggot at school." In fact, school officials often tacitly support discrimination against gay students when they set policies, such as eliminating all student groups on campus in order to keep gay student groups from forming.

Regardless of how difficult it can be to effect change, homosexual activists point out that public schools have a responsibility to ensure the safety of all students. These advocates maintain that schools need to enact antiharassment policies and strictly enforce them. They want teachers to provide accurate and positive information on homosexuality and intervene when they hear antigay remarks in their classrooms. Many mental health experts urge school counselors to get training on how to deal positively with gay teens' problems. Gay youth supporters also exhort principals to be supportive of gay teens.

Not everyone agrees that schools need to change their policies in order to protect gay and lesbian teens, however. Even analysts who agree that harassment against gays and lesbians is a serious problem on American campuses argue that schools do not need more disciplinary rules because they cannot enforce the ones they already have. These commentators point out that most parents—who finance public schools with their tax dollars—disapprove of homosexuality and would rightly protest policies that seemed to condone it. Similarly, these analysts argue that requiring counselors and other school personnel to support gay students is often asking them to act against their own religious or personal convictions. As one school counselor put it, "Gay/lesbian [sic] turn me off based on my own beliefs/prejudices. I find this morally reprehensible." Another counselor explained, "I just feel that if a person is ill, one trys [sic] to cure the illness not accept it and even promote it in society by telling the person the act and life style is 'ok.'" Those who disapprove of gay-friendly policies on campus argue that schools should not be in the business of making gay students feel good about themselves—the school's sole mission is to teach basic subjects such as math and English.

Some critics go so far as to suggest that homosexual activists have exaggerated the problem of antihomosexual bias in America's schools in order to further their campaign for more civil rights and social acceptance for gays and lesbians. For instance, critics claim that statistics on gay teen suicide have been manufactured by those sympathetic to homosexuals. In fact, the Centers for Disease Control and Prevention, the National Institute of Mental Health, the American Psychological Association, and the American Association of Suicidology concluded in 1994 that "there was no population-based evidence that sexual orientation and suicidality are linked in some direct or indirect manner." In other words, it has so far been impossible to prove that gay teens commit suicide at higher rates than other teens.

Whether or not schools want to change their policies regarding gay students, they may soon find that they have to. Increasing numbers of gay and lesbian students are filing lawsuits against school districts for allowing harassment of homosexual students. Jamie Nabozny won the first major victory in a gay student harassment suit in 1996, when a federal jury found Wisconsin high school officials liable for not protecting him from extensive physical and verbal abuse. The U.S. Court of Appeals applied the Equal Protection Clause to sexual orientation in the school setting and required the state to "treat each person with equal regard, as having equal worth, regardless of his or her status." Nabozny settled the case for nearly 1 million dollars.

Public schools are in a difficult position. Because they are part of society, schools often reflect the negative attitudes held by the general public about homosexuality. At the same time, schools are public institutions whose purpose is to provide a safe place for all students to learn. On the one hand, parents do not want schools espousing beliefs about homosexuality that they do not share. On the other hand, schools are in a unique position to educate students about homosexuality and possibly help stop discrimination and hate crimes. Whether schools should encourage acceptance of gay and lesbian students is one of the issues debated in *Homosexuality: Current Controversies* in the following chapters: What Are the Origins of Homosexuality? Do Homosexuals Face Serious Discrimination? Should Society Encourage Increased Acceptance of Homosexuality? and Should Society Sanction Gay and Lesbian Families? What public schools decide to do on behalf of their homosexual students will surely have an enormous impact on gay teens, their families, and society.

# Chapter 1

# What Are the Origins of Homosexuality?

# Emerging Research on Homosexuality: An Overview

**by Melissa Healy**

**About the author:** *Melissa Healy writes for the* Los Angeles Times.

It is not the most cherished childhood photo in his mother's collection, but it may be the most prescient.

The little boy, not quite 2, is perched on a potty seat. A mop of brown hair frames a face with delicate features and big brown eyes. He is wearing a pretty white sundress purloined from his older sister's closet, a "very girly" frock, according to his mother, that is one of his two favorites. Secreted away elsewhere in the house are the little boy's other passions: his mother's fancy shoes and jewelry, his sister's Barbie doll. And behind the lens is mom, a college professor from Toronto, "collecting evidence" that she can take to the pediatrician.

The boy in the photo, now nearly 15, is contemplating his sexual orientation with the same secretiveness that he once used to hide his penchant for cross-dressing. On the phone, he gabs with his many girlfriends about their current crushes, adopting their incredulous, eye-rolling gestures and their distinctive, sing-song mode of speech. About his own crushes, however, he is mum.

His mother, who demanded anonymity in the interests of her son's privacy, has no doubt about the young man's future sexual orientation. "I'm sure he'll end up being gay," she says matter-of-factly. As a parent, she wishes it were otherwise; being straight is simply an easier life for a young adult, she said. But she loves her son, and it's clear to her that even before she and her husband adopted him 20 days after the child's birth, this, simply, was the way he was made.

## A Curious Mystery

While scientists have pondered the mystery of homosexuality for centuries, the secret of how homosexuals are made is only now beginning to yield to their inquiries. Long branded a mental illness, attraction to those of the same sex was expunged in 1973 from the list of psychiatric disorders recognized by practicing clinicians. And American society has fitfully followed suit, emboldening many in this long-closeted minority to declare and celebrate their sexual orientation openly.

The drive toward societal acceptance has not dampened many scientists' zeal to explain one of evolution's most curious mysteries: Why has a trait that inhibits sexual reproduction endured? To these researchers, homosexuality remains an evolutionary oddity that demands to be explained. Intriguing new research is finding there may be many different pathways to gayness. Those seeking to explain homosexuality traditionally looked for instances of early sexual abuse, emotionally distant parents and other socialization factors to explain a child's later same-sex attraction.

But researchers from unexpected disciplines such as brain science and audiology are bringing new perspectives to a field long dominated by Freudians, social workers and, more recently, by gay activists. They are uncovering a wide range of possible physical markers for homosexuality—from the way one's inner ear responds to sound to the shape of one's hand—that are evident from a child's first days. These insights not only point to the mechanisms at work in homosexuality: They offer the intriguing and controversial prospect that perhaps in the not-too-distant future, parents like the mother in Toronto could do more than brace for a child's sexual awakening; they could do something about it.

## Gender-Crossing

Still, the science of homosexuality remains in its infancy. For now, there exists only one childhood trait—often exhibited before a child can walk—that strongly predicts homosexuality later in life. It is early behavior that departs markedly and persistently from the boys-and-trucks, girls-and-dolls stereotypes of years past.

For the cross-dressing toddler in Toronto and other boys who show "pervasive and persistently" effeminate behavior, the odds of being gay lie at about 75%, according to J. Michael Bailey, a psychologist and sexuality researcher at Northwestern University in Evanston, Ill. That is a probability of homosexuality 20 times as high as that in the broad population of boys; it is estimated (though hotly disputed) that 3% to 4% of males will grow up to

> *"Intriguing new research is finding there may be many different pathways to gayness."*

be gay. Among girls, this so-called gender-atypical behavior also is a good predictor of later lesbianism, though the pattern is weaker.

That may disappoint those who hoped science would have disproved a painful stereotype. But strong and sustained gender-crossing behavior is, says Bailey, "about as strong a predictor as exists in the developmental literature."

Strong as the relationship may be, however, it has major limitations. Most important, researchers stress there is no evidence that early gender-bending behavior is the *cause* of later homosexuality: In fact, many argue, the early onset of such predictive behavior suggests that for many, sexual orientation may be fixed at birth. The fact that such behavior is more likely to be greeted with horror than encouragement by family and friends is seen as further evidence for that position.

Beyond that, researchers caution, such behavior is far from conclusive. Many adult gay men and lesbians were gender-conformers as children. And many boys derided as "sissies" and girls labeled as tomboys grow up to be straight.

## Consistently Fighting Traditional Roles

The distinction, say researchers, is gender-bending behavior that is neither subtle nor temporary. It isn't "just a phase," say parents like Angela and James, a couple who spoke on condition their last names not be used.

By the time he was 18 months old, their son, now almost 7, was drawn to his mother's shoes and scarves. From 3 years old, he "would obsess" about the Little Mermaid and Cinderella, mimicking their dresses, their songs and their gestures, according to his parents.

"Being the progressive, modern-thinking parents we were, we thought, 'Let's not stereotype,'" said Angela, explaining why the couple bought

*"Strong and sustained gender-crossing behavior is . . . 'about as strong a predictor [of homosexuality] as exists.'"*

their son a Barbie doll (and a Ken, whom the child pointedly ignored) when he asked for it.

It was a poignant moment of epiphany—the day their then-4-year-old son stood up in a shopping cart and wept at the realization that he would not grow up to be a mommy—that drove the couple to seek treatment for the child's "gender-identity disorder." A certain type of treatment, called "reparative" or "conversion" therapy, seeks to steer a gay person toward heterosexual behavior. By contrast, however, treatment for gender-identity disorder focuses on an individual's confused sense of self, seeking to make them comfortable with their actual gender.

The American Psychiatric Assn. continues to view it as a mental disorder. But because it affects many in the homosexual community, gay activists object sharply to the labeling and treatment of what they call "transgender" behavior, denouncing clinicians' efforts as "genocide."

All of which underscores a key point: As a field of research, homosexuality lies at the dangerous intersection of science and minority politics. In this world, every new finding carries added weight. Both gay activists and their detractors—largely Christian conservatives who view homosexuality as contrary to biblical teachings—dissect the work of researchers for political meaning. If gays and lesbians are "born that way"—if homosexuality can definitively be traced to genes or prenatal environment—is being gay a choice? Do lesbians and gay men follow the same pathways to homosexuality? And if scientists can uncover how homosexuals are made, will they not be an important step closer to finding how they can be *un*made?

> *"As a field of research, homosexuality lies at the dangerous intersection of science and minority politics."*

To homosexuals struggling to protect and extend their rights, the answers to these questions may mean the difference between acceptance and intolerance, cultural vibrancy and decline—life and death, even. For even as a majority of Americans tell pollsters they believe homosexuals should enjoy job protections and basic human rights, roughly half of Americans, according to the Gallup Poll, continue to believe homosexuality "should not be considered an acceptable alternative lifestyle." And only 29% say they would like to see homosexuality "more accepted" in this nation.

## Worry for a Child's Status in Society

For parents in particular, the dilemma of anticipating a child's homosexuality can be acute. The Toronto mom, whose son started playing with her fancy shoes at about 10 months, is typical: Like many who see the early glimmerings of a child who will grow up to be gay, she insists that as an intellectual, ethical and political matter, she would never consider trying to change her son's sexual course. But as she assesses the social challenges a gay son will face in life, she echoes the sentiment of virtually all parents interviewed for this article: If her child could magically be remade, she would wish a heterosexual life for him. "It's tougher to be a gay kid in high school," said James, whose 7-year-old has been treated for gender-identity disorder. "Geez, it's not easy being a straight adolescent!"

Although hypothetical for today's parents, the possibility that future parents may be able to take a pill or tinker with a gene to steer their offspring toward heterosexuality is no pipe dream.

"It's not a matter of whether" we'll find homosexuality's basic mechanisms, "it's a matter of when," said Dennis McFadden, a University of Texas specialist on auditory perception. "And parents are going to rush to influence them, possibly before a child is born."

Indeed, scientists are finding that an individual's sexual orientation may be most powerfully shaped before birth—both by genes and, as more recent research is showing, by prenatal environment.

In the last two decades, researchers have established beyond much doubt that, like high intelligence, green eyes or a propensity for certain diseases, homosexuality runs in some people's genes. Northwestern's J. Michael Bailey, who has conducted much of this research, notes that a male with a gay brother is three to seven times more likely to be gay himself; and a woman with a gay sister is four to eight times likelier to be a lesbian than a female drawn from the broader population.

"The data definitely are not as strong as for other traits such as intelligence or schizophrenia," said Bailey. But he added that researchers from various disciplines are nearing consensus on this point: Some genetic component to homosexuality clearly exists.

Studies of identical twins—siblings with the same DNA—illustrate both the power and the limitations of genes in homosexuality. A man or a woman is at least 10 times likelier to be gay if his or her identical twin is homosexual; in other words, his or her probability of being homosexual lies between 20% and 50%. But flip that figure over, and it looks far less impressive: Those probabilities still mean that, among identical twins in which one is homosexual, between half and 80% have a heterosexual twin. Having a "gay gene," if such a thing exists, carries no certainty of being gay.

How else, then, to account for homosexuality?

In the last several years, a welter of new research has begun to point strongly to a developing fetus' intrauterine environment as a possible incubator of gayness. This new line of research has been scattered broadly across the peer-reviewed journals that collectively make up science's bazaar of evidence and ideas. But it all started with a little-understood birth-order peculiarity long observed among adult gay men: They tended to be little brothers, frequently in a household full of older boys.

"When I first encountered these early studies, I thought they were so preposterous that I dismissed them out of hand," said Ray Blanchard, a psychologist at the University of Toronto's Department of Psychiatry. "It struck me as the most bizarre example of pseudoscience."

Later, "by accident," Blanchard said, he happened upon evidence in his work that there might be something to this anecdotal oddity. He began scouring dozens of databases containing data on both birth order and sexual orientation. By the late 1990s, he had established one of the strongest associations with homosexuality in the field.

For a male child, Blanchard found, the more older brothers in his family, the higher the probability that he would be gay. A firstborn male has a likelihood of homosexuality of about 2%. But for a boy with four older brothers, those odds jump to 6%, Blanchard found. In all, he estimated, one in seven gay men owed his sexual orientation to this "fraternal birth order" effect.

## An Immune Response That May Grow Stronger

What force was at work here? An intriguing parallel suggested an explanation. "Blue babies," or babies born with anemia due to incompatibilities with their mother's blood type, were much more likely to be latter-born males, too. And researchers had established that the "blue baby" effect was the result of a maternal immune reaction to the presence of foreign cells—male cells—in her blood during pregnancy. With each male child a woman carries, that immune reaction grows stronger and so does the probability of a maternal reaction to the blood incompatibility that causes a newborn to look blue from low oxygen.

Blanchard hypothesized that a pregnant woman carrying a male child has an analogous kind of immune response, which grows stronger with each subsequent male fetus she carries. While he is unclear how, exactly, that immune response affects the baby, many researchers coming to the same conclusion surmise that it affects the chemistry of the amniotic soup in which a fetus develops. At a crucial period of fetal brain development, a higher-than-average concentration of certain hormones—say, the powerful hormone estradiol—could cause changes in the way the developing baby's brain is wired. The implications of that chemical shift would likely be evident early. And they would likely last a lifetime.

By the end of the 1990s, other researchers were beginning to posit similar hypotheses on the bases of wildly different data. Researchers already had established that compared with their heterosexual counterparts, gay men and lesbians were more likely to be left-handed. But in Berkeley and in Liverpool, England, a psychologist and a biologist, working independently, were finding that the shape of the hands—a key measure of in-utero exposure to sex hormones—tended to be different, too.

> *"Like high intelligence, green eyes or a propensity for certain diseases, homosexuality runs in some people's genes."*

Simply put, the ring finger of a heterosexual man's right hand tends to be much longer than his index finger; in straight women, the two fingers typically appear nearly the same length, with the pointer dipping just slightly below the ring finger.

But John T. Manning, a biologist at the University of Liverpool, found that as a group, lesbians have a hand pattern that looks more like a man's than like that of a typical straight female, though still not quite as pronounced. "The finding," Manning concluded, "strongly tells us that female homosexuals have had high levels of exposure to testosterone before birth."

## Texas Researcher Takes Another Tack

Manning seemed to be zeroing in on a defining moment in the development of sexual orientation. In the meantime, in Austin, Texas, a very different route brought psychologist Dennis McFadden to the same conclusion.

A psychoacoustics specialist, McFadden has studied group differences in two measures of hearing: otoacoustic emissions—tiny clicking sounds produced by the auditory system in response to stimulus—and auditory-evoked potential, the brain-wave peaks that an individual produces when presented with sound.

From their earliest days, boys and girls score differently on each measure—no surprise, perhaps, since a fetus' auditory system develops at the same time that hormonal differences peak in the womb and gender differences emerge. But McFadden found that lesbians fell between heterosexual men and women on both measures—a strong sign that they were exposed to higher-than-normal levels of male hormone in utero.

*"For a male child . . . the more older brothers in his family, the higher the probability that he would be gay."*

But like Manning in Liverpool and University of California psychologist Marc Breedlove, McFadden turned up a confounding pattern when he tested gay males. In one auditory measure, but not both, homosexual men were "hypermasculinized" compared with heterosexual men: Essentially, their brain-wave peaks produced in response to sound were more "manly" than those of the average straight man.

Breedlove, surveying hand shapes with a portable photocopy machine at a San Francisco street fair, had come up with a similar finding. Writing in the journal *Nature* in 2000, Breedlove reported that he had been unable to establish a direct relationship between the overall average finger lengths of men and their sexual orientation. But on the basis of their finger lengths, he found that some gay men appeared to have been exposed to greater-than-normal levels of male hormones prenatally.

McFadden and Breedlove had run headlong into one of homosexuality's most entrenched stereotypes and some of its strongest research. In many cognitive measures, gay men tend to fall between men and women on the continuum of gender differences—they are, according to researchers, "feminized." Gay men tend to have better language skills, an area where girls generally fare better than boys. And they tend to be weaker in activities that take great spatial acuity, like maze-running and mathematics—areas where boys, as a group, outperform girls.

But here, by contrast, was evidence that some gay men were more "male" than the average male. And it tracked with other, sketchy indications of "hyper-masculinization" among a group of male homosexuals: Their average number of sex partners was greater than that of their straight counterparts, the levels of testosterone that circulated in their blood was higher and their genitalia were larger. "This calls into question all of our cultural assumptions that gay men are feminine," said Breedlove.

Evidence like this has confounded and unsettled the community of researchers as well. With new findings scattered across many disciplines and, at best, a patchwork of explanations for homosexuality emerging, little is settled in this most incendiary of fields.

Within the gay activist community, the jumbled state of research is greeted with conflicting reactions: There is fascination "because these studies help us understand who we are," said David Smith, a spokesman for the Human Rights

Campaign, a Washington-based gay-rights group. And there is a kind of grudging sympathy for the challenges facing researchers, since gay men and lesbians know how complicated and diverse they are. And finally, Smith added, there is a sense that whatever the outcome of research, "it shouldn't matter, because everyone deserves to be treated with dignity and respect."

## Many Factors at Work

Indeed, the fact that no one researcher has unlocked the mystery of all homosexuals' orientation suggests there may be many different factors at work.

Gay men and lesbians, in short, come in all varieties, scattered widely across our conventional notions of masculinity and femininity, said Northwestern's Bailey. "That suggests possibly that there are different bases for homosexuality" in different people, he said.

If they are to continue to uncover homosexuality's roots, scientists acknowledge, they increasingly will have to look at gay men and lesbians not just as groups, but as individuals. In that sense, they say, they are mirroring the challenges of the larger society. And the sentiments of parents like Angela and James.

"It's not on my mind that I'm watching our son grow up gay," said James. His 7-year-old is, he added, simply who he is: a shy child with a backyard fort and, yes, an attraction to Barbie dolls. If he ends up being gay, they will not worry so much about whether it was the fraternal birth order effect or an infancy traumatized by premature birth and kidney problems.

"If he decides he wants to come out," said Angela, "I'll simply be the biggest advocate out there."

# Homosexuality Is Biologically Determined

## by Simon LeVay

*About the author: Simon LeVay, a neurobiologist, has authored several books, including* The Science of Sex *and* Queer Science. *In 1991, LeVay claimed to have found a link between brain structure and homosexuality.*

Sexual orientation, like any other durable aspect of our mental lives, must have some structural or chemical representation within the brain, for it survives the temporary extinction of all brain activity (as when the brain is cooled to near-freezing for certain surgical procedures). In that sense, sexual orientation must be "biological"—as must our preference for one soccer team over another, which also survives brain cooling. The question, though, is whether one can best understand how some people end up gay, some straight, and some bisexual by looking for these brain representations and how they develop. In the case of soccer partisanship, that would probably not be a good strategy.

### Gay Rats?

Animal research has provided the strongest hints that sexual orientation may be fruitfully studied at a biological level. This work starts with the observation that most laboratory animals show a preference for sex acts with partners of the other sex, just as most humans do. This preference comes about as a result of hormone exposure during a "critical period" when the brain circuits for sexuality are first assembling themselves. During this period, which in rats extends from a few days before birth to a few days after birth, the brains of male rat fetuses are exposed to high levels of "androgenic" (male-making) hormones, especially testosterone, which is secreted by the fetus's own testes. Testosterone has both direct and indirect effects on the development of neurons throughout the brain, but its effects are strongest in the hypothalamus, a zone at the base of the brain that plays a key role in the regulation of sexual behavior. Under the influence of testosterone, a group of neurons in the rat's hypothalamus known as the *sexually dimorphic nucleus* or SDN, as well as some other structures in the vicinity, grow to a relatively large size. ("Sexually dimorphic" means "differing in structure between the sexes" and a "nucleus" is an anatomically distinct cluster of neurons.) If testosterone levels are low during the critical period, as is generally true of female fetuses, the SDN remains small.

In an important series of experiments begun by researchers at the University of Kansas in 1959, it has been shown that manipulating the levels of testosterone during the critical period influences the sexual behavior shown by the animal in adulthood, and also influences the size of SDN. Thus, removal of testosterone from a male fetus during the critical period (by surgical or chemical castration) results in an adult rat that is less willing than untreated males to engage in sex with females and more willing to have sex with males. Administration of testosterone to female rats during the critical period has the converse effects. High levels of hormones in adulthood are necessary to trigger sexual behavior, but the levels of hormones during the critical period determine what kind of sexual behavior can be triggered.

These early hormonal manipulations affect the size and molecular characteristics of the SDN, in a way that roughly parallels the behavioral effects. An animal of either chromosomal sex will have a large SDN and show a sexual orientation towards females if testosterone levels were high during the critical period, and conversely an animal of either sex will have a small SDN and be sexually oriented towards males if testosterone levels were low during the critical period. It has even been found that, if one examines a large number of untreated male laboratory rats, their SDN's vary somewhat in size, and the individual variation can be correlated with individual differences in sexual behavior.

> "Manipulating the levels of testosterone during the critical period [of fetus development] influences . . . sexual behavior."

One other point worth making is that androgen levels in fetal life influence not just the rat's sexual behavior but many other traits that are sexually differentiated in that species. Rats have a "gender," in the sense that there are many things you can predict about a rat if you know its sex, and most of these traits are controlled by early testosterone levels. Examples include aspects of reproductive behavior but also traits that have no immediate connections to reproduction, such as aggressiveness or the differing strategies male and female rats use to find their way through mazes.

## Observations on Humans

We think of rats as wind-up toys and humans as creatures of reason, emotion, and morality. Yet in the area of sexuality at least there may be some basic similarities between humans and non-human animals. Although we obviously cannot perform the same kind of experiments on humans that have been done on laboratory animals, analogous experiments are sometimes done for us, either a whim of nature or by human misadventure.

An example of an experiment of nature is the syndrome known as congenital adrenal hyperplasia (CAH). This is an "inborn error of metabolism" in which the adrenal gland secretes excessive amounts of androgens during the latter part of fetal life. Girls born with CAH often display some degree of virilization of the external genitalia, such as an enlarged clitoris or partial fusion of the labia. After

*"When . . . girls [exposed to higher levels of male hormones in the womb] grow up they have a much greater likelihood of experiencing same-sex attraction."*

birth, androgen levels can be returned to normal by pharmacological means, and the genital abnormalities if present can be corrected or reduced. Even so, several studies have reported that when these girls grow up they have a much greater likelihood of experiencing same-sex attraction than do comparison groups of women (such as their unaffected sisters). It is not the case that all CAH girls become lesbians; on the contrary, they still tend to be closer to the heterosexual end of the spectrum than to the homosexual end, but the difference between CAH women and controls is very marked and highly significant in a statistical sense.

Some researchers have argued that this effect is a psychological consequence of the growing girls' realization that their genitalia are not entirely normal, or of their parents' reaction to their condition. The broader consensus, however, is that the atypical sexual orientation of CAH women results from the atypical levels of androgens to which their brains were exposed during fetal life.

The fact that CAH women are not usually out-and-out lesbians can be interpreted in various ways. One possible reason is that the timing and amounts of androgen exposure in female CAH fetuses does not entirely match that observed in normal male fetuses. Another possibility is that early hormone exposure, though influential, is not the only determinant of adult sexual orientation. The "messiness" of experiments of nature prevents us from resolving this issue.

A broader criticism of studies involving CAH and other unusual conditions is to ask: What do they have to do with the sexual orientation of the vast majority of gay or lesbian individuals, who did not suffer from any overt endocrinological condition during fetal life? In fact, isn't dragging CAH into the argument equivalent to "pathologizing" the homosexuality of most gays and lesbians?

## Inner Ears and Softballs

One way researchers have attempted to answer this criticism is to work in the other direction: that is, to seek out normal homosexual or bisexual people and to study whether they carry any indicators of atypical fetal development as compared with heterosexual controls. An interesting study of this kind was performed recently by two auditory physiologists at the University of Texas, Dennis McFadden and Edward Pasanen. These researchers study "otoacoustic emissions," which are weak sounds produced by the inner ear in the process of transforming external sounds into electrical signals. The emissions are generally stronger in women than in men. The reason for this basic sex difference probably has to do with sex hormones during fetal life: high levels of testosterone, as are usually found in male fetuses, cause the ear to develop in such a way as to produce relatively weak emissions, while low levels of testosterone, as are usually found in female fetuses, cause the ear to develop in such a way as to produce relatively strong emissions. McFadden and Pasanen found that the otoacoustic emissions measured in lesbian and bisexual women were significantly weaker than in heterosexual women, though not as weak as in heterosexual men. They conclude that lesbian and bisexual women were exposed to relatively high levels of androgenic hormones during fetal life, and they suggest that these high levels influenced both their sexual orientation and their auditory physiology.

Another study of the same kind was done by Jeff Hall and Doreen Kimura, who were then at the University of Western Ontario. Hall and Kimura studied throwing skills: a sample of gay men, straight men, straight women, and lesbians were tested in their accuracy in throwing a ball to a target. In general, men do significantly better than women on such tests, and this male superiority exists already in very young children, at an age before sports experience begins to differ between the sexes. It is believed that this basic sex difference is set up before birth by differential androgen exposure and that it reflects a long evolutionary history of male responsibility for hunting and warfare. Hall and Kimura confirmed the basic sex difference, but also found differences related to sexual orientation: the gay men performed significantly worse than the straight men and at about the same level as the straight women. The lesbians performed better than the straight women, although the difference was not significant with the sample size used in the study. Hall and Kimura interpret their result to suggest that the brains of gay men were exposed to relatively low levels of testosterone-like hormones during the period of fetal life when brain circuits responsible for targeting skills are developing.

> *"Lesbian and bisexual women were exposed to relatively high levels of androgenic hormones during fetal life."*

Of course, one can always argue that throwing skills, and even perhaps otoacoustic emissions, are influenced by postnatal experiences to a greater degree than the researchers acknowledge. To circumvent this kind of criticism, Hall and Kimura examined a trait that is unarguably set up during fetal life and is completely unaffected by postnatal life experiences. This trait is fingerprint patterns, which remain unaltered after the end of the second trimester of fetal life.

Hall and Kimura compared the fingerprint patterns of a large number of gay and straight men. They counted the "ridges" on the fingers of the left and right hands, and calculated the ratio of the ridge count on the two sides. Most people are "right-biased," that is, they have a somewhat higher number of ridges on the fingers of the right hand. According to Hall and Kimura, there is a sex difference in this trait, with women being on average slightly less right-biased than men. The gay men too were significantly less right-biased than the straight men. Again, the researchers interpreted this result to mean that gay men were exposed to atypically low levels of androgenic hormones during the period of fetal life when fingerprint patterns are being set up (the second trimester). . . .

## Brain Structure

If the prenatal differentiation of the brain proceeds differently in "gay" and "straight" fetuses, then by analogy with the animal experiments mentioned earlier one might expect to see structural differences between the brains of gay and straight adults. I tested this hypothesis in 1990, when I examined the hypothalamus of the brains of gay and straight men that I obtained at autopsy. My research took its origin in earlier work of Laura Allen, Roger Gorski, and their colleagues at UCLA, who had reported the existence of two sexually dimorphic nuclei in the human hypothalamus, which they named INAH2 and INAH3. Both these nuclei were on average larger in men than in women, but the difference was much more robust for INAH3 than for INAH2. Furthermore, recent work by William Byne suggests that INAH3 may be homologous to the SDN of rats. (Another cell group, INAH1, was previously reported as sexually dimorphic by a Dutch research group and named by them the "sexually dimorphic nucleus," but several subsequent studies have failed to replicate their observations.)

> *"Gay men were exposed to atypically low levels of androgenic hormones during . . . fetal life."*

In my study, INAH3 was on average 2–3 times larger in the heterosexual men than in the gay men, and this difference was highly significant. In fact, there was no significant difference between its size in the gay men and in the women in my sample. I concluded that, for men, at least one brain structure is sex-atypical in homosexual individuals. I consider it most likely that this structural difference comes about as a consequence of differences in fetal neuroendocrinological development.

Of course, there are inevitable shortcomings in human autopsy studies. For one thing, because the subjects are deceased, it is impossible to obtain a detailed sex history. One also has to be concerned about the possibility that disease processes (specifically, AIDS complications in the case of many of my subjects) might be responsible for the differences I saw, rather than differences in sexual orientation. For a number of reasons I am confident that disease effects did not contaminate my results, but the final answer to such concerns must wait for the development of imaging techniques that would allow us to visualize these very small brain structures in living people. Such a technical advance would also allow us to look for differences related to sexual orientation in women. An autopsy study comparing lesbians and heterosexual women would be difficult or impossible, because women's sexual orientation is rarely mentioned in their medical records.

> *"[The] INAH3 [region of the hypothalamus] was on average 2–3 times larger in the heterosexual men than in the gay men."*

Showing structural differences between the brains of gay and straight adults does not tell us unequivocally when these differences arose. Some brain regions retain a degree of anatomical plasticity into adult life. It is conceivable that the INAH3 of the gay men in my sample might have started out the same size as in the heterosexual men and become smaller in consequence of the particular sexual feelings or sexual behaviors that these men experienced. Nevertheless, all the animal research points to the early "critical period" (which in humans would be entirely before birth) as being the time when the size of this nucleus could easily be influenced by endocrinological events. In adult animals, even radical interventions such as castration have little or no effect on the size of the SDN. My inclination is therefore to believe that the difference in size between the INAH3 of gay and straight men in my study resulted from prenatal developmental processes.

I do not mean to argue that INAH3 is necessarily a "sexual orientation center" of the kind originally hypothesized by Hirschfeld. Most likely, a number of interconnected brain regions play a role in sexual orientation. Since my research was published, Laura Allen and her colleagues reported on a second brain structure (the anterior commissure—a bundle of fibers that interconnects the left and right cerebral hemispheres) that is different in size between gay and straight men. Another research group has reported on a brain nucleus that apparently differs between transsexual and heterosexual men. Most likely, there will turn out to be numerous differences between the brains of heterosexual, gay, and transsexual individuals, some related directly to sexuality and some to the more peripheral differences such as the differences in spatial and targeting skills mentioned earlier.

## Genes

The observations mentioned so far suggest that there are endocrinological differences between fetuses who ultimately become gay or straight adults, but they do not explain how such differences arise. One can imagine three kinds of mechanisms. One might be a direct genetic mechanism, whereby genes possessed by "gay" fetuses cause hormone levels to be different from "straight" fetuses, or cause the brain to respond to hormones in a different way. Another mechanism might be non-genetic but still intrinsic to the fetus: some kind of random biological process that affects endocrinological development. A third mechanism would involve external events that somehow affect fetal development.

Concerning the first possibility, are there genes that influence sexual orientation, and if so, do they work through endocrinological pathways in fetal life? The evidence for a genetic influence on sexual orientation comes primarily from family and twin studies. Homosexuality runs in families: if you are a man and you have a gay brother, your own chances of being gay are increased about five-fold. Similarly, if you are a woman and you have a lesbian sister your own chances of being lesbian are increased about five-fold. This clustering is largely sex-specific: e.g., a man who has a lesbian sister is only slightly (if at all) more likely to be gay than a man who does not have a lesbian sister, and vice versa. Thus, if the family clustering is genetic in origin, there would seem to be different genes that influence sexual orientation in men and women.

## Family Clustering

Of course, family clustering can be caused by non-genetic factors. To address the question of genes more directly, researchers have studied twins. Monozygotic (or "identical") twins have all the same genes, while dizygotic (or "fraternal" twins) are like regular brothers or sisters: they have about half their genes in common. If one member of a twin pair is gay, the chances that the other twin is also gay (the so-called "concordance rate") depends on zygosity. Thus, in studies by Richard Pillard of Boston University, Michael Bailey of Northwestern University, and their colleagues, the concordance rate was about 50% for male monozygotic twins but only about half that (20–25%) for male dizygotic twins. The results from these studies suggested that there was a substantial genetic influence on sexual orientation, particularly in men. The data suggested a genetic influence in women too, but more recent studies have cast some doubt on this finding.

If genes have an important influence on sexual orientation, one might expect that monozygotic twins reared apart would have a good chance of sharing the same sexual orientation. In one study from Thomas Bouchard Jr.'s group at the University of Minnesota, six pairs of monozygotic twins reared apart were identified in which at least one twin in each pair was gay, lesbian, or bisexual. Of the two male pairs, one was fully concordant for homosexuality and the second was partially concordant (both twins were bisexual

> *"A number of interconnected brain regions play a role in sexual orientation."*

to some degree). These two cases supported the idea that genes influence sexual orientation in men. The four female cases, however, were all discordant: all four twins of the lesbian subjects turned out to be completely heterosexual.

Again, this finding tends to diminish the possible significance of genes in the sexual orientation of women. Unfortunately, the small numbers of such cases that have been ascertained reduce the reliability of any conclusions one might want to draw from them.

Given that the concordance rate for male monozygotic twins raised together is no more than about 50%, non-genetic factors evidently contribute to the sexual orientation of monozygotic twins. What these non-genetic factors might be was the subject of a recent study by Lynn Hall of Brown University: she examined the fingerprint patterns of 9 pairs of male monozygotic twins who were discordant for sexual orientation, and found that in every pair the gay twin was left-shifted in his ridge counts in relation to his straight co-twin. Hall concluded that the twins' sexual orientation was strongly influenced by endocrinological factors operating prenatally, and that different postnatal life experiences had little influence. Hall also found a difference between the fingerprint patterns of discordant monozygotic *female* twin pairs: the total ridge counts were lower in the lesbian than in the heterosexual twins, again supporting the notion that prenatal events influence the sexual orientation of discordant female twins.

## The X Chromosome Factor

Molecular geneticist Dean Hamer of the National Cancer Institute has attempted to close in on the actual genes that might be influencing human sexual orientation. Hamer reported that, among the more distant relatives of gay men, only those male relatives linked to the gay man through females (e.g., maternal uncles and cousins who were the sons of maternal aunts) had a better-than-chance likelihood of being gay themselves. This suggested to Hamer that there might be genes influencing male sexual orientation on the X chromosome, for this is the only chromosome that men inherit exclusively from their mothers. He therefore used the techniques of DNA linkage analysis to study the genomes of pairs of gay brothers, and found evidence that such brothers had an above-random likelihood of sharing DNA markers in a certain region of the X chromosome named Xq28. This meant that the two brothers had inherited genes in this region from the same one of their mother's two X chromosomes. Other, straight brothers in the same families generally did not share the same markers in this region. Thus, Hamer argued, a gene or genes in the Xq28 region comes in two alternative forms, one predisposing its owner to become gay and the other predisposing its owner to become straight.

So far, Hamer has not identified the actual genes that might be involved—the Xq28 region probably contains several hundred genes, none of which are particularly obvious candidates to be a "gay gene." Furthermore, a Canadian group has reported failing to replicate Hamer's result. Thus the possible involvement of the Xq28 region in the development of male sexual orientation remains uncertain. Neither Hamer nor any other group has homed in on genes influencing sexual orientation in women, and in fact Hamer has become skeptical that such genes exist.

If genes do influence sexual orientation—in men at least—how might such genes work? One possibility is that they might influence the level of androgens circulating in the blood of fetuses during a critical period of prenatal life. Another possibility is that they influence the brain mechanisms that respond to androgens. (The gene that codes for the androgen receptor molecule, however, does not seem to differ between gay and straight men.) Finally, they may operate through some quite different or indirect path. In general, we do not understand human brain development in sufficient detail to make confident predictions as to how behavioral genes exert their effects. When the genes themselves have been identified and sequenced, however, as will eventually happen as a part of the Human Genome Project, their mode, time, and location of action may be revealed. [A working draft of the entire human genome sequence was announced in June 2000.]

# Homosexuality Is Part of Nature's Diversity

**by Bruce Bagemihl**

**About the author:** *Bruce Bagemihl is a biologist, researcher, and author of several books on biology and sexuality, including* Biological Exuberance: Animal Homosexuality and Natural Diversity, *from which this excerpt was taken.*

Titus and Ahab—male Gorillas—often courted and had sex with one another in the mountains of Rwanda, while Marchessa sought out her own sex during her pregnancy. In Florida, Bottlenose Dolphins Frank, Floyd, and Algie participated in homosexual activity with each other, as did Gabe and Moe-Miller, West Indian Manatees. Les and Sam (Siamangs) were doing the same in Milwaukee, while Kiku, a female Bonobo living in Congo (Zaire), had sex with her female "mentor" Halu more often than with anyone else in the new troop she joined. Cato and Mola (male Crested Black Macaques), Depp and Nice (male Rhesus Macaques), as well as Saruta and Oro (male Japanese Macaques) and Daddy and Jimmy (Crab-eating Macaques), also mounted one another. On the isle of Corsica, Le Baron and Le Valet (Asiatic Mouflons) were inseparable, as were Marian and her female Grizzly companion in the high mountains of Wyoming. Apolli and Arima—Long-eared Hedgehogs in Vienna—each refused to mate with males after they were separated from one another. In Austria, Greylag gander Pepino had a brief liaison with Florian but was later courted by Serge, while Max, Odysseus, and Kopfschlitz formed a threesome and went on to raise a family with Martina. A White-handed Gibbon named Floyd became sexually involved with George (his father) in Thailand, while Sibujong and Bobo, male Orangutans, had sexual interactions with one another in Indonesia.

As these examples show, zoologists sometimes bestow names upon the animals they study, lending an unintentionally—and eerily—human quality to their reports of homosexual activity. Although most scientists are careful to avoid anthropomorphizing their subjects, their use of human names such as these reminds us at once of each creature's individuality as well as the dangers of projecting human qualities onto animals. Such naming also demonstrates the nearly universal human preoccupation with seeking connections between ourselves and other species. Where animal behavior—especially sexual behavior—is concerned, it seems that comparisons will inevitably be made between animals and people (even by scientists). . . .

## Uniquely Human?

Comparisons between animals and people almost inevitably focus on behaviors that are supposed to be uniquely human. As biologist James Weinrich points out, nearly every behavior that was at one time believed to be practiced only by people has been found to have an analogue among animals—including homosexuality:

> There is a long and sordid history of statements of human uniqueness. Over the years, I have read that humans are the only creatures that laugh, that kill other members of their own species, that kill without need for food, that have continuous female receptivity, that lie, that exhibit female orgasm, or that kill their own young. Every one of these never-never-land statements is now known to be false. To this list must now be added the statement that humans are the only species that exhibit "true" homosexuality. Does anyone ever state that we alone exhibit true heterosexuality?

While many scientists now accept that animals engage in homosexuality, claims about human uniqueness continue to be made regarding the *specifics* of homosexual interactions: people, but not animals, engage in exclusive homosexuality, for example; people, but not animals, exhibit greater variety or "genuine" sexual motivation in their homosexuality; people, but not animals, react with hostility toward homosexuality and live in groups segregated by sexual orientation; and so on.

As we come to understand more and more about animal behavior, premature blanket statements like these have generally proven to be naive, if not incorrect— and this is especially true where homosexuality is concerned, since so much still remains to be learned regarding such activities in animals. . . .

## Exclusive Homosexuality

An oft-repeated claim about homosexuality is that exclusive, lifetime, or "preferential" homosexual activity is unique to human beings, or at least rare among animals (especially among primates and other mammals). This is really a question of sexual orientation—that is, to what extent do animals engage in sexual and related activities with members of the same sex without also engaging in such activities with members of the opposite sex? In fact, exclusive homosexuality of various types occurs in more than 60 species of nondomesticated mammals and birds, including at least 10 kinds of primates and more than 20 other species of mammals. We'll consider these various forms of homosexual orientation and compare them to the wide variety of bisexualities that are also found throughout the animal world.

When discussing the question of exclusive homosexuality, several factors need to be distinguished: the length of time that exclusivity is maintained (short-term versus long-term, including lifetime), the social context and type of same-sex activity involved (pair-bonding versus promiscuity in nonbreeding animals, for example), the type of animal involved (e.g., mammal versus bird), and the degree of exclusivity (e.g., absolute absence of opposite-sex activity versus primary homosexual associations with occasional heterosexual ones, and vice versa). These factors combine in various ways and interact with each other to produce a number of different patterns. To begin with, we will consider long-term or extended exclusivity, since this pattern appears to be the most contested as to its existence among animals. Because species vary widely as to their life expectancy, onset of sexual maturity, and period of adulthood, it is difficult to come up with an absolute definition of *long-term* that has wide applicability. For the purposes of this discussion, though, we will somewhat arbitrarily consider homosexual activity that continues for less than two consecutive years (or breeding seasons) to be short-term, while anything continuing longer is considered extended or long-term, with the understanding that the latter category includes a wide spectrum of possibilities, anywhere from 3 years to a life span of over 40 years.

## A Difficult Task

The only way to absolutely verify lifetime exclusive homosexuality is to track a large number of individuals from birth to death and record all the various homosexual or heterosexual involvements they have. Needless to say, this is a difficult task to accomplish (especially in the wild) and has been achieved for only a few species—indeed, in many cases the comparable evidence for lifetime exclusive *heterosexuality* is not available either, for precisely the same reasons. Nevertheless, in at least three species of birds—Silver Gulls, Greylag Geese, and Humboldt Penguins—fairly extensive tracking regimes have been conducted, and individuals who form only homosexual pair-bonds throughout their entire lives have been documented. In some cases these are continuous pair-bonds that last upward of 15 years in Greylag Geese and 6 years in Humboldt Penguins (until the death of the individuals involved), while in other

> *"Many scientists now accept that animals engage in homosexuality."*

cases (e.g., Silver Gulls) individuals may also have several same-sex partnerships during their lives (either because of "divorce" or death of the partners).

While absolute verification of lifetime homosexuality is not directly available for other species, extended periods of same-sex activity, perhaps even lifelong, are strongly suggested. In Galahs, Common Gulls, Black-headed Gulls, Great Cormorants, and Bicolored Antbirds, for example, specific homosexual partnerships have been documented as lasting for as long as six years (or individuals having several consecutive homosexual associations for that length of time); in most of these cases the absence of heterosexual activity for at least one partner has been documented or is highly likely. In many other bird species, same-sex partnerships that last anywhere from several years to life probably also occur: Black Swans, Ringbilled Gulls, Western Gulls, and Hooded Warblers, for instance. Although these durations have not been confirmed in specific individuals, homosexual pairs that continue for at least two years or birds who consistently form same-sex pairs for that time have been verified. In still other cases, long-term same-sex bonds undoubtedly occur because homosexual pairs in these species typically follow the pattern of heterosexual pairs, which are usually lifelong (or of many years duration): Black-winged Stilts, Herring Gulls, Kittiwakes, Blue Tits, and Red-backed Shrikes, among others. Finally, it must also be remembered that in many animals (e.g., Pied Kingfishers), same-sex (and opposite-sex) pair-bonds that last two to three years can still be lifelong, owing to the relatively short life span of the species.

In mammals, cases of long-term, exclusively homosexual pairing are indeed rare. One example is male Bottlenose Dolphins: the majority of males in some populations form lifelong homosexual pairs, specific examples of which have been verified as lasting for more than ten years and continuing until death. Although the sexual involvements (both same- and opposite-sex) of such individuals have not in all cases been exhaustively tracked, it is

> *"Exclusive homosexuality of various types occurs in more than 60 species of nondomesticated mammals and birds."*

quite likely that at least some of these animals have little or no sexual contact with females (since breeding rates tend to be low in Bottlenose communities, with many individuals not participating in reproduction each year and, by extension, possibly throughout their lives). Absolute verification in this species, however, may not be forthcoming, since it is virtually impossible to continuously monitor the sexual behavior of all individuals within a given population of an oceangoing species. Bottlenose Dolphins are exceptional, however, in that the homosexual pattern in this species is distinct from the heterosexual one: opposite-sex pair-bonding does not occur among Bottlenose Dolphins. In most other species, homosexual and heterosexual activities tend to follow the same basic patterns, whether this means pair-bonding, polygamy, promiscuity, or some other arrangement. Lifetime homosexual couples are not prevalent among mammals, therefore, for the same reason that lifetime heterosexual couples are not: monogamous pair-bonding is simply not a common type of mating system in mammals (it is found in only about 5 percent of all mammalian species). . . .

"Preference" for same-sex activity is, admittedly, a rather elusive concept to measure when dealing with nonhumans (though not nearly as slippery as "identity"). Although we cannot access their internal motivations or "desires," animals do offer a number of other clues as to their individual "preferences" in addition to the proportion of their behaviors or partners that are same-sex. These include homosexual activity being performed in (spite of) the presence of members of the opposite sex, individuals actively competing for the attentions of same-sex partners (rather than "resorting" to such activity), advances of opposite-sex partners being ignored and/or refused, and "widowed" or "divorced" individuals continuing to pair with same-sex partners after the loss of a homosexual mate (even when opposite-sex partners are available). These types of behaviors have

> *"Because of the wide prevalence of bisexuality— both within and across species—exclusive* **heterosexuality** *is . . . certainly less than ubiquitous."*

in fact been reported in more than 50 mammals and birds, indicating that for at least some individuals in these species, same-sex activity has "priority" over opposite-sex activity in some contexts. The converse is also true for species such as Canada Geese, Silver Gulls, Bicolored Antbirds, Jackdaws, and Galahs: in situations where opposite-sex partners are not available, only a fraction of the population engages in same-sex activity, indicating more of a heterosexual "preference" in the remainder of the population. Animals who do participate in same-sex activity in such a situational context could perhaps be said to exhibit a "latent" bisexuality; i.e., a predominantly heterosexual orientation with the potential to relate homosexually under certain circumstances. Another factor to be considered when evaluating individual "preferences" or degrees of bisexuality is the consensuality of the sexual interaction. Female Canada Geese and Silver Gulls in homosexual pairs, for example, may engage in occasional heterosexual copulations under duress; i.e., they are sometimes forcibly mated or raped by males. Likewise, heterosexually paired males in Common Murres, Laysan Albatrosses, Cliff Swallows, and several Gull species may be forcibly mounted by other males. Technically, all such individuals are "bisexual" because they engage in both homosexual and heterosexual activity, but the sort of bisexuality they exhibit is far different from that of a female Bonobo or a male Walrus, for instance, who willingly mates with animals of both sexes.

Broad patterns of sexual orientation across individuals show almost as much variation as that within individuals. In some species, the majority of animals are exclusively heterosexual, but a small proportion engage in bisexual activities (e.g., Mule Deer) or exclusively homosexual activities (e.g., male Ostriches). In others, the vast majority of individuals are bisexual and few if any are exclusively heterosexual or homosexual (e.g., Bonobos). Other species combine a pattern of nearly universal bisexuality with some exclusive homosexuality (e.g., male Mountain Sheep). In still other cases, the proportions are more equally distributed, but still vary considerably. In Silver Gulls, for instance, 10 percent of females are exclusively homosexual during their lives, 11 percent are bisexual, and 79 percent are heterosexual. Homosexual-bisexual-heterosexual splits for specific populations of other species include: 22-15-63 percent for Black-headed Gulls; 9-56-35 percent for Japanese Macaques; and 44-11-44 percent for Galahs. . . .

It is true that exclusive homosexuality in animals is less common than bisexuality—but it is not a uniquely human phenomenon, for it occurs in many more species than previously supposed. Moreover, because of the wide prevalence of bisexuality—both within and across species—exclusive *heterosexuality* is also certainly less than ubiquitous. Animals, like people, have complex life histories that involve a wide spectrum of sexual orientations, with many different degrees of participation in both same- and opposite-sex activities. To the question "Do animals engage in bisexuality or exclusive homosexuality?" we must therefore answer "both and neither." There is no such thing as a single type of "bisexuality" nor a uniform pattern of "exclusive homosexuality." Multiple shades of sexual orientation are found throughout the animal world—sometimes coexisting in the same species or even the same individual—forming part of a much larger spectrum of sexual variance.

## Nonchalance and Acceptance

An aspect of animal homosexuality that has received little attention in both popular and scientific discussions is the position or "status" of homosexual, bisexual, and transgendered individuals in the larger society. What kind of social response do they evoke from the animals around them? What is their spatial relation to the rest of the population—are they segregated, fully integrated, or somewhere in between? Primatologist Paul L. Vasey suggests that homosexual behavior in primates is characterized by a noticeable lack of hostility and segregation from the animals around them, and by and large this does appear to be true—not only for primates, but also for the vast majority of other species in which homosexual activity occurs. Almost without exception, animals with "different" sexualities and/or genders are completely integrated into the social fabric of the species, eliciting little of the attention, hostility, segregation, or secrecy that we are accustomed to associating with homosexuality in our society. Observer after scientific observer has commented on how homosexual behavior in animals is greeted with nonchalance from nearby animals. Individuals move effortlessly between their homosexual activities and other social interactions or behaviors without eliciting so much as a second glance from the animals around them.

*"Homosexual behavior in animals is greeted with nonchalance from nearby animals."*

Where individuals engaging in homosexual activity do attract attention, it is usually out of simple curiosity (e.g., African Buffalo, Musk-oxen), or else because other animals want to participate. In a number of species such as Bono-bos, Killer Whales, West Indian Manatees, Giraffes, Pronghorns, Common Murres, and Sage Grouse, homosexual interactions between two animals often develop into group sessions as more and more animals are drawn to the activity

> *"In a few cases [individual animals] actually do appear to rise in status . . . specifically because of their homosexual activities."*

and join in. This is also true for het-erosexual interactions in many of these species, and sometimes homo-sexual and heterosexual activity are part of the same group interaction. This illustrates an important point concerning the integration of homo-sexual activity within the larger so-cial framework: when bisexuality is prevalent in a species, or when a large pro-portion of the population engages in homosexual activity (as is often the case), the distinction between "homosexual" and "heterosexual" animals melts away, as does the potential for aggressive responses based on those categories. An "observer" of homosexual activity could just as easily be a participant at some other time, and any separation between animals that engage in same-sex activ-ity and those that don't becomes essentially arbitrary.

Even in species where homosexuality, bisexuality, or transgender are not widespread, animals that participate in same-sex behaviors (or transgendered individuals) are not generally treated to adverse reactions from the majority around them. Rather, homosexual activity is regarded as routinely as heterosex-ual activity is. In fact, in many species it is heterosexual, not homosexual, be-haviors that draw a negative response. In numerous primates and other animals, for example, male-female copulations are regularly harassed and interrupted by surrounding animals. Same-sex activity in these species is either disregarded al-together (e.g., Stumptail Macaques), or else is subject to a much lower rate of harassment and interruption than opposite-sex matings (e.g., Hanuman Lan-gurs, Japanese Macaques). Adult male Bonobos interfere with the heterosexual pursuits of younger males while ignoring (or even participating in) their homo-sexual activities, while heterosexual breeding pairs of Jackdaws, rather than same-sex pairs, are sometimes terrorized by nonbreeding heterosexual pairs (who may even kill their young). And in Guianan Cock-of-the-Rock, heterosex-ual courtship interactions are routinely interrupted and harassed by other males while homosexual activities are not. In fact, females defer to males engaging in same-sex courtship or copulation (by leaving or avoiding the display grounds while this activity is going on), and males may actually interrupt heterosexual interactions by initiating homosexual ones.

Not only are homosexuality and transgender largely devoid of negative re-sponses from other individuals, in some cases they actually appear to confer a positive status on the animals involved. In species that have a ranked form of so-cial organization, for instance, homosexual activities are often found among the highest-ranking individuals (e.g., Gorillas, Bighorn Sheep, Takhi, Gray-capped Social Weavers). Likewise, transgendered animals sometimes have high status in a population (e.g., Savanna Baboons) or are more successful than other animals at obtaining sexual partners (e.g., Red Deer, Common Garter Snakes). While the benefits experienced by these individuals are not necessarily a direct result of their transgender or homosexuality, in a few cases individuals actually do appear to rise in status or obtain other positive results specifically because of their homosexual activities. Black Swans and Greylag Geese who form homosexual partnerships, for example, often become powerful, high-ranking forces in their flocks, in part because the combined strength of the paired males gives them an advantage that single males and heterosexual pairs do not have. In fact, Black Swan male pairs sometimes acquire the largest and most desirable territories in their domain, relegating other birds to a distinctly disadvantaged status. . . .

## Humans Are Animals, Too

Homosexuality is part of our evolutionary heritage as primates: anyone looking at the prevalence and elaboration of homosexual behavior among our closest relatives in the animal kingdom will be led, eventually, to this conclusion. In fact, primatologist Paul L. Vasey traces the occurrence of homosexuality in primates back to at least the Oligocene epoch, 24–37 million years ago (based on its distribution and characteristics among contemporary primates). Some of the most organized and developed forms of homosexuality among animals can be found in the more than 30 species of monkeys and apes where this behavior occurs. Bonobos, for instance, engage in both male and female homosexual interactions with disarming frequency and enthusiasm, and they have also developed many unique forms of sexual expression, including a type of lesbian tribadism known as genito-genital rubbing.

> *"Homosexuality is part of our evolutionary heritage as primates."*

Similar elaborations of homosexual patterns are found among Stumptail Macaques, Gorillas, Hanuman Langurs, and many other monkey and ape species. In addition to highly developed systems of same-sex interaction and diverse sexual techniques, a number of other aspects of homosexual activity in primates are particularly salient. Among these are various forms of pair-bonding such as consortships, "favorite" partners, or sexual friendships; evidence for exclusive or preferential homosexual activity in some individuals (as discussed in the preceding section); female orgasm in monkeys and apes, in both homosexual and heterosexual contexts; female-centered or matrifocal societies, as well as male alliances and other groups of cooperating males in some species; and the wide range of nonreproductive heterosexual activities found in many primates.

# Homosexuality Is Linked to Childhood Gender Nonconformity

## by Daryl J. Bem

**About the author:** *Daryl J. Bem teaches in the department of psychology at Cornell University.*

Exotic Becomes Erotic (EBE) theory attempts to account for three major observations: First, most men and women in our culture have an exclusive and enduring erotic preference for either males or females; gender is, in fact, the overriding criterion for most people's erotic choices. Second, most men and women in our culture have an exclusive and enduring erotic preference for persons of the opposite sex. And third, a substantial minority of men and women have an exclusive and enduring erotic preference for persons of the same sex. In seeking to account for these observations, EBE theory provides a single unitary explanation for both opposite-sex and same-sex desire—and for both men and women. In addition, the theory seeks to account for sex differences in sexual orientation and for departures from the modal patterns, such as bisexual orientations, orientations that are not enduring but fluid and changeable, and sexual orientations that are not even based on the gender of potential partners.

## Overview of EBE Theory

The central proposition of EBE theory is that individuals can become erotically attracted to a class of individuals from whom they felt different during childhood. This phenomenon is embedded in the overall sequence of events that leads to an individual's erotic attractions—the component of sexual orientation addressed by the theory.

• According to the theory, biological variables such as genes or prenatal hormones do not code for sexual orientation per se but for childhood temperaments, such as aggression and activity level.

• A child's temperaments predispose him or her to enjoy some activities more than other activities. One child will enjoy rough-and-tumble play and competitive team sports (male-typical activities); another will prefer to socialize quietly or play jacks or hopscotch (female-typical activities). Children will also prefer to play with peers who share their activity preferences; for example, the child who enjoys baseball or football will selectively seek out boys as playmates. Children who prefer sex-typical activities and same-sex playmates are referred to as gender conforming; children who prefer sex-atypical activities and opposite-sex playmates are referred to as gender nonconforming.

• Gender-conforming children will feel different from opposite-sex peers, and gender-nonconforming children will feel different from same-sex peers.

• These feelings of being different produce heightened physiological arousal. For the male-typical child, it may be felt as antipathy or contempt in the presence of girls ("girls are yucky"); for the female-typical child, it may be felt as timidity or apprehension in the presence of boys. A particularly clear example is the "sissy" boy who is taunted by male peers for his gender nonconformity and, as a result, is likely to experience the strong physi-

> *"Individuals can become erotically attracted to a class of individuals from whom they felt different during childhood."*

ological arousal of fear and anger in their presence. However, the theory claims that every child—conforming or nonconforming—experiences heightened, nonspecific physiological arousal in the presence of peers from whom he or she feels different. For most children, this arousal [is not] consciously experienced.

• Regardless of the specific source of the childhood arousal, it is subsequently transformed into erotic attraction.

It is important to emphasize that [this sequence] is not intended to describe an inevitable, universal path to sexual orientation but the modal path followed by most men and women in a gender-polarizing culture like ours, a culture that emphasizes the differences between the sexes by pervasively organizing both the perceptions and realities of communal life around the male-female dichotomy.

## Evidence for the Theory

The central proposition that individuals can become erotically attracted to a class of individuals from whom they felt different during childhood is very general and transcends erotic orientations that are based on gender. For example, a light-skinned person could come to eroticize dark-skinned persons through one or more of the processes described by the theory. To produce a differential erotic attraction to one sex or the other, however, requires that the basis for feeling different must itself differentiate between the sexes; that is, to arrive at a sex-based erotic orientation, an individual must feel different for sex-based or gender-related reasons. Simply being lighter-skinned, poorer, more intelligent, or more introverted than one's childhood peers does not produce the kind of feeling different that produces differential homoerotic or heteroerotic attraction.

Data consistent with this analysis comes from an intensive, large-scale interview study conducted in the San Francisco Bay Area by the Kinsey Institute for Sex Research. Using retrospective reports from adult respondents, the investigators compared approximately 1,000 gay men and lesbians with 500 heterosexual men and women to test several hypotheses about the development of sexual orientation. The study (hereinafter, the "San Francisco study") yielded virtually no support for current experience-based theories of sexual orientation, including those based on processes of learning or conditioning or on family psychodynamics.

The study did find, however, that 71% of the gay men and 70% of the lesbians in the sample reported that they had felt different from their same-sex peers during childhood, a feeling that was sustained throughout childhood and adolescence for most respondents. When asked in what ways they had felt different, they overwhelmingly cited gender-related reasons. Gay men were most likely to say that they had not liked boys' sports; lesbians were most likely to say that they had been more masculine than other girls were and had been more interested in sports than other girls. In contrast, fewer than 8% of heterosexual men or women said that they had felt different from same-sex childhood peers for gender-related reasons. Those who had felt

> *"Every child . . . experiences heightened, nonspecific physiological arousal in the presence of peers from whom he or she feels different."*

different from their peers tended to cite such reasons as having been poorer, more intelligent, or more introverted.

Several other studies have also reported that gay men and lesbians recall having felt different from same-sex peers on gender-related characteristics during childhood. The major weakness in all these studies, including the San Francisco study, is that they rely on adults' retrospective reports of childhood feelings. On the other hand, the respondents in some of the studies were relatively close in time to their childhood years; in one study, for example, 88% of gay male youths as young as 14 years reported having felt different from other boys on gender-related characteristics throughout their childhood years. Moreover, the link between childhood gender nonconformity and sexual orientation has been confirmed in over 50 studies, including prospective ones

## The Antecedents of Feeling Different

Feeling different from one's childhood peers can have any of several antecedents, some common, some idiosyncratic. The most common antecedent is gender polarization. Virtually all human societies polarize the sexes to some extent, setting up a sex-based division of labor and power, emphasizing or exaggerating sex differences, and, in general, superimposing the male-female dichotomy on virtually every aspect of communal life. These gender-polarizing practices ensure that most boys and girls will grow up feeling different from opposite-sex peers and, hence, will come to be erotically attracted to them later in life. This, according to the theory, is why gender becomes the most salient category and, hence, the most common criterion for selecting sexual partners in the first place and why heteroeroticism is the modal preference across time and culture. Thus, the theory provides a culturally based alternative to the assumption that

> *"Seventy-one percent of . . . gay men and 70 percent of . . . lesbians . . . reported that they had felt different from their same-sex peers during childhood."*

evolution must necessarily have programmed heterosexuality into the species for reasons of reproductive advantage. . . .

How, then, does a child come to feel different from same-sex peers? As cited earlier, the most common reasons given by gay men and lesbians in the San Fransisco study for having felt different from same-sex peers in childhood were sex-atypical preferences and behaviors in childhood—gender nonconformity. In fact, in the path analyses of the San Francisco study, childhood gender conformity or nonconformity was not only the strongest but the only significant childhood predictor of later sexual orientation for both men and women. The effects are large and significant. For example, compared with heterosexual men, gay men were significantly less likely to have enjoyed boys' activities (e.g., baseball and football) during childhood, more likely to have enjoyed girls' activities (e.g., hopscotch, playing house, and jacks), and less likely to rate themselves as having been masculine. These were the three variables that defined gender nonconformity in the study. Additionally, gay men were more likely than heterosexual men to have had girls as childhood friends. The corresponding comparisons between lesbian and heterosexual women are also large and significant.

It is also clear that relatively more women than men reported enjoying sex-atypical activities and having opposite-sex friends during childhood. As these data confirm, enjoying male-typical activities is common for a girl in our society, implying that being a tomboy is not sufficient by itself to cause her to feel different from other girls. In fact, we see the difference between the percentages of lesbians and heterosexual women who report having enjoyed boys' activities during childhood (81% vs. 61%, respectively) is less than half the size of the difference between them in their aversion to girls' activities (63% vs. 15%). Moreover, this latter difference is virtually identical to that between gay men and heterosexual men in their reported childhood aversions to boys' activities (63% vs. 10%). . . .

EBE theory proposes that exotic becomes erotic because feeling different from a class of peers in childhood produces heightened nonspecific physiological arousal, which is subsequently transformed into erotic attraction. To my knowledge, there is no direct evidence for the first step in this sequence beyond the well-documented observation that novel ("exotic") stimuli produce heightened physiological arousal in many species, including our own; filling in this empirical gap in EBE theory must await future research. In contrast, there are at least three mechanisms that can potentially effect the second step, transforming generalized arousal into erotic attraction. Only one of these, the extrinsic arousal effect, is discussed here.

In his first-century Roman handbook, *The Art of Love*, Ovid advised any man who was interested in sexual seduction to take the woman in whom he was interested to a gladiatorial tournament, where she would more easily be aroused to passion. However, he did not say why this should be so. A contemporary version of Ovid's claim was introduced by E. Walster, who suggested that it constitutes a special case of the 2-factor theory of emotion [proposed by S. Schachter and J.E. Singer]. This theory states that the physiological arousal of our autonomic nervous system provides the cues that we feel emotional but that the more subtle judgment of which emotion we are feeling often depends on our cognitive appraisal of the surrounding circumstances. According to Walster, then, the experience of erotic desire results from the conjunction of physiological arousal and the cognitive causal attribution (or misattribution) that the arousal is elicited by a potential sexual partner.

## Physiological and Sexual Arousal

Although not all investigators agree that it arises from a cognitive attribution process, there is now extensive experimental evidence that an individual who has been physiologically aroused will show heightened sexual responsiveness to an appropriate target person. In one set of studies, male participants were physiologically aroused by running in place, by hearing an audio tape of a comedy routine, or by hearing an audio tape of a grisly killing. No matter how they had been aroused, these men reported more erotic interest in a physically attractive woman than did men who had not been aroused. This effect has also been observed physiologically. In two studies, preexposure to a disturbing (nonsexual) videotape subsequently produced greater penile tumescence in men and greater vaginal blood volume increases in women when they watched an erotic videotape than did preexposure to a nondisturbing videotape.

> *"Childhood gender conformity or nonconformity was . . . the only significant childhood predictor of later sexual orientation."*

In other words, generalized physiological arousal, regardless of its source or affective tone, can subsequently be experienced as erotic desire. At that point, it is erotic desire. My proposal, then, is that an individual's protracted and sustained experience of feeling different from same- or opposite-sex peers throughout childhood and adolescence produces a correspondingly sustained physiological arousal that gets eroticized when the maturational, cognitive, and situational factors coalesce to provide the critical defining moment.

The precise timing of this moment, however, is influenced by several factors, including actual sexual experience with opposite- and same-sex peers. A recent review suggests that, in general, men and women recall their first sexual attractions, whether same-sex or opposite-sex, as occurring when they were between 10 and 10.5 years of age. Nevertheless, social norms and expectations inevitably influence an individual's awareness and interpretation of early arousal. Most individuals in our culture are primed to anticipate, recognize, and interpret opposite-sex arousal as erotic or romantic attraction and to ignore, repress, or differently interpret comparable same-sex arousal. We should also expect to see secular changes and cohort effects. For example, the heightened visibility of gay men and lesbians in our society is now prompting individuals who experience same-sex arousal to recognize it, label it, and act on it at earlier ages than in previous years.

## The Biological Connection

EBE theory proposes that to the extent biological factors such as the genotype, prenatal hormones, or brain neuroanatomy influence an individual's later sexual orientation, they do so only indirectly, by intervening earlier in the chain of events to influence a child's preference for sex-typical or sex-atypical activity and peer preferences—his or her gender conformity or nonconformity.

*"Generalized physiological arousal, regardless of its source . . . , can subsequently be experienced as erotic desire."*

More specifically, the theory specifies that any link between, say, the genotype and gender nonconformity is composed of two parts: a link between the genotype and childhood temperaments and a link between those temperaments and gender nonconformity. This implies that the mediating temperaments should possess three characteristics: First, they should be plausibly related to those childhood activities that define gender conformity and nonconformity. Second, because they manifest themselves in sex-typed preferences, they should show sex differences. And third, because they are hypothesized to derive from the genotype, they should have significant heritabilities.

One likely candidate is aggression and its benign cousin, rough-and-tumble play. Gay men score lower than heterosexual men on measures of childhood aggression, and parents of gender-nonconforming boys specifically rate them as having less interest in rough-and-tumble play than do parents of gender-conforming boys. Second, the sex difference in aggression during childhood is one of the largest psychological sex differences known. Rough-and-tumble play in particular is more common in boys than in girls. And third, individual differences in aggression have a large heritable component.

Another likely candidate is activity level, considered to be one of the basic childhood temperaments. Like aggression, differences in activity level would also seem to characterize the differences between male-typical and female-typical play activities in childhood.

> *"Girls are punished less for being gender-nonconforming."*

Moreover, gender-nonconforming boys and girls are lower and higher on activity level, respectively, than are control children of the same sex. Second, the sex difference in activity level is as large as it is for aggression. Even before birth, boys in utero are more active than girls are. And third, individual differences in activity level have a large heritable component. . . .

## Sex Differences

One of the more audacious claims made for EBE is that it provides a single unitary explanation for both opposite-sex and same-sex desire—and for both men and women. Not everyone is convinced, however, and I have been challenged to defend the theory against the charge that it is androcentric: valid for men, perhaps, but not for women.

To be sure, there is now substantial evidence that men and women differ from one another on several aspects of sexuality, irrespective of their sexual orientations. As I tell my students, if you want to understand the sexuality of gay men, think of them as men; if you want to understand the sexuality of lesbians, think of them as women. But most of these differences have to do with the primacy or intensity of erotic desire, the relative emphasis on the physical attributes of potential partners, and the willingness to engage in impersonal sex without romantic involvement. Such differences are not pertinent to EBE theory's account of how erotic orientations develop.

There is, however, one sex difference that is pertinent to EBE theory: Women's sexual orientations are more fluid than men's. Many studies, including a national random survey of Americans, have found that women are more likely to be bisexual than exclusively homosexual, whereas the reverse is true for men. Non-heterosexual women are also more likely to see their sexual orientations as flexible, even "chosen," whereas men are more likely to view their sexual orientations in essentialist terms, as inborn and unchangeable. For example, men who come out as gay after leaving heterosexual marriages or relationships often describe themselves as having "finally realized" their "true" sexual orientation. Lesbians in similar situation, however, are more likely to reject the implication that their previous heterosexual relationships were inauthentic or at odds with who they really were: "That's who I was then, and this is who l am now."

The greater fluidity of women's sexual orientations is consistent with EBE theory. In our society, women grow up in a (phenomenologically) less gender-polarized culture than do men. Compared with boys, girls are punished less for being gender-nonconforming, and they are more likely than boys to engage in both sex-typical and sex-atypical activities and are more likely to have childhood friends of both sexes. This implies that girls are less likely than boys to feel differentially different from opposite-sex and same-sex peers and, hence, are less likely to develop exclusively heteroerotic or homoerotic orientations.

It is even possible that some of today's nonheterosexual women may be giving a preview of what sexual orientations would look like in a less gender-polarized future. It is possible that we might even begin to see more men and women who, instead of using gender as the overriding criterion for selecting a partner, might base their erotic and romantic choices on a more diverse and idiosyncratic variety of attributes. As I [have] remarked, "Gentlemen might still prefer blonds, but some of those gentlemen (and some ladies) might prefer blonds of any sex."

# Studies Proving the Biological Origin of Homosexuality Are Flawed

**by Trudy Chun**

**About the author:** *Trudy Chun writes for Concerned Women for America, an organization that works to strengthen the traditional family according to Judeo-Christian moral standards.*

The debate over homosexual "rights" often spirals into a discussion over whether homosexuality is a learned behavior or a genetic trait. Many homosexual activists insist that they cannot help their sexual behavior. They have argued that scientists have "proven" homosexuality is biological through studies that link sexual orientation to everything from differences in portions of the brain, to genes, finger length and inner ear differences.

With all this scrambling for scientific evidence, one would think the issue has been settled. But if we take an intellectually honest look at the research, we may find more questions raised than answered.

## The Hypothalamus

The first frenzy of this trend erupted in 1991 when Simon LeVay published a study in *Science*. His study noted a difference in a brain structure called the hypothalamus when evaluating homosexual and heterosexual men. LeVay found that in the specimens he studied, the hypothalamus was generally larger in heterosexual men than in homosexual men. Therefore he concluded that these findings "suggest that sexual orientation has a biologic substrate."

While LeVay's study hit the media with a splash that rippled from coast to coast, it was anything but conclusive. An analysis of the study and its methodology reveals some serious flaws. The first problem, which LeVay himself readily admits, is that all 19 of his homosexual subjects had died of complications associated with AIDS. Therefore the difference in the hypothalamus might well be attributed to the AIDS rather than homosexuality. LeVay attempted to compensate for the weakness by including a few heterosexuals who died of AIDS complications in the heterosexual sample. However, LeVay did not know for sure whether all subjects in his heterosexual sample were indeed heterosexual; all of these subjects were simply "presumed heterosexual."

Moreover, Dr. William Byne argued in *Scientific American* that "[LeVay's] inclusion of a few brains from heterosexual men with AIDS did not adequately address the fact that at the time of death virtually all men with AIDS have decreased testosterone levels as the result of the disease itself or the side effects of particular treatments. . . . Thus it is possible that the effects on the size of the INAH3 [hypothalamus] that he attributed to sexual orientation were actually caused by the hormonal abnormalities associated with AIDS."

## Exceptions and Alternate Interpretations

Another weakness of LeVay's study is that even in his sample there were "exceptions"—that is, there were some homosexuals who had larger hypothalamus structures than some of the heterosexuals examined. Even LeVay admits that these exceptions "hint at the possibility that sexual orientation, although an important variable, may not be the sole determinant of INAH3 [hypothalamus] size."

LeVay is an open homosexual, and his interview with *Newsweek* suggests he had an agenda from the outset. LeVay lost his gay partner to AIDS, an event that made him re-evaluate what he was doing with his life. As a result, he took on this project. LeVay believes America must be convinced that homosexuality is determined biologically. "It's important to educate society," he told *Newsweek.* "I think this issue does affect religious and legal attitudes."

Since LeVay released his study, other researchers have found that brain structures can change as a result of life experiences. In 1997, University of California at Berkeley psychologist Marc Breedlove released a study that showed that sexual activities of rats actually structurally changed aspects of the brain at the base of the spinal chord. "These findings give us proof for what we theoretically know to be the case—that sexual experience can alter the structure of the brain, just as genes can alter it," Breedlove commented.

> *"You can't assume that because you find a structural difference in the brain [of homosexuals], that it was caused by genes."*

"You can't assume that because you find a structural difference in the brain, that it was caused by genes. You don't know how it got there."

Breedlove is not an activist out to prove homosexuality is not biological. In fact, he does believe a genetic component exists somewhere, but he, unlike LeVay, seems willing to take a more honest approach to research.

In 1993 a group of medical researchers at the National Cancer Institute, led by Dr. Dean H. Hamer, released a study that linked homosexuality to the X chromosome. While the study won a great deal of media attention, it also offered little proof of a biological link to homosexuality.

Hamer's results are often misunderstood. Many believe that the study found an identical sequence (Xq28) on the X chromosome of all homosexual brothers. In reality, what it found was matching sequences in each set of brothers who were both homosexual. Dr. Byne argues that in order to prove anything by this study, Hamer would have had to examine the Xq28 sequence of gay men's heterosexual brothers. Hamer insisted that such an inclusion would have confounded his study. Byne responded, "In other words, inclusion of heterosexual brothers might have revealed that something other than genes is responsible for sexual orientation."

Hamer's motives are also questionable. Although his research is sponsored by the National Cancer Institute, his work has had little to do with cancer. This study alone took $419,000 of the institute's taxpayer-backed funds, according to *The Washington Times*.

One of Hamer's researchers told the *Times* that homosexuality is "not the only thing we study," but it is "a primary focus of study." Hamer reportedly stated he has pushed for an Office of Gay and Lesbian Health inside the National Institutes of Health, and he testified in opposition to Colorado's Amendment 2, which sought to keep homosexual activists from winning minority class status. Sen. Robert C. Smith (R-New Hampshire) accused the doctor of "actively pursu[ing] . . . a gay agenda."

Another fact that casts doubt on Hamer's conclusions is that his study has not been replicated by other researchers, which would help to confirm his theory. In 1999, Drs. George Rice, Neil Risch and George Ebers published their findings in *Science* after attempting to replicate Hamer's Xq28 study. Their conclusion: "We were not able to confirm evidence for an Xq28-linked locus underlying male homosexuality." Moreover, they added that when another group of researchers tried to replicate Hamer's study, they too failed to find the genetic connection to homosexuality.

## The Twin Study

Another study that has advanced the theory that homosexuality is a biological phenomenon is the famed "Twin Study" by J. Michael Bailey and Richard C. Pillard. Bailey and Pillard examined identical and fraternal twin brothers and adopted brothers in an effort to establish a genetic link to homosexuality. The study results yielded some statistics that seem to support the hypothesis and other statistics that appear to refute it. Fifty-two percent of the identical twins shared the same homosexual sexual orientation, while only 22 percent of fraternal twins fell into the same category. This finding appears to support the argument for biology, since identical twins share the same genes. However, the rate of non-twin conformity should mirror that of fraternal twins. In the Bailey and

Pillard study, the rate was only 9.2 percent. And the rate in adopted—which, if the biological hypothesis were true, should have been even lower than non-twin brothers—was actually higher (11 percent).

In his analysis of the medical evidence supporting a biological cause of homosexuality, Dr. Byne noted other twin studies. He wrote, "Without knowing what developmental experiences contribute to sexual orientation . . . the effects of common genes and common environments are difficult to disentangle. Resolving this issue requires studies of twins raised apart."

> *"Science has yet to produce a conclusive study that shows homosexuality has a biological cause."*

Other physicians have also criticized the study for overvaluing the genetic influence.

Dr. Byne's arguments might lead some activists to label him a "homophobe." He is, in reality, quite the contrary. Byne readily advocates societal acceptance of homosexuality, but nevertheless concludes, "Most of the links in the chain of reasoning from biology to social policy [regarding homosexuality], do not hold up under scrutiny."

As a matter of fact, Bailey did conduct another study in 1999, published in the March 2000 issue of the *Journal of Personality and Social Psychology*, that revealed the genetic influence on homosexuality he supposedly found earlier may actually be less. He sent a questionnaire to the entire Australian Twin Registry. Only three pairs of identical male twins were both homosexual out of a total of 27 male identical twin pairs in which at least one was homosexual. Of the 16 fraternal male twins, in none of the pairs were both homosexual. Bailey found similar results for lesbians.

## Hormones

The determination to find a biological link to homosexuality continued, as researchers examined exposure to certain hormones as a biological cause of homosexuality.

In 1998, researchers Dennis McFadden and Edward G. Pasanen published a study that evaluated the auditory systems of heterosexuals and homosexuals. Specifically the study considered differences in echo-like waveforms emitted from an inner ear structure of people with normal hearing. These waves are higher in women than in men, often attributed to the person's exposure to androgen (a male hormone) in his or her early development as a fetus.

The McFadden study found the level of these waveforms in the ears of self-acknowledged lesbian women ranged between those of men and those of heterosexual women. The researchers concluded that this evidence suggests that female homosexuality could be a result of increased exposure to the male hormone androgen in the womb (homosexual men did not show the same variation).

The media eagerly jumped on this bandwagon, touting the evidence that homosexuality is indeed biological. But even the researchers themselves are not too quick to draw definitive conclusions. They caution that the results are only tentative. In the published study, they point out that exposure to "intense sounds, certain drugs, and other manipulations" can lower the level of these auditory waveforms. "Thus, it may be that something in the lifestyles of homosexual and bisexual females leads them to be exposed to one or more agents that have reduced the [waveforms], either temporarily or permanently." Moreover, even if the hearing differences were caused by an increased exposure to androgen in the womb, scientists would still be a far cry away from proving that this exposure is a cause of homosexuality—especially since the difference was not apparent in the male homosexual sample.

## Finger Length

In March 2000, yet another study on a biological link to homosexuality hit the media with fanfare. This time researchers weren't looking at ears, but fingers. Scientists believe finger length indicates how much exposure a person had to androgen while in the womb.

Typically, people's index finger is slightly shorter than the ring finger—a difference that is seen more clearly on the right hand due to exposure to higher levels of androgen while the human is developing in the womb. In females, the ring finger and index finger are almost the same size, but in men the ring finger is generally shorter.

In this study, Berkeley's Dr. Breedlove, who had in 1997 shown how sexual activity can change brain structure, found that homosexual women's finger length had a tendency to follow the male pattern. But again, the media was more eager than the researcher to draw definitive conclusions as to what this means. In fact, Breedlove told CNN, "There is no gene that forces a person to be straight or gay. . . . I believe there are many social and psychological, as well as biological, factors that make up sexual preference."

## Fact or Spin?

Homosexual activists have been working to legitimize their sexual behavior for decades. Now they have found a strategy to win a foothold in America's heart. "If homosexuality is biological, how can society condemn it?" they argue. Unfortunately, their "proof" is based on flawed studies and media spins. Science has yet to produce a conclusive study that shows homosexuality has a biological cause.

As homosexual activists vie for legitimacy in American society, citizens and legislators would do well to avoid putting their confidence in political rhetoric and take some time to examine the facts.

# Homosexuality Is Caused by Societal Dysfunction

**by Jeffrey Satinover, in an interview by the National Association for Research and Therapy of Homosexuals**

**About the author:** *Jeffrey Satinover, a diplomat of the American Board of Psychiatry and Neurology, wrote the book* Homosexuality and the Politics of Truth. *The National Association for Research and Therapy of Homosexuals (NARTH) provides psychological understanding of the cause, treatment, and behavior associated with homosexuality.*

*The following text is taken from a radio interview [with the National Association for Research and Therapy of Homosexuals] in which Dr. Satinover was a guest. He spoke to the interviewer as follows:*

In America of late, truth has become subject to terrible political pressure. The question isn't just homosexuality, but rather, freedom from all sexual constraint. This has been an issue for civilization for thousands of years.

## No Moral Compass

I think many people have a sense, especially in America, that too many barriers have come down. We now have so little of a moral compass that we're really completely at sea. We're awash in the tide of unconstrained instinctive behaviors which are all being labeled "okay" because nobody really has a sense, any more, as to what's right and what's wrong. In [mythology expert] Joseph Campbell's words, "Follow your bliss." This has led us into a growing barbarism.

We are now looking at a generation of young people who are exposed to a sometimes explicit, and sometimes implicit set of values that says that homosexuality is perfectly okay—it's just a complement to heterosexuality.

The implication of such a set of values to an impressionable, possibly confused and certainly exploring youngster, is that there is no reason whatsoever not to go out and try it and see whether it fits. It's simply that a door has been opened and a certain number of people will walk through that door and thereby expose themselves to terrible risks at an age where they are not really capable of making intelligent judgments about the risks.

## No "Gay Gene"

In the news, now, we're hearing so many overblown claims of a genetic foundation for homosexuality. The whole subject of behavioral genetics is complex. It does not lend itself to sound bites at all.

The real genetic question is—what is it in the background of people who become homosexual that opens that door for them, whereas the door is essentially closed for other people?

In a nutshell, every behavioral trait in human nature has a genetic component. For example, basketball playing is clearly genetic. If you were to perform on basketball players the kinds of studies that have been done on homosexuality, you would find an unequivocal genetic association—very powerful, probably much stronger than there is with homosexuality. But if you ask yourself what that's about—it's clear that it's NOT that there is a gene for basketball playing. . . .

The reason there's a genetic association is that there's an *intermediate* trait which allows people who carry these traits to become basketball players in greater numbers than those who do not have those traits—namely, height, athleticism, and so on. So it's not surprising that there is a growing number of studies that show a genetic association to homosexuality. But that is a far cry from saying that homosexuality is genetic in the way that eye color is genetic.

Of course, there is a political implication to the misuse of the idea that there is a heritable component to homosexuality—that is, the false notion that if it is "genetic," then it must be unchangeable. But I think the most important point that one can make about homosexuality is that it *is* significantly changeable—although statistically, not for everyone.

As a matter of fact, there is an extremely interesting statistic in the more detailed version of the *Sex in America* survey (*The Social Organization of Sexuality*), which showed that 2.8% of the men in their sample were essentially homosexual. But a much larger percentage had been homosexual at some point in their lives previously. Somewhere between 10% and 16% had apparently gone through a homosexual phase. By gay activist standards they would be people who would have a supposed— and supposedly fixed—"gay identity,"

> *"We're hearing so many overblown claims of a genetic foundation for homosexuality."*

yet by the time they were adults and were sampled in the survey, they had given homosexuality up. In fact, the largest proportion by far had given it up.

There are also case reports in the psychiatric literature of single individuals as well as groups of individuals who in a variety of settings actually do spontaneously leave a homosexual identity.

The debate over homosexuality has been profoundly affected by the current culture of complaint. Many, many areas of political life, social life and scientific life today are being profoundly influenced by the various competing claims and cross-claims to victimhood.

A recent article in a psychiatric publication informed us that 30% of all 20-year-old homosexual men will be HIV-positive or dead by the age of thirty. You would think that the objective, ethical medical approach would be: let's use anything that works to try to take these people out of their posture of risk. If it means getting them to wear condoms, fine. If it means getting them to give up anal intercourse, fine. If it means getting them to give up homosexuality, fine. But that last intervention is the one intervention that is absolutely taboo.

There is no doubt that a cold, statistical analysis of this epidemic would lead you to the conclusion that this attitude of political correctness is killing a substantial portion of those people. I think there is an element of denial, in the psychological sense, of what gay-related illnesses really mean.

## Pressure to Normalize

The normalization of homosexuality was a classic example where the American Psychiatric Association (APA) knuckled under [when, in 1973, they removed homosexuality from their list of mental illnesses] to a victim group's pressure tactics. In that instance, no substantive data was presented either to "prove" that homosexuality is an illness, or to "prove" that it is not.

Actually, many of the diagnoses that exist in psychiatry are labeled as illnesses for reasons that have nothing to do with medicine. Instead, psychiatric diagnoses are very subject to intellectual fads that come and go.

The reason the APA talks about disorders—rather than illnesses—is precisely because there are very, very few mental illnesses where underlying pathophysiology is even suspected. In most cases, if you are going to use the term illness, you would have to use it as a metaphor. They are possibly spiritual illnesses, or they are ways of life that are consensually undesirable. But they don't necessarily reflect some underlying disorder in the hardware that backs up the mind.

And so the whole question of what constitutes psychiatric illness is already so weak that it opened the door for activists to come in and make a change in the nomenclature without even having to appeal to rigorous scientific standards. Had they done so, there simply would have been no data one way or another. . . .

## National Association for Research and Therapy of Homosexuals (NARTH) Interviews Dr. Satinover

*National Association for Research and Therapy of Homosexuals: How did you get involved in the issue of homosexuality?*

Jeffrey Satinover: I had been reading Leanne Payne's *The Healing Presence.* The book describes a sophisticated system of depth psychology from a religious context, where psychological insights are united with healing prayer. After striking up a correspondence with Leanne, I was invited to a conference of hers and I accepted. At that time, I did not even know that the conference was related to homosexuality.

There I met hundreds of people struggling with that issue, and many who had successfully emerged on the other side and were married with children. As I got to know them, I found them to be quite remarkable. The struggle to be healed had left an indelible imprint. I saw a humility, an empathy and a fearlessness about life. They knew exactly what it meant to stand up for what they believed in, since the struggle to become who they truly were had exacted such a cost in suffering.

The struggle against homosexuality is like so many of the desperate challenges that are common to our modern age—so many people are wrestling with the results of emotional deprivation within the family, because damaged childhoods are so endemic. The life story of a homosexual has parallels for anyone struggling with spiritual, moral and character issues . . . which is to say, all of us!

These people's particular problem happened to be homosexuality, but that was incidental. Their battle was a microcosm for the identity problems of so many people today, who are struggling with what it means to be a man or a woman—with the way that men and women can best relate to one another in the world—as well as with the larger problem of personal identity.

These people had found their way back from the greatest degree of brokenness to embody the values that our culture has always held dear (at least, until recently). They've lived

> *"The most important point that one can make about homosexuality is that it is significantly changeable."*

through the most extreme possible crisis and come out the other side. They've wrestled with self-deception to find the truth, and come out with an assurance and self-possession which makes them exemplars of what the therapeutic process ought to produce, but only rarely does. I wanted to be around these people as much as I could, because I knew I had a lot to learn from them.

## Homosexuality Is Not Good

*Before going to this conference, what had you believed about homosexuality?*

I had always been somewhat of an iconoclast and I had therefore been wary of the extent to which the psychiatric profession consistently sold itself out to political fashion on a lot of issues. So I had not bought the PC line entirely. Yet, I was still uncertain. But after meeting these people who were struggling successfully, I realized that to some extent, the wool had been pulled over my eyes by both our culture and the psychiatric profession. Clearly homosexuality was not good, and was changeable. . . .

*Should the American Psychiatric Association have de-pathologized homosexuality?*

In some ways I think the psychiatric establishment was right—homosexuality is not a disease the way that, say, pneumonia or cancer or schizophrenia are diseases. Homosexuality makes a certain kind of sense as an understandable adaptation to some types of life circumstances. If you grow up in a Cosa Nostra family [an American branch of the Mafia], it makes sense to be a sociopath. By the same token, it's profoundly confusing to label the sociopathic responses, of, say, war orphans as "disordered" when a war orphan must become a sociopath in order to survive; if he fails to, he may die. So, under the circumstances of war, which response is "healthier"—that is to say, "adaptive"?

## Adapting to Adverse Circumstances

Homosexuality, too, is a method of adapting to adverse circumstances. But like sociopathy, it exacts a cost in terms of constrictions in relationships.

There are many psychological "illnesses" which cannot be adequately or convincingly explained using the medical model of psychiatry. Being homosexual is not like having a tumor. We should throw out the Diagnostic and Statistical Manual (DSM) and start carefully rethinking all of these so-called illnesses. Right now, the DSM is mostly a collection of problems labeled illnesses because they are simply consensually undesirable within our present culture. But at base, they are *really* issues of values, philosophy, and character.

How can we "prove" to the psychiatric establishment that homosexuality is psychologically unhealthy? When we tried to defend the idea that homosexuality is a disorder as evidenced by the higher associated suicide rate, gay activists said that the suicide was not due to the inherently dissatisfying nature of the condition—it was due to the stresses of homophobia. When we point to the high level of gay promiscuity, they said we were using a narrow, "heterosexist" and outdated definition of promiscuity. Gays could be emotionally faithful to one partner, they argued, while being sexually active with many partners.

And you can't get around those arguments unless you're actually willing to say that promiscuity is an inferior way of life. You need to be able to say that some certain standard is better.

If we can't settle on a shared higher vision, then it's amazing what we must be prepared to accept. For example, there is actually a growing body of literature in sexological journals arguing that the psychological and emotional benefits of promiscuity more than outweigh the risks to life from AIDS.

So that is the fundamental flaw of psychology—it is meaningless without the backdrop of a framework of values.

There I believe homosexuality—like narcissism—is best viewed as a spiritual and moral illness.

Now psychology as a discipline must step up to the table and accept responsibility for the extent to which it has been propagating an amoral ethos. Fyodor Dostoevsky put it best in *The Grand Inquisitor:* "Without God, everything is permissible."

# Searching for a Gay Gene Will Harm Homosexuals

## by Mark Schoofs

**About the author:** *Mark Schoofs writes for the* Village Voice.

Historian James Steakley is describing how doctors used to lobotomize gay men. The instrument "looked like a knitting needle," he says, "a mechanical scalpel-like thing that would mush up your gray matter. They would target the sexual center of the brain. Later they changed to an electronic tip, so they could burn it out."

Lobotomy was only one "cure" for homosexuality. Castration was another. In the U.S., doctors practiced hormone "therapy" on gay men and removed the clitoris from lesbians. American doctors also tried electroshock therapy and, as late as the 1970s, "aversion therapy," in which gay men were shown male pornography while being injected with drugs that caused them to vomit.

Most of these techniques were meant to be helpful, even kind. Homosexuals would be happier if they could change, doctors commonly thought. Fortunately, the science behind these "cures" was wrong, so all of them failed. But what if researchers found something that really does influence sexual orientation? In fact, scientists are searching for precisely that—a genetic component. Their research, combined with the revolution in reproductive technology, could converge like pincers on gay men and lesbians.

"Once you identify the gene, it's really a routine thing" to manufacture a test for it, says Simon LeVay, the researcher who made headlines when he found brain differences between gay and straight men. Soon, he says, "abortion won't be like it is now, where you pull out a recognizable lump of tissue that looks like a person." Rather, it will be possible to run genetic tests on embryos when they have only a few cells. "What we're talking about here is a democratic, do-it-yourself eugenics," says LeVay. "It could have horrifying consequences."

In his mind's eye, Ronald M. Green, director of the Dartmouth Ethics Institute, keeps seeing a series of human embryos, all fertilized in test tubes, none bigger than a few hundred cells. That's the time when parents choose: Which embryos should be transferred into the mother's uterus to have a chance at life, and which should be discarded?

This is already what happens with in-vitro fertilization. Women take "super-ovulation" drugs that make them produce about 12 eggs in one cycle, of which only four or five are implanted back into the womb. But as soon as science figures out how to freeze human egg cells—which, Green predicts, will happen by 2002—women will be able to store their eggs until they are ready to have a child.[1] The proportion of pregnancies conceived through in-vitro fertilization will then soar, he says, and couples will be able to select from perhaps 100 fertilized eggs.

Choosing an embryo is simple now, because genetic testing is in its infancy. Only major diseases (such as cystic fibrosis) and abnormalities (such as extra chromosomes) can be detected. But this age of innocence is swiftly drawing to an end. The National Human Genome Research Institute is mapping every gene.[2] If parents knew which embryos were likely to turn out gay, would they discard them?

"Sexual orientation offers the most serious potential for eugenics," says Green, who is heterosexual and the father of two children. "I'm more concerned about it than about the choice of IQ or anything else."

> *"Sexual orientation offers the most serious potential for eugenics."*

Religion teaches that homosexuality is not just a sin but a disorder, he notes, and many believers "look to AIDS as evidence that this is against God's will." Secular parents might also be tempted. "Even well-intentioned parents often see being gay as a source of suffering, and their instinct to want the best for your child is a powerful one." (Indeed, this is what motivated doctors to attempt previous "cures.") He concludes that if couples from either of these groups "are given the choice of checking a box for which of 12 embryos are chosen, they might well choose the ones that aren't gay or lesbian."

## Bulwarks to Disaster

Green insists he's "not apocalyptic." Both he and LeVay believe disaster can be averted through activism and education. "Look at feminism," says LeVay. "If we could have done sex-selective abortions a generation ago, we would have had what we're seeing now in India," where fetuses are commonly aborted because they are female. "But sex selection doesn't happen in America because we've convinced people that a girl's life is worth as much as a boy's. I'm very optimistic we can prevent people from aborting gay kids not by outlawing it, but by changing the world so that people don't want to change sexual orientation."

1. At press time, human eggs have been frozen with some success, but the quality of frozen eggs remains poor. 2. A working draft of the entire human genome sequence was announced in June 2000.

Ironically, religious belief may actually protect gays. Fundamentalists are convinced life starts at fertilization, so they might feel constrained from aborting an embryo. ("They'd just torture it after it was born," quips gay activist Benjamin Schatz.) But no article of faith would restrain them from "curing" a fetus of its homosexual predisposition.

"I would favor changing [gays] to heterosexuals," says Vinson Synan, dean of Pat Robertson's Regent University. Why? "Because homosexuality is wrong, of course." The former chief rabbi of England, Lord Jakobovits, has given his blessing to eliminating homosexuality through genetic engineering. And Mahdi Bray, president of the National Muslim Political Action Center, an Islamic lobby, says that would offer "another way to help in dealing with the problem of homosexuality."

These religious leaders may yet have a chance to put their beliefs into practice. Scientists are working on ways to *change* human genes, fixing the genetic codes that cause a wide variety of diseases, including cancers and inherited conditions such as hemophilia. Called "genetic therapy" or "genetic surgery," this same technology could be used for genetic enhancement, the term for maximizing supposedly desirable traits, such as height, or the need for only a few hours of sleep per night.

If there are genes that influence sexual orientation, "we will learn how to interfere with or modify them," says genetic-therapy pioneer Theodore Friedmann. "It's inevitable that's going to happen."

## The Activist Breach

Despite this ominous prospect, not a single major gay organization is mobilizing to cope with these advances. And without activist prodding, the scientific community is keeping a studied silence. Eric Meslin, a director of the Human Genome Research Institute's Ethical, Legal and Social Implications branch, says it would be "inappropriate" to discuss the ethics of genetic testing or therapy for sexual orientation, because his department has funded no work in this area.

Among those who have leaped into this breach is openly gay journalist Chandler Burr, who wrote a book on the biology of sexual orientation. In 1996 he published a cover story in the conservative *Weekly Standard* arguing "that a conservatism unremittingly hostile to homosexuality . . . can, and should, embrace the gay gene." One of the main reasons, Burr writes, is the ability to change homosexuality to heterosexuality, something he "would not be opposed to considering" for himself.

## Studies of Sexual Orientation

As of yet, no one has found a specific gene or set of genes that influence sexual orientation. Most scientists ridicule the popular notion that there is a "gene for" any behavioral trait, or that genes mechanistically cause a complex human behavior. What a gene does is produce a protein, which then interacts with millions of other proteins in the body, and with environmental factors from diet to mental stimulation. For sexual orientation, the most genes can probably do is tilt the odds that someone will be gay or straight.

Still, evidence suggests that such genes exist, at least in men. To summarize the findings: Identical twins are more likely to have the same sexual orientation than either fraternal twins or brothers, who are in turn more likely to have the same orientation than adopted brothers.

(These studies sometimes uncover remarkable details, such as the pair of twin brothers who, living in separate cities and without knowing that the other was doing the same, photographed older shirtless construction workers and masturbated to the pictures.)

Studies of women are fewer and less clear. One showed results similar to what was found in gay men, but another produced no evidence that sexual orientation is inherited. Indeed, sexual orientation appears to be quite different in males and females. For example, while men are likely to describe themselves as straight or gay, many women say their orientation can change over time. And there is a clear-cut divergence between men and women in the most startling genetic research conducted so far.

In two studies, geneticist Dean Hamer found a correlation between a particular region on the X chromosome, called Xq28, and male homosexuality. The first study showed that gay brothers were much more likely to share genetic markers from this region than would have been expected by chance. In his second study, Hamer detected no linkage between lesbianism and the Xq28 markers, or any others. But he found again that gay brothers were more likely to share the telltale markers.

He also looked at straight brothers. "Sure enough, more often than not they had opposite DNA markers than their gay brothers," Hamer says. "This tells you there's a sexual orientation gene—get one version and you're more likely to be gay, get another and you're more likely to be straight."

> *"For sexual orientation, the most genes can probably do is tilt the odds that someone will be gay or straight."*

Hamer has not found this gene. In his book *The Science of Desire* he writes, "We narrowed the search to the neighborhood, the X chromosome—and even the block, Xq28—but we didn't find the house." The "block" probably contains about 200 genes. Once the genome project is complete, then, says LeVay, "it will be very easy for Dean to go back into his stored blood samples and see exactly which genes" correlate with male sexual orientation.

"It's highly unlikely" that Hamer's research will hold up, insists Stanford researcher Neil Risch. He points to other ballyhooed discoveries, such as a gene for alcoholism, that were later discredited. Indeed, a Canadian team has found no linkage so far between male homosexuality and the X chromosome. This "failure to replicate" is a major reason why scientists are reserving judgment.

## Correlation and Cause

Hamer's findings are controversial for other reasons. Some critics question whether homosexuality and heterosexuality are really stable and definable traits. Historian Jonathan Ned Katz points to a New Guinea tribe's rite of passage, in which boys fellate older men and swallow their semen, but then grow up to have sex with women. How can the terms *homosexuality* and *heterosexuality* define "this variability of historical and social custom?" he asks. "I believe sexuality can never be pinpointed in this way. It's too complex."

Even if Hamer has found a correlation, he may not have found a cause. As researcher William Byne has pointed out, genes might "cause the brain to be wired specifically for homosexual orientation." But it is just as likely that these genes "might influence personality traits that could in turn influence the relationships and subjective experiences that contribute to the social learning of sexual orientation."

*"In the future, genes for sexual orientation could be not only identified but altered."*

It's conceivable that both Hamer and his critics are right. Hamer found men without the "gay" Xq28 markers who nevertheless were homosexual—and straight men with the gay markers. "It's not like a switch," he explains. "Understand what a genetic test will be like. It'll say a fetus has maybe a 7 or 15 per cent chance of being gay instead of the usual 4 per cent chance. That's not much of a test."

But it could be enough. If a couple is staring at a panel of 12 embryos, says Green, "and one has Xq28 markers and the others don't, I think people will begin to engage in that sort of statistical analysis."

## Genetic Therapy

In the future, genes for sexual orientation could be not only identified but altered.

Already, scientists are developing ways to correct genetic defects that cause some diseases and cancers. Their main tool? Viruses, which are little more than chunks of DNA or RNA wrapped in a protein sheath. What scientists do is strip the virus of the elements that cause disease. Next they load it with the genetic "cargo" they want to deliver, such as a gene that corrects a mutation. The altered virus "infects" the proper cells, fixing the genetic flaw.

For adults who might want to change their sexual orientation, the dangers are profound. That's because after a certain point in childhood, the ability to acquire some complex behaviors—such as language—gets foreclosed. In a famous case written about by Oliver Sacks, a 50-year-old blind man was given his sight—but all he could "see" was a chaos of color and light. If the genetic basis of sexual orientation were changed in an adult, "that person would probably feel uncomfortable with their newfound sexuality," speculates LeVay. "All the socially constructed parts, which are substantial, would be out of sync with their new feelings."

"The poor guy would be trying to pick up chicks at Barneys and the opera," Hamer quips. "It would be awful," he says, getting serious. "One couldn't do that in isolation without all sorts of unpredictable consequences."

Since genetic therapy would probably work best on fetuses or newborns, the ramifications are similar to embryo abortion. If a "gay gene" is found, gay people will depend upon the kindness of parents.

Most parents are not that "Orwellian," [a term that refers to George Orwell's book *1984,* in which authority figures controlled all aspects of each individual] says Hamer, the father of a 12-year-old girl. "Part of the fun of having kids is that you can't predict everything."

But when push comes to shove, Hamer doesn't trust the world with a genetic test for sexual orientation. "I feel very deeply that such a test should never be developed," he says. "I don't underestimate the power of homophobia, so that's why I believe we will need rules and regulations" governing what genetic tests are allowed. But Congress hasn't even passed a gay rights bill, making it dubious that it would ban genetic testing for homosexuality.

Even "if this choice were available," says Green, "I'm not sure enough people would use it to make a significant impact." Yet, like many experts, his fears keep surfacing. It is "reasonable to assume," Green says, that many parents would terminate their gay embryos, a practice "that can reasonably be called genocidal."

"Given the stigma around homosexuality," says veteran gay activist Urvashi Vaid, the worst fears "are absolutely realistic." Merely a reduction of gay people could cause great suffering. Green says, "If enough people choose not to have gay and lesbian children, the political power of the community might dwindle," leaving those who live on more vulnerable to "majoritarian tyranny."

Green also worries that "collective harm" might befall the entire human race if the proportion of gay people shrank. He says, "We don't have the wisdom" to know what "the systematic elimination of a naturally occurring gene"

> *"It is 'reasonable to assume'*
> *. . . that many parents would*
> *terminate their gay embryos."*

would mean to our biological and cultural future. Indeed, studies have shown that homosexuality is linked to childhood gender nonconformity, a technical way of saying that gay boys are often "sissies" and lesbian girls "tomboys." American culture tends to denigrate such nonconformity, but it might leaven both masculine machismo and feminine meekness, making society overall less sexist. For boys, notes sexual-orientation researcher Richard C. Pillard, one of the "gender atypical traits" is fewer fistfights. "I'd like to believe," he says, "that gay people blend the best of male and female."

Of course, not all gay people manifest these traits. But as Elizabeth Birch, head of the Human Rights Campaign, a national gay political group, wonders: "What else are you flushing when you flush sexual orientation?"

## Ten Steps Behind

Despite the colossal stakes, "we have never taken it up as an institution, and we have no formal policy," says Birch. Similarly, the National Gay and Lesbian Task Force [NGLTF] is sponsoring a talk on the subject, but is taking no other specific measures. "I could give you some PR answer," says Benjamin Schatz, executive director of the Gay and Lesbian Medical Association, "but it would be bullshit. We haven't taken a policy line on this."

Says Vaid, "I don't know of any gay organization that is monitoring the bioethics or regulation of all this." Why isn't her own group—a strategic think tank sponsored by NGLTF—taking action? "I don't know!" she answers, taken aback. "We should. We will."

There is a lot to do. People with AIDS have muscled their way into the design of every trial, the approval of every drug, the debate over every law and regulation remotely affecting the disease. "That's what will be required here," says Birch, "becoming activist-experts who are absolutely steeped in the science and 10 steps ahead of it."

But activists are 10 steps behind, despite the fact that many of the leading researchers in this field—such as LeVay and Hamer—are gay. For example, one reason the genome project hasn't funded any investigations into ethical implications of gay-related research is that not a single proposal addressing sexual orientation has been submitted. What about a consensus statement signed by leading scientists declaring that all sexual orientations are healthy and should not be tampered with? "That's a good idea," says Hamer. But no one is doing it.

"There's a lot of policy obstacles we could put up," Vaid says, starting to brainstorm. "Insurance doesn't pay for cosmetic surgery, and homosexuality is not an illness or ailment that should be corrected. So I think we have some really good grounds to block" reimbursement for a test for sexual orientation or a "cure" via genetic surgery.

Perhaps the biggest obstacle to political activism is mustering urgency. The danger, after all, seems far in the future, and gay resources are limited.

> *"'Collective harm' might befall the entire human race if the proportion of gay people shrank."*

"I have a hard time faulting gay organizations for not prioritizing this when we're still in the middle of an HIV crisis and a hate-violence crisis," says Vaid. But scientists have a different view. "It seems distant," says Pillard. "But, you know, it's later than you think."

# Chapter 2

# Do Homosexuals Face Serious Discrimination?

# Chapter Preface

In October 1998, gay college student Matthew Shepard was brutally murdered outside Laramie, Wyoming. Shepard met his attackers, twenty-one-year-old Russell Henderson and twenty-two-year-old Aaron McKinney, at a Laramie bar the night of the murder. After telling Shepard that they were gay, the two men lured him out of the bar, and Henderson pistol-whipped him with a .357-caliber Magnum. Then the two men drove Shepard to a deserted area, strung him on a roadside fence, and beat him as he begged for his life. Shepard died at the hospital the next day.

The Shepard murder immediately led to increased calls for the enactment of state and federal hate crimes legislation that would increase the penalties for crimes motivated by bias. After Shepard's murder, the Wyoming legislature voted on several hate crimes bills in February 1999, but all were defeated. A majority of states have some kind of hate crimes laws on the books, but most of the laws do not cover sexual orientation, and enforcement is spotty. At the federal level, the Hate Crimes Statistics Act of 1990 requires the FBI to collect statistics on bias-motivated crimes, but it does not establish sentencing guidelines. The Hate Crimes Sentencing Enhancement Act of 1994 allows for stiffer sentences for hate crimes committed on federal property, but the act does not include sexual orientation. Efforts to pass the 1999 Hate Crimes Prevention Act—which would have added sexual orientation to the list of hate crimes covered by existing federal law—failed.

Supporters of hate crimes laws believe that hate crimes are uniquely harmful and should be punished more severely than other crimes. They claim that hate crimes, unlike random violence, targets groups of people in order to intimidate, which can fragment communities. As syndicated columnist Deb Price explains, "A hate crime isn't just an act of violence—it's a message. To the targeted victim, it says, 'How dare you think you have a right to be here.' And to the members of that targeted community, it says, 'You may be next.'" At the root of the argument for hate crimes laws is the assumption that harsher punishment for those who commit hate crimes will deter others from committing violence against individuals of hated groups.

Paradoxically, while many advocates of hate crimes legislation were exploiting Shepard's murder to pressure government to pass new laws protecting gays and lesbians, Shepard's parents were asking that his death not be used to further political goals. While many demanded increased punishment, in the end, the Shepards called for mercy. During the trial of Aaron McKinney, Judy and Dennis Shepard asked the court—which was considering giving McKinney the death penalty—to spare the life of the man who killed their son. In court, Dennis Shepard said to McKinney, "I too believe in the death penalty. I would like nothing better than to see you die, Mr. McKinney. However, this is the time to begin the healing process. To show mercy to someone who refused to show mercy." The court agreed, and McKinney was sentenced to two life sentences without appeal. In another trial, Henderson also received two life sentences.

What the nation will ultimately do about violence and discrimination against gays and lesbians remains to be seen. The campaign to enact federal hate crimes laws will certainly continue. Many feel that current state and federal laws are not sufficient to protect gays and lesbians in a nation where homophobia is the last accepted prejudice. But the Henderson and McKinney sentences also seem to suggest that special laws protecting gays and lesbians may not be necessary. After all, the two men received harsh punishment in a state that has no such laws. Opponents of hate crimes legislation reason that what needs to change is society's attitudes toward homosexuality, not sentencing laws.

To be sure, events in Wyoming have made violence against gays and lesbians more visible than ever. As Dennis Shepard said of his son's murder, "My son paid a terrible price to open the eyes of all of us" to the intolerance faced by the gay community. However, those concerned about discrimination against gays and lesbians will continue to disagree about the best way to reduce it, such as enacting hate crimes legislation. The authors in the following chapter debate whether discrimination against gays and lesbians is a serious problem and what actions should be taken to combat it.

# Discrimination Against Gays and Lesbians Is a Serious Problem

## by Byrne Fone

**About the author:** *Byrne Fone, professor emeritus at City University in New York, is the author of several books on homosexuality, including* Homophobia: A History, *from which this excerpt was taken.*

The new confidence and social visibility of homosexuals in American life have by no means conquered homophobia. Indeed, it stands as the last acceptable prejudice. In July 1993, *Newsweek* ran a report on American sexual diversity, in which homosexuality was positively discussed. One outraged reader responded: "Homosexuality is abnormal behavior. In no way, shape, or form is it a moral equivalent of heterosexuality. If this makes me a homophobe, I wear the label with pride." She was not alone.

### Homosexuals and the Church

As activist gay people battled homophobia, homophobes fought the social acceptance of homosexuality. Determined to protest any attempt to change traditionally antihomosexual positions, homophobes made their voices heard in houses of worship, science and medicine, and law enforcement. Religious institutions have always considered homosexual practice a matter for discipline, though some groups have made reforms. The Episcopal Church, for example, looks kindly on homosexuals, informally sponsoring gay religious groups, such as Integrity; some Episcopal priests perform "ceremonies of union" between gay couples. Some Reform Jewish groups sponsor gay synagogues and even support the right of gays and lesbians to enjoy civil marriage. The United Church of Christ allows noncelibate homosexuals to be ordained. The United Methodist Church, while insisting that it does not "condone the practice of homosexuality and consider[s] this practice inconsistent with Christian teaching," nevertheless concedes that homosexuals are people of "sacred worth."

For the most part, however, practicing homosexuals are not welcomed at God's table. The Roman Catholic Church continues to treat homosexuality as a violation of "moral" and "natural" law. An article in the Vatican's official newspaper, for example, urged Christians not to support political candidates who endorse same-sex marriages. The author, one Reverend Gino Concetti, insisted that all who support such candidates are open to "moral censure," since homosexual marriage would "undermine the foundation of the family model upon which human civilization was built." Concetti drew on the authority of Pope John Paul II, who has called such marriages catalysts for "moral disorder": "If the unions of homosexuals are a moral disorder, neither can they ever be legitimate on the legal or civil level."

Like conservative Catholics, most conservative Protestants (as well as Orthodox Jews) condemn homosexuality on the basis of the biblical prohibition. They argue that practicing homosexuals, having willfully chosen perversion, stand outside the divinely created natural order. So long as they persist in engaging in homosexual acts, they will be foreclosed from God's grace. While claiming to hate the sin but love the sinner, most conservative religious sects do the latter only if the homosexual agrees to reject the "homosexual lifestyle." That rejection can take many forms. Heterosexual marriage is one prescription for sexual salvation. Once homosexuals are, as it were, out of practice, they will supposedly cease to be homosexual. The practice of heterosexuality washes away homosexuality as

> *"Practicing homosexuals are not welcomed at God's table."*

baptism does sin. Homosexuals unable to find suitable partners can still achieve forgiveness, either through abstinence or through treatment by a number of "transformation ministries" dedicated to changing sexual orientation by a combination of prayer and "reparative therapy." It does not disturb the reparative therapists that at least thirteen ministries of one recovery group, Exodus, have closed because their directors reverted to homosexuality. Those who persist in homosexual activity, the conservatives affirm, deserve the judgment that God has surely intended for them.

## Religious Homophobes

Religious homophobes use any means that come to hand to punish homosexuals on earth, while confidently proclaiming that God's last judgment will fall upon them from heaven. And numerous religious leaders have preached against homosexuals from the pulpit, excoriated them in the media, initiated antigay programs in the schools, sponsored and funded attacks on their rights in the courts and the legislature. They have condoned—by silence—violence against homosexuals; some extreme sectarian homophobes actually incite and participate in antihomosexual violence. Some have even advocated a return to ancient punishments. George Grant, in *Legislating Immorality: The Homosexual Movement Comes out of the Closet* (1993), approvingly cites biblical and historical precedents for the execution of homosexuals. "Sadly," as Grant notes, "the 20th century saw this remarkable 2,000-year-old commitment suddenly dissipate." Grant's opinions are not unique. The antigay preacher Reverend Fred Phelps, prompted by the death penalty given one of the men who bombed the Federal Building in Oklahoma City in 1995, announced that "homosexuals, also, should have the death penalty." A

> *"[Homophobes] argue that homosexuals should be classified as psychological deviants and urged—or compelled—to seek treatment."*

Topeka, Kansas, religious organization that holds antigay demonstrations near the funerals of people who have died from AIDS carries placards asserting, "Gays Deserve to Die."

Perhaps in obedience to injunctions like this, a religious group calling itself STRAIGHT (Society to Remove All Immoral Gross Homosexual Trash) has dedicated itself to the cause of a "fag free America," and a Southern Baptist leader has threatened "the wrath of God on our nation if the government pursues civil rights for homosexuals." In the 1990s a bomb exploded in a lesbian bar in Atlanta, injuring a number of patrons; in Washington, five black gay men were murdered by someone authorities believe to be an antigay serial killer; two lesbians in Oregon were murdered "execution style," and the murder rate of gay men in Texas has risen so high that a magazine article in *Vanity Fair* refers to "The Killing Fields." The murder of Matthew Shepard—bound, tied to a fence, and beaten to death with a pistol by two men on a bleak winter night in 1998 in Wyoming because he was gay—was celebrated by a Kansas minister who praised God for the murder on his Web site, godhatesfags.com.

## Using Science and Law to Discriminate

Not every homophobe relies on religious doctrine. Many turn to science instead. Pointing to homosexuals' "abnormal" sexual practices, the real or imagined promiscuity of the "homosexual lifestyle," or their supposed gender-role confusion or effeminate manner, they argue that homosexuals should be classified as psychological deviants and urged—or compelled—to seek treatment. In this perspective, homosexuality is not a sin but a psychological fault, neither a choice nor an inherent condition, but the result of something going terribly awry in early childhood. As Charles Socarides, a conservative psychiatrist and author of *Homosexuality: A Freedom Too Far* (1995) puts it: homosexuality is a "neurotic adaptation" resulting from "smothering mothers and abdicating fathers." There are several variations on the theme that nurture is at fault, and although the American Psychiatric Association removed homosexuality from its official list of mental illnesses in 1973, a number of vocal practitioners still insist that homosexuality is a sickness, which can be cured through counseling or extensive psychoanalysis.

Other homophobes look to the law to control—and to criminalize—homosexuals, enlisting what could be called official or state-sponsored homophobia. For them, homosexuals pose an imminent—and constantly growing—danger to the institutions of society. Many claim that the government has the right and the duty to control homosexuals, to cast a watchful eye over their private as well as public activities, and to punish them for their sexual infractions. This attitude has infected even the U.S. Supreme Court, which in 1986 heard the case of *Bowers v. Hardwick,* brought under a Georgia law that defined as "sodomy" and declared criminal "any sexual act involving the sex organs of one person and the mouth or anus of another." That is, anyone, male or female, heterosexual or homosexual, could be prosecuted as a sodomite. In *Bowers v. Hardwick* the person discovered in such an act—Hardwick—was a homosexual; the act took place in his home. The illegal entry of police into his bedroom brought the case to the attention of gay civil rights lawyers, who argued that Hardwick's rights as an individual—not as a homosexual—had been violated. To much shock and outrage, the Supreme Court ruled that the invasion of Hardwick's privacy was justified on the grounds that what the court called "homosexual sodomy" was not protected even in private, because "the majority of the electorate of Georgia" believed "that homosexual sodomy is immoral." Though the Georgia sodomy statute does not penalize homosexuals per se, and though Hardwick did not appear before the court *as* a homosexual, it was as a homosexual that he was judged. His homosexuality as much as his homosexual activity figured in the decision of the court, which essentially asserted that no fundamental right of privacy attaches to consensual homosexual sodomy.

## Government's Role

On behalf of its armed forces, the U.S. government has also translated homophobia into law. Evidence of homosexual acts or of homosexuality had always been a legal reason for dishonorable discharge from the armed services. In 1996 the federal government allowed homosexuals to serve on the following terms: they would not be asked about their orientation, but they must not state it—the now infamous "don't ask; don't tell" compromise. Under this law, uniformed homosexuals must continue to hide if they wish to continue to serve. Obviously, the "don't ask; don't tell" policy is blatantly discriminatory, nor should anyone be surprised to learn that since its inception, witch-hunts to find evidence of gay sexual activity have continued and the number of men and women discharged for homosexuality has dramatically in-

> *"Homophobia is especially evident in antihomosexual legislation . . . , which [denies] to homosexuals the rights granted to other citizens."*

creased. Between 1998 and the end of 1999, more than 1,600 military careers were ended because of "don't ask; don't tell," and harassment of gay soldiers doubled. This law collaborates in sustaining the most oppressive kind of homophobia by creating the most oppressed kind of homosexuals: forced to be both invisible and silent.

Homophobia is especially evident in antihomosexual legislation, such as anti–gay rights initiatives, which deny to homosexuals the rights granted to other citizens. Bills prohibiting same-sex marriages have been introduced in more than half the state legislatures. In 1996 federal legislators passed, and the president signed, the "Defense of Marriage Act" (DOMA). DOMA turns heterosexuality into law. It declares that, legally, marriage may be defined only as the union of one man and one woman. Its effect is to ban same-sex marriage in the United States. Same-sex marriage would give to some homosexuals a chance to solemnize a lifelong union. That is the emotional and spiritual issue. Legally recognized same-sex marriage would obtain for gay and lesbian partners the legal benefits enjoyed by heterosexual couples, which they are now denied. That is the legal issue. The moral issue is that the Defense of Marriage Act—like all attempts to deny same-sex couples or gay or lesbian individuals equal rights— valorizes blatant heterosexism even as it promotes homophobia.

> *"Only some of the freedoms available to the heterosexual many are available to the homosexual few."*

In 1999, the Arizona legislature considered a bill to bar domestic partner benefits and strip them from gay couples who already enjoyed them. Judicial decisions favoring gay marriage have been handed down in Hawaii and Alaska; but in both states, popular initiatives effectively overturned the courts' decision. Nearly two-thirds of each state's voters chose to uphold only heterosexual marriage. A ruling by the Vermont Supreme Court in December 1999 sweepingly declared that under the state's constitution the Vermont legislature must legalize gay marriage or offer gay couples the benefits that heterosexual couples enjoy. Strangely, the court was unwilling to rule that gay people should be given marriage licenses. Instead, it handed the choice to the state legislature—that is, in effect, to the voters. By the end of 1999, thirty state legislatures had enacted laws against gay marriage, and antigay groups in twenty other states were moving to introduce statutes against both gay marriage and domestic partnerships benefits. Maine attempted to reverse a state law that prohibited discrimination against gay people in housing and employment. Forty states still allow employers to fire homosexuals summarily.

A much decorated and honored officer loses her commission on the grounds that homosexuals who reveal the fact are no longer fit to serve; a lesbian couple is denied custody of a child, who goes to the abusive father; the inheritance of the surviving partner of a long-term gay relationship is challenged by a distant and hostile family. The murderer of a gay man claims outraged manhood, and homophobia itself, as a defense: "Being a verry [*sic*] drunk homophobik [*sic*] I flipped out and began to pistol whip the fag with my gun." When homophobia taints the law, the government's claim to represent all of the people is fatally vitiated; only some of the freedoms available to the heterosexual many are available to the homosexual few.

## Saying "No" to the Gay Crusade

For students of homophobia—and most gay people are such students, however unwilling—the evidence of prejudice is everywhere. In June 1995, as gay people celebrated the anniversary of the 1969 Stonewall Rebellion [in which gays protested a police raid on the Stonewall Inn, a gay establishment], the *New York Post* published an editorial headlined "Saying No to the Gay Crusade." It praised a court decision to exclude gay groups from the St. Patrick's Day parade and argued that "there are plenty of other parades in which gay activists can prance about to their heart's content"; they should not use the St. Patrick's Day parade in "a deliberate attempt to secure legitimacy for a lifestyle millions of Americans consider unnatural and unhealthy." Though homosexuals "should not be subjected to illegal discrimination," the *Post* admits, yet the decision of the court has "significance" that "extends beyond constitutional law," since "society has sound reason not to treat their relationships as morally equivalent to heterosexual bonds." "In our view," the editorial continued, "the goal of the homosexual litigants is to secure judicial affirmation of homosexuality as a morally valid alternative lifestyle. . . . There's only one kind of family society should actively encourage: two-parent homes featuring a mother and father. Such arrangements are crucial to social cohesion."

Calling upon the terrors of the unnatural and the epidemic, conjuring the danger of an uncontrolled populace engaged in a destructive and perversely chosen lifestyle, the *Post* pictures homosexuals as an immoral minority crusading against the moral precepts and family values that millions of Americans, a moral majority, believe to be immutably true.

Homosexuals are confirmed in this inequality not by mere constitutional law, but by a higher tribunal—the moral law itself—from which there is no appeal. Society has "sound reason" not to treat homosexual relations as equivalent to heterosexual "bonds." That sound reason is the protection of "millions of Americans," of the heterosexual family, and of social cohesion. Such an overwhelming imperative can support a final, chilling implication—one all too familiar in the history [of homophobia]: to protect itself, society has equally sound reason to take whatever action may be necessary against those whose presence endangers it.

In daily life homophobia finds a habitation in newspaper editorials like the one in the *Post,* another in a declaration by U.S. senator Trent Lott that homosexuals are akin to alcoholics, sex addicts, and kleptomaniacs. Homophobia resides in fulminations against homosexuals delivered by TV evangelists, in slurs hurled from passing cars, in graffiti scrawled on walls, in a discharge from the armed forces after a painful investigation, in a summary eviction from an apartment, or in the loss of a job. Homophobia is a national issue and a national threat when politicians approve it, lobby for it, and legislate it, as has now happened in a majority of state legislatures and in Congress. A homophobic lobby in the House of Representatives has helped pass one measure denying federal housing money to a city because it supports homosexual domestic partners, and forced through another measure that takes away federal money from housing programs for people with AIDS so as to allocate it elsewhere. Homophobia threatens the fabric of the nation when school boards mandate that school districts shall "neither implement nor carry out any program or activity that has either the purpose or effect of encouraging or supporting homosexuality as a positive lifestyle alternative." Homophobia touches our lives when a group called the Family Research Council declares its intention on its Web page to "wage war on the homosexual agenda."

> *"It is in physical violence against lesbians and gay men that homophobia shows its most vicious face and its most terrible consequences."*

## Physical Violence

It is in physical violence against lesbians and gay men that homophobia shows its most vicious face and its most terrible consequences. Homophobes in federal and state legislatures have opposed legislation that would punish *all* hate crimes, because the proposed laws would punish violence based on sexual orientation. Indeed, in only eleven states is discrimination against homosexuals actually illegal; barely half have enacted any hate-crime laws directed against antigay violence. Across America, even as gay people registered political and social progress in the nineties, antigay violence increased. In 1995, the National Coalition of Anti-Violence Programs predicted that 1996 would show an increase in violence against gay men. The prediction was fulfilled. Antigay violence rose by 6 percent when general violence seemed to decline. In 1998 antigay violence rose 7 percent over the previous year—even as crime nationwide dropped by 4 percent. At this writing, the preliminary statistics for 1999 are no better.

Antigay violence increased not only against gay white men but against lesbians, gay people of color, and gay people younger than eighteen and older than sixty-five. Violence directed against gay people with AIDS increased by 32 percent. Nearly half of the perpetrators are white males (47 percent), with Latinos and African Americans being responsible for 22 percent and 21 percent of assaults respectively. Street attackers are usually groups of two or more young males in their teens and twenties, though violence committed by males under eighteen has increased by 21 percent. There is also an increase in the number of women willing to attack lesbians and gay men.

Not only did violence increase, but the intensity of the violence increased also. More and more of the attacks were physical assaults intended to inflict serious injury or death. Thirty-five percent of attacks *did* end in severe injury or death, while the incidence of simple harassment decreased. If words were used less, weapons were used more. The bricks and bottles of the past became clubs, baseball bats, lead pipes, and guns. Since the murder of Matthew Shepard in October 1998, thirty gay men have been murdered in America. In July 1999, Pfc Barry Winchell, an openly gay soldier who had been harassed by members of his U.S. Army company, was murdered by one of them, an eighteen-year-old private who beat him to death with a baseball bat while he slept. As the National Coalition of Anti-Violence Programs report observes: "The threat of homophobic violence exists everywhere—on the streets, in people's homes and at their place of work. This means that lesbians and gay men are being attacked by people they know and see on a regular basis, as well as by complete strangers. This reality robs lesbians and gay men of any safe places—even their homes— where they can feel free of the threat of violence."

# Homosexuals Seek Equal Rights, Not Special Rights

**by John Gallagher**

**About the author:** *John Gallagher is senior news editor for the* Advocate, *a national gay and lesbian newsmagazine.*

On February 16, 1998, Charley Mitchell went for a jog in Falmouth, Maine. He almost didn't come back. After Mitchell completed his five-mile run, he returned to his van, which is adorned with a rainbow flag, a pink triangle, and a bumper sticker for Maine Won't Discriminate, a group that had just failed in its attempt to defeat a referendum that removed the state's antidiscrimination protections from the books.

## Anti-Gay Backlash

"I remember reaching for my keys to the van, and the next thing I know, I was in a CAT scanner at Maine Medical Center," says Mitchell. While he wasn't looking, someone sneaked up on him and hit him over the head, possibly with a bat or a two-by-four. He suffered two fractures in his face, a concussion, a black eye, and cuts.

Mitchell was not robbed and has no known enemies. A psychiatrist who does outreach at soup kitchens and homeless shelters, he has lived quietly with his partner of eight years and the three children they have adopted. The only explanation that police can come up with for the attack is that Mitchell's van gave him away as gay.

As is common in the wake of antigay campaigns, reports of bias attacks are up. "The fact of the matter is, there is not just one bigot out there who would hit people and vote to take away our rights," says Mitchell. "There's a lot, a lot, a lot. You can't put all of them in jail. The point is that people have to understand what we are talking about. They've been fooled by the rhetoric of the religious right."

According to those who fought to repeal Maine's antidiscrimination law, gays like the bruised and bloodied Mitchell are seeking "special rights." It would be hard to imagine the campaign against Maine's gay rights law without the phrase special rights. From radio programs to voter pamphlets to direct-mail appeals, the Maine Christian Civic League and other supporters of the referendum drive repeatedly hammered home the belief that nondiscrimination protections for gays amounted to an unfair and undue advantage denied other people.

## The "Special Rights" Mantra

"'Special rights' was just the mantra of their camp," says Tracey Conaty, field organizer at the National Gay and Lesbian Task Force (NGLTF), who worked with Maine Won't Discriminate. "It permeated any sort of interview or spin they were doing."

With great success, as it turned out. On February 10, 1998, voters went to the polls in a special election to determine whether to retain the nondiscrimination protections passed by the legislature in 1997. When the results were in, the protections were repealed, by a slim margin of about 6,000 votes. Afterward Gov. Angus King, who appeared in commercials against the referendum, provided his own explanation about the loss. "I think people were concerned about the phrase special rights," he said.

After a decade of remarkable advances and increased acceptance, gay and lesbian activists continue to be dogged by the idea that they are somehow asking for more than anyone else. Protection from being unjustly fired from a job or from being thrown out of an apartment are beliefs to which most Americans subscribe. Yet when those same protections for gay men and lesbians are tagged as "special rights," many people readily agree with that assessment.

"It makes perfect sense that people are not in favor of special rights," says David Boaz, an analyst at the libertarian Cato Institute, a Washington, D.C., think tank. "In America we're in favor of equal rights." (Indeed, the pro-referendum forces in Maine recognized as much. The title of their campaign committee was YES TO EQUAL RIGHTS.)

At the same time, notes Boaz, the appeal of the "special rights" phrase is not based purely on principle. "I think among some parts of the population, there's a feeling we've been creating too many rights and have to draw a line somewhere," he says. For many people, it's easiest to draw the line at gay rights. "There is an animus against gays that is touched upon by the campaigns against special rights," says Boaz.

"'Special rights' is an Achilles' heel for us right now," concedes Conaty. "We haven't been successful as a movement in countering it, and we're paying the price."

## Appealing to the Dispossessed

In Maine—as elsewhere—"special rights" played best to certain groups of people. "The people to whom the 'special rights' argument was made were not a large portion of the population, but it was significant," says William Coogan, a professor of political science at the University of Southern Maine. "It basically appeals to white men who have a high school education or less, people who are insecure in their jobs, and people who feel that all kinds of other groups are getting a break. They see this not as an equal-protection question but as a zero-sum game, one in which the gains of one group will come at their expense."

The argument is often given a boost by the claims that gays and lesbians come from a privileged background to begin with. Citing surveys about the appeal of the gay market, opponents of gays rights are able to characterize gays as holding professional positions, earning above-average wages, and owning their own homes. They cite such claims that gays take more vacations than other consumers and are twice as likely as the general population to have a college education.

> *"Gay and lesbian activists continue to be dogged by the idea that they are somehow asking for more than anyone else."*

"There's a reservoir of belief that gay people as a whole are very privileged economically," says Mary Bonauto, an attorney at Gay and Lesbian Advocates and Defenders, a legal group in Boston that provided legal assistance to Maine Won't Discriminate. "There are people who are still anxious about the future and their ability to hold a job. Those factors animate part of the 'special rights' rhetoric. It's what gives the rhetoric any force."

To make the rhetoric still easier to take, opponents of the Maine nondiscrimination law were able to recruit Alveda King, niece of [civil rights activist] Martin Luther King Jr., to claim that gay rights falls outside the realm of acceptable civil rights. "No one is enslaving the homosexual or making them sit in the back of the bus," she said during her visit to the state. "Homosexuality is a moral, and not a civil rights, issue."

## Decided by Ideologues

How much the "special rights" rhetoric mattered in Maine is a subject of debate among political analysts. The unique nature of the referendum in Maine—a single-issue special election held at an unusual time of year—meant that only motivated voters were likely to show up. Paul Volle, a leader of the referendum movement, predicted that the election would be "decided by ideologues" on both sides of the issue.

Only 30% of the registered electorate voted, about half the usual turnout in Maine elections. "People have their day-to-day lives," says Bill Nemitz, a columnist for the *Portland Newspapers*. "Many people turned on the 11 o'clock news that night and said, 'Damn, I forgot to vote.'"

The "special rights" rhetoric had the power to energize conservative Christians, the referendum's core of supporters. Indeed, most of the Christian Civic League's focus was on getting those voters to the polls. With an advertising budget that was, at best, one third that of Maine Won't Discriminate's, the group did little to target a mass audience. Instead, in effect, it preached to its own choir. For example, the Christian Coalition of Maine distributed 240,000 fliers at 900 conservative churches. The fliers underscored the implicit threat of pedophilia with such questions as "Do you want to send your children or grandchildren to day cares, preschools, and schools that are forced to hire homosexuals?"

> *"The 'special rights' rhetoric [has] the power to energize conservative Christians."*

Sometimes the implied threat is made explicit. In Fairhaven, Mass., Leo and Jackie Pike hung signs on their porch when they discovered that two of their neighbors, Brad Sousa and David Brunelle, were gay. In a kind of vigilante warning system that equated homosexuality with pedophilia, the Pikes' signs informed passersby with the message WARNING!! THERE ARE KNOWN HOMOSEXUALS IN THE NEIGHBORHOOD. WATCH YOUR YOUNG BOYS AT ALL TIMES. THEY ARE LOOKING FOR CHICKENS.

On February 11, 1998, the Pikes were convicted of violating Sousa's and Brunelle's civil rights under a statute covering anyone protected under state law. The conviction was only possible because Massachusetts has a law prohibiting discrimination against gays and lesbians—exactly the kind of law repealed in Maine.

"I think they were able to scare some people," says Robin Lambert, a gay activist in Portland. "They talked about whether homosexuality should be taught in school."

## Using Jesus

The referendum forces made no secret of the fact that they were running against homosexuality in general, not just the legislation on the ballot. "We said homosexuality is immoral and it's wrong," said Michael Heath, head of the Christian Civic League. For the most part and by design, that message was only by conservative Christians.

"The Christian Civic League used Jesus a lot," says Lambert. "They said Jesus would not approve of our lifestyle. Their core of supporters was very energized by this. I don't think they changed many minds."

"The primary argument was based on religious grounds," says Coogan. "I think that 'special rights' could be more powerful." Coogan says that when conservatives mounted an antigay initiative in 1995, the argument was used to greater effect among voters. The effort failed in the general election that year. "The argument was met at the time by a strong argument of the economic impact of turning down civil rights," he says. "That argument wasn't made this time."

The "vote no" effort was hampered by a number of other strategic missteps. Although the Christian Civic League began gathering signatures for a referendum last summer, the campaign against the referendum did not get off the ground until after the special election was called. Activists around the state complained that rural counties were written off, allowing the antigay side to go unchallenged and rack up huge vote margins. Similar problems contributed to the gay activists' loss in battling Colorado's antigay Amendment 2 in 1992.

The Maine referendum's success provided a much-needed boost for the Christian Coalition, which has been reeling from financial woes and an uncertain sense of direction since the departure last year of its director, Ralph Reed. The week after the election, the coalition announced a Families 2000 plan to recruit 100,000 church liaisons in time for the November 2000 elections. Among the issues the strategy plans to target is gay rights.

## The Same Old Story

For gay activists, perhaps the most frustrating aspect of the Maine loss is that the same argument, and especially the "special rights" charge, has been used with devastating effect over and over again during the past ten years. The phrase has been employed continuously in contemporary gay rights battles since 1988, when Lon Mabon of the Oregon Citizens Alliance formed the No Special Rights Committee to run one of his antigay campaigns. Despite its long history, activists have yet to develop an adequate response to "special rights" rhetoric.

"It's brilliant," says Donna Red Wing, national field director of the Human Rights Campaign (HRC), a national gay group, who first encountered the phrase in 1990 as head of the Lesbian Community Project in Portland, Oregon. "I remember the first time I saw the banner that said, NO SPECIAL RIGHTS FOR HOMOSEXUALS," she recalls. "I remember thinking, right, no special rights for anybody. It resonates with everyone."

Since Oregon, "special rights" has been used regularly in the battle over gay rights. The phrase was a staple of the 1992 antigay campaigns in Colorado and Oregon. The name of the 1993 referendum effort to repeal Cincinnati's nondiscrimination ordinance was EQUAL RIGHTS, NOT SPECIAL RIGHTS. "It was the only billboard the Right had during the campaign," says Betsy Gressler, former president of Stonewall Cincinnati, a gay group. The phrase has also been employed in statewide electoral battles in Washington and Idaho as well as in numerous local controversies and is enshrined as the title of the antigay video *Gay Rights/Special Rights.*

> *"The 'special rights' charge ... has been used with devastating effect over and over again."*

The expression has even shown up in presidential campaigns. In 1996, for example, Senator Bob Dole, the Republican nominee, announced, "I don't favor creating special rights for any group."

The phrase plays on the belief, borne out in polls, that gays and lesbians are already protected under current law. "When you hear about gay rights and you think gays are already protected, it's not a huge leap to think it's special rights, especially if someone is feeding you that phrase," says Red Wing.

## Equal Rights, Not Gay Rights

Useful as shorthand as it may be, the phrase gay rights may only fuel the "special rights" argument. "It reached the point whenever I wrote about it, I made a very conscious effort to get away from gay rights," says Nemitz. "Every time I referred to it, I would write 'equal rights for gay people.' Gay rights implies something different from other rights."

"I think we have to get away from calling it gay rights," agrees Lambert. "It wasn't called black rights. It was called civil rights or equal rights. Gay rights feeds into the 'special rights' rhetoric."

Boaz says that, as a libertarian, he believes that nondiscrimination laws in general are inappropriate. "There are unfortunate things that happen in our lives that the coercive force of government should not be applied to," he says. "On the other hand, it seems we continue to create new special rights for groups ranging from the disabled to people of Appalachian origin, and none of those create the backlash that creating rights for gays and lesbians does."

> *"The phrase ['special rights'] plays on the belief . . . that gays and lesbians are already protected under current law."*

"Special rights" was dealt a severe blow in 1996 when the Supreme Court explicitly rejected the idea as an accurate depiction of the protections gays are seeking. In his majority opinion striking down Colorado's Amendment 2, Justice Anthony Kennedy wrote, "We cannot accept the view that Amendment 2's prohibition on specific legal protections does no more than deprive homosexuals of special rights. To the contrary, the amendment imposes a special disability upon those persons alone. Homosexuals are forbidden the safeguards that others enjoy or may seek without constraint."

Few are acquainted with the opinion, however. "The lawyers are all gratified that the phrase was exposed as ridiculous," says Bonauto. "But Justice Kennedy doesn't work on the stump."

## A Movement's Shortcomings

One reason the phrase has remained potent lies with its use in campaigns, where strategies are short-term. "In the heat of a campaign, you often don't have the opportunity to do education work," says Red Wing. "But the fact is, for ten years we have had the opportunity. An education campaign should probably be much further along. It's not as though we heard 'special rights' for the first time in Maine."

Some gays are more pointed in their criticism of the movement's shortcomings. "Homosexuals are the least effective minority group in presenting their point of view to the majority," says David Brudnoy, an openly gay radio talk show host in Boston. "Blacks have marched and died for their rights. Gay people just simply will not speak up. Defeat is caused as much by the lassitude of the homosexual population as it was by the craziness of the religious right."

Activists believe that the loss in Maine is a call to redouble basic education efforts. "We have made tremendous cultural progress, but politically we lag behind," says Kerry Lobel, executive director of NGLTF. "We need to get back to the basics of telling our stories in ways we don't often do anymore. You tell your story for a long enough time, and you think that surely everyone understands. But clearly people don't understand it unless we tell them over and over again."

"We have to get back out ahead on this," agrees Elizabeth Birch, executive director of HRC. "That message of 'special rights' is very, very potent, and we have to be more muscled and more clever in dealing with it."

Ultimately, the phrase special rights may best be countered not with another, equally catchy sound bite but with increased gay visibility, something that relies more upon individuals than organizations. "We say it over and over again, but it's absolutely true," says Birch. "When someone knows someone who is gay, their support goes way up. The more people come out, the more we will be on a quicker path to protection."

Mitchell agrees that given the proper knowledge, most people will back protections for gay men and lesbians. He points to a patient of his, "a good-hearted guy," who voted for the repeal because he believed the Right's assertion that teachers would be teaching students homosexuality. At the same time, the patient, who only discovered Mitchell's sexual orientation after the publicity surrounding his beating, told him, "The next time somebody bothers you, call me up, and I'll beat the crap out of him."

"He doesn't wish us harm, but he doesn't know enough," says Mitchell. "It seems to me there are lots of innocent people who hear things and don't know how to interpret them. There are probably more people who are uninformed than there are those who are hateful. If we can convince the uninformed, the hateful can do what they want. We'll be OK."

# Gays and Lesbians Face Discrimination in the Military

**by Carl Rowan**

**About the author:** *Carl Rowan was a former diplomat and prize-winning journalist whose work was syndicated around the country.*

I can't believe that President Bill Clinton did not know that it was morally wrong, and absolutely unworkable, to say to gay Americans that to fight for their country they, in effect, had to stay "in the closet."

I can't believe that first lady Hillary Clinton did not tell the president privately, even then, that it was insulting and a violation of every concept of equal justice to force homosexuals to live a lie, even as they tolerated circumstances of second-class citizenship.

When the Pentagon first adopted its "don't ask, don't tell" policy, I wrote that it was an abomination that contradicted all the Clinton administration rhetoric about justice and its opposition to hate crimes. All that policy did was set gays' apart as soldiers who were less than soldiers and foster the hatred and physical attacks that this administration professed to deplore.

Now, after Mrs. Clinton dared to say publicly that the policy has been a failure, the president agreed. He and Defense Secretary William Cohen have asked the Pentagon for a full review of the policy.

We don't need to guess what some in the military hierarchy will say: Letting openly declared homosexuals serve alongside straight military people will be destructive to morale. I know that the issue of racial desegregation of the military is different in many ways, but I cannot escape the memory that some admirals and generals were using the "morale" argument to justify Jim Crow in the military during and right after World War II. Dwight Eisenhower and others said that if blacks and whites were put in the same units, they would fight forever over women and whisky.

The doomsayers were wrong about racial integration, and they are wrong in their predictions of a calamity if homosexuals are treated as human beings.

I know the argument that if homosexuals serve as openly declared gays they will be sexual harassers and predators. Well, most of us have worked at radio and TV stations, in government agencies, or somewhere, with gay people. We have found them to be good colleagues, not mindlessly aggressive predators.

The word "review" makes me fear that the Pentagon is searching for a new scheme that will fall short of what is right: to simply treat gays the way everyone else is treated. Enforce the rules regarding harassment, sexual activity, dating and everything else the same way with gays as with straights.

There is hope in the fact that both Democratic candidates for the presidency, Vice President Al Gore and former Senator Bill Bradley, have disavowed "don't ask, don't tell." But the winner of the Democratic nomination is likely to face Texas Governor George W. Bush, who has said that he will not meet with gay groups. No one can be sure what stance he would take as commander in chief on the issue of gays in the military.[1]

This means that political posturing and passions are likely to dominate decisions that ought to be based only on national security interests. Certainly we need the brains and brawn of all able-bodied Americans in our defense establishment, and a homosexual serving openly is no security threat compared with one who fears

> *"[The policy] was insulting and a violation of every concept of equal justice to force homosexuals to live a lie."*

being "outed" or having his or her sexual orientation used against him or her in any way.

Our military must say not only, "We don't ask," but that it doesn't give a damn as long as soldiers and sailors do their jobs and live by the military codes.

Sometimes justice is so simple we feel compelled to kill it with complications and stupid games.

---

1. George W. Bush did not overturn the "don't ask, don't tell" policy when he became president in 2000.

# Hate Crime Laws Are Necessary to Protect Gays and Lesbians

## by the Human Rights Campaign

**About the author:** *The Human Rights Campaign works for lesbian, gay, bisexual, and transgender equal rights.*

Lesbian, gay, bisexual and transgender Americans are frequent targets of vicious hate crimes. Yet only in rare circumstances can the federal government assist in the investigation and prosecution of hate crimes committed against someone because of his or her real or perceived sexual orientation or gender. This prevents federal law enforcement authorities from assisting in these cases in the same fashion as hate crimes based on race, color, religion or national origin. The Human Rights Campaign (HRC) advocates for the addition of actual or perceived gender, sexual orientation and disability to the laws governing prosecution of hate crimes, and believes that these hate crimes should be investigated and prosecuted on an equal basis as other categories of hate crimes currently covered by state and federal law.

### Hate Crimes Affect More than Just the Individual Attacked

All violent crimes are reprehensible. But the damage done by hate crimes cannot be measured solely in terms of physical injury or dollars and cents. Hate crimes rend the fabric of our society and fragment communities because they target a whole group and not just the individual victim. Hate crimes are committed to cause fear to a whole community. A violent hate crime is intended to "send a message" that an individual and "their kind" will not be tolerated, many times leaving the victim and others in their group feeling isolated, vulnerable and unprotected. According to a study funded by the Department of Justice's Bureau of Justice Statistics, 85 percent of law enforcement officials recently surveyed recognized this type of violence to be more serious than similar crimes not motivated by bias.

Statistics support that gay, lesbian and bisexual Americans are often targeted for violence. Under the Hate Crimes Statistics Act, *the Federal Bureau of Investigation (FBI) consistently reports hate crimes based on sexual orientation are the third highest reported category of hate crimes,* behind race and religion, respectively. "Sexual orientation" is currently not included in any federal criminal civil rights laws. Since many times gays and lesbians are not "out" to their families, coworkers or even friends, they feel they have no one to seek assistance from or even discuss the hate violence they have experienced.

Hate crimes are often inordinately severe, sometimes going well beyond the force needed even to kill someone. For example, in a hate crime in Texas, a gay man died after being stabbed 35 times.

## An Underreported Problem

Law enforcement experts agree that when compared to other crimes, hate crimes are underreported to the police. Minority groups, including gays, lesbians, bisexuals and transgender individuals, have historically had strained relations with law enforcement and fear what is called "re-victimization" when they go to the police. For gays and lesbians, re-victimization can consist of the police verbally or physically attacking the individual who reports the crime, blaming the victim ("if you weren't outside a gay bar, you wouldn't have been beaten up") or unwillingness to write up a police report.

> *"Hate crimes rend the fabric of our society and fragment communities because they target a whole group and not just the individual victim."*

In a study funded by the National Institute of Mental Health, researchers found that only one-third of victims of anti-gay hate crimes reported the incident to police compared to 57 percent of the victims of random crimes. As this study indicates, many victims of anti-lesbian and anti-gay incidents do not report the crimes to local law enforcement officials because they fear that their sexual orientation may be made public—that they will be "outed" to family, employers or in some other way—or that they would receive an insensitive or hostile response, or they would be physically abused or otherwise mistreated. The National Bias Crimes Training for Law Enforcement and Victim Assistance Professionals calls this phenomena "secondary injury" which is the victim's perceived rejection by and lack of expected support from the community.

A graphic example of this occurred as a result of the bombing of the predominantly lesbian bar, The Otherside Lounge, in Atlanta in February 1997. Five bar patrons were injured severely enough to be taken to the hospital by ambulance. However, one victim who had shrapnel wound refused to be treated when she saw media swarming the hospital emergency room.

Further, in jurisdictions where people know that there are no hate crime laws covering sexual orientation or real or perceived gender, they are less motivated to report such crimes to authorities. If a perpetrator cannot be prosecuted, victims may think it a waste of time and energy to report the crime. A Department of Justice report released in October 2001 confirms that hate crimes are underreported; that a disproportionately high percentage of both victims and perpetrators of hate violence are young people under 25 years of age; and that only 20 percent of reported hate crimes result in arrest.

## Hate Crimes Statistics

Even though hate crimes based on sexual orientation are underreported, the number of hate crimes reported suggest an appalling amount of bias-motivated violence against gays and lesbians. Since the Federal Bureau of Investigation began collecting hate crime statistics in 1991, more than 9,700 hate crimes based on sexual orientation have been reported. Since 1991, reported hate crimes based on sexual orientation have more than tripled and consistently rank as the third highest category after race and religion, which made up 53.8 and 18.3 percent, respectively, of the total, 8,063 in 2000.

The FBI's 2000 Uniform Crime Reports—the most recent year we have statistics—showed that as overall serious crime decreased slightly nationally, with the Crime Index at its lowest level since 1978, reported hate crimes have continued to rise and increased 2.3 percent from 1999 to 2000. Reported hate crime based on sexual orientation comprised 16.1 percent of all hate crimes for 2000 for a total of 1,299. At the same time, the number of law enforcement agencies participating in reporting hate crimes decreased from 12,122 to 11,690. In addition, 1,317 were reported to the FBI for 1999; 1,260 were reported in 1998; 1,102 were reported in 1997; 1,016 such incidents were reported in 1996; 1,019 such incidents were reported in 1995; and 685 and 860 such incidents were reported in 1994 and 1993, respectively.

The National Coalition of Anti-Violence Programs (NCAVP), a non-profit organization that tracks bias incidents against gay, lesbian, bisexual and transgender people, reported 2,151 incidents for 2,000 from only 11 jurisdictions, compared to the 11,690 jurisdictions reporting to the FBI. The NCAVPs reported 1,992 incidents for 1999; 2,552 in 1998;

> *"The number of hate crimes reported suggest an appalling amount of bias-motivated violence against gays and lesbians."*

2,445 incidents in 1997; 2,529 in 1996; 2,395 in 1995; 2,064 in 1994; and 1,813 in 1993.

A December 2001 report by the Southern Poverty Law Center (SPLC), a non-profit organization that monitors hate groups and extremist activity in the United States, in its year-end Intelligence Report (Winter 2001) went so far as to say that the system for collecting hate crime data in this nation is "in shambles." SPLC estimates that the real number of hate crimes being committed in the United States each year is likely closer to 50,000, as opposed to the near 8,000 collected by the FBI.

## Current State Laws Are Inadequate

Only twenty-seven states and the District of Columbia currently have hate crime laws that include "sexual orientation" in the list of protected categories. Forty-five states have hate crime laws, but their listing of categories do not all include "sexual orientation." Five states have no hate crime laws whatsoever.

In May 1997, South Carolina Attorney General Charles Condon drafted a hate crime bill for his state in response to the burning of numerous African-American churches there. His draft bill did not include sexual orientation because, according to Condon's legislative lobbyist, "Nobody has demonstrated to us that there's a problem [with people being attacked because of their sexual orientation], so we decided to take action against race-based hate crimes." There were at least four documented reports of anti-gay hate crimes in the state in the previous year. A hate crime victim from South Carolina also testified before the Senate Judiciary Committee in June 1997 about a violent beating that occurred in April 1996 that left him without hearing in one ear, broken ribs and forty-seven stitches in his face. He had been beaten by thugs screaming "we're going to get you, faggot" and was left for dead in a trash bin outside a primarily heterosexual bar in Myrtle Beach, S.C.

## Federal Law Is Also Inadequate

Currently, only two federal hate crime statutes include "sexual orientation":

The Hate Crimes Statistics Act (PL 101-275) became law in 1990 and was reauthorized in 1996. This law requires the FBI to collect statistics on hate crimes on the basis of race, religion, ethnicity, sexual orientation and disability. Although the FBI is required to collect and analyze the statistics from local and state law enforcement agencies, the local and state agencies are *not* required to provide statistics to the FBI. *This law does not allow federal assistance in investigation and prosecution of hate crimes or enhance penalties for hate crime perpetrators, it simply compiles statistics from the various local and state jurisdictions that report to the FBI.*

The Hate Crimes Sentencing Enhancement Act (PL 103-322) was passed as a part of the Violent Crime Control and Law Enforcement Act of 1994. This law directs the U.S. Sentencing Commission to provide sentencing enhancements of "not less than three offense levels for offenses that the finder of fact at trial determines beyond a reasonable doubt are hate crimes." This law is considered the federal counterpart to state hate crime penalty statutes, to be used for hate crimes committed on only federal property, such as national parks. Because the law can only be used when a crime is perpetrated on federal property, it is only very rarely used.

A broad coalition of groups, including 175 civil rights, civic, religious, state

and local government associations and law enforcement organizations, supp
legislation to amend current federal criminal civil rights law under 18 U.S.C.
245. These changes would provide authority for federal officials to investigate
and prosecute cases in which the violence occurs because of a victim's actual or
perceived gender, sexual orientation and disability, and would eliminate an
overly restrictive jurisdictional obstacle to prosecution. This legislation, the
Hate Crimes Prevention Act, was originally introduced in 1997 after a White
House Conference on Hate Crimes.

Since then, the majority of the U.S. Congress voted in support of the legislation when a revised version, the Local Law Enforcement Enhancement Act,
[LLEEA], was offered as an amend-
ment to the Senate Department of
Defense Authorization bill in June
2000. The bill passed the Senate in a
bi-partisan vote, 57 to 42, including
13 Republicans. In September 2000,
the House passed a motion to instruct

> *"Forty-five states have hate crimes laws, but their listing of categories do not all include 'sexual orientation.'"*

in support of the measure, 232 to 192, including 41 Republicans. Despite these
strong votes, opponents of the legislation were able to strip the bill from the
DoD bill before the end of the 106th Congress. The bill has been reintroduced
in the 107th Congress with a record number of original cosponsors
(S. 625/H.R. 1343). The Human Rights Campaign supports this bill and will
work for its passage.

18 U.S.C. 245 is one of the primary statutes used to combat racial and religious
violence. The statute currently prohibits intentional interference with enjoyment
of a federal right or benefit, such as going to school or employment, on the basis
of the victim's race, religion, national origin or color. Under this statute, the government must prove the crime occurred because of the victim's race (or other protected category) and because he or she was enjoying a specifically enumerated
federally protected right. These dual requirements have severely restricted the
ability of the federal government to act in appropriate cases.

While state and local authorities have and will continue to play the primary
role in the investigation and prosecution of hate violence, federal jurisdiction
would provide an important backstop to ensure that justice is achieved in every
case. The LLEEA limits the federal government's jurisdiction to only the most
serious violent crimes directed at persons, resulting in death or bodily injury,
and not property crimes. This bill would allow states with inadequate resources
to take advantage of Department of Justice resources and personnel in limited
cases that have been authorized by the attorney general and enables federal,
state and local authorities to work together as partners in the investigation and
prosecution of bias-related crimes. [As of June 2002, the Local Law Enforcement Enhancement Act had not been passed.]

# Americans Have Become More Accepting of Homosexuality

## by Jeni Loftus

**About the author:** *Jeni Loftus is a Ph.D. candidate in the department of sociology at Indiana University.*

Since the Stonewall riots in 1969 [during which patrons of The Stonewall Inn, a gay establishment, resisted a police raid], there have been many steps both forward and backward for gays and lesbians in the United States. They have gained social acceptance among certain subgroups of the population while facing increased hostility from others. But what major gains, if any, have been made in Americans' attitudes toward homosexuality?

Research suggests that Americans have become increasingly liberal in their opinions about civil liberties, especially those regarding African Americans and females. Research suggests that this liberalization is beginning to be extended to gays and lesbians. Yet the research on attitudes toward homosexuality is contradictory and has not systematically explored the causes and patterns of opinion change over time.

## Demographics and Ideology

Two factors might account for changes in American attitudes toward homosexuality. First, the changing demographic makeup of the population might explain these changes. Research demonstrates, for example, that those with more education are more liberal in their attitudes toward homosexuality, and thus increasing educational levels may account for an increasing liberalism in attitudes toward homosexuality. Second, shifts in cultural ideologies might explain these changes. If so, attitudes toward homosexuality are embedded within other attitude beliefs, such as attitudes toward sexuality generally. Thus, any increasing or decreasing liberalization in attitudes toward homosexuality would be a function of changes in other attitudes.

If increasingly positive attitudes toward homosexuality can be largely accounted for by changes in the demographic makeup of the United States, this would suggest no major attitude change has occurred in relation to homosexuality. That is, there would only be more people in the population with demographic characteristics that are associated with more liberal attitudes. If, on the other hand, changing demographics cannot account for changes in attitudes toward homosexuality, but changes in other attitudes can, this would suggest that the change is part of a larger cultural ideological shift. Overall, Americans may be becoming more liberal, and homosexuality may be but one aspect of this trend. Finally, if changing attitudes toward homosexuality cannot be accounted for by changes in demographics or attitudes, this would indicate that the change in these attitudes is independent of demographic and cultural ideological shifts. In this case, perhaps there is something unique about Americans' attitudes specifically toward homosexuality, and the gay liberation movements have had some success in gaining acceptance for gays and lesbians.

I address three main questions: (1) Over the past 25 years, what has been the pattern of change in attitudes toward homosexuality? (2) To what extent can these changes in attitudes be attributed to demographic changes in the population? (3) To what extent can these changes in attitudes be attributed to changes in other attitudes generally?

## Attitudes Affect Behavior

Are shifts in attitudes worth studying? Debate surrounds the issue of whether attitudes are indicative of behavior. Richard LaPiere argued that one's responses to a question about an object are too abstract and have no context to allow us to predict how the individual will behave when he or she encounters the actual object. Therefore, how one responds to a survey question concerning attitudes toward a group will not accurately reflect how the respondent will act when encountering an individual from that group. Martin Fishbein and Leek Ajzen argue, however, that attitudes do impact behavior. In their theories of "Reasoned Action" and "Planned Behavior," they posit that beliefs about an object impact attitudes toward an object, which impact intention toward an object, which impact behavior toward an object. Thus, one's attitudes toward a group will affect one's behavior toward that group.

> *"Those with more education are more liberal in their attitudes toward homosexuality."*

Mary Jackman argues that the putative liberal shift in American attitudes is superficial—individuals may report liberal attitudes but they do not act on them. Jackman subsequently argues that dominant groups develop liberal ideologies to justify their social positions, but liberalization in attitudes generally does not lead to social change. This body of work questions the importance of studying public opinion, arguing that such opinions do not usually lead to action. If this is true, why study changes in attitudes toward homosexuality?

Research suggests that, contrary to Jackman's arguments, attitudes do matter. The treatment of a group is affected by the attitudes held by others about that group. Fishbein and Ajzen argue that although one cannot necessarily predict a particular behavior based on a particular attitude, one can expect the valence of one's behaviors to be in accordance with the valence of one's attitudes. Thus, attitudes will impact behaviors.

Recent research suggests that broader shifts in attitudes are reflected in broader shifts in behavior. Reynolds Farley documents the changes in American attitudes toward African Americans and the changes in their legal treatment. Since World War II, Americans have become increasingly more likely to support equal rights for African Americans, and during this time, numerous laws and policies that denied equal rights to African Americans were overturned. Farley does not argue that all Americans support equal rights for, or hold positive attitudes toward African Americans; however, there has been a trend in this direction that corresponds with changes in law and policy.

Clem Brooks finds that changing attitudes have had a significant impact on vote choice and on the outcome of presidential elections since 1972. Thus, the increasingly liberal attitudes held by Americans are not superficial, because Americans do act on these attitudes. Furthermore,

> *"One's attitudes toward a group will affect one's behavior toward that group."*

Mary Burstein argues that governments pay attention to, and act on, the opinions of their citizens, therefore attitudes affect public policy. Thus, changes in attitudes toward homosexuality in the United States may be genuine changes with significant implications.

## Prior Research on Attitudes Toward Homosexuality

Several studies have examined changes in attitudes using the National Opinion Research Center General Social Surveys (GSS), the best data available for studying shifts in these attitudes. Analyzing data from 1973 to 1977, Norval D. Glenn and Charles N. Weaver find a small but significant increase in positive attitudes regarding the morality of homosexuality. Edmund F. Dejowski finds a decline from 1973 to 1988 in American's willingness to restrict the civil liberties of homosexuals, which he partially attributes to increasing levels of education. Robert C. Smith reports a decline from 1973 to 1991 in the willingness of respondents to restrict the civil liberties of homosexuals but he finds an increase in the belief that homosexuality is always wrong. While Smith finds that age is becoming a less important determinant over time of attitudes toward homosexuality, he did not explore whether changes in the age structure of the population accounted for changing attitudes. Other demographic and cultural ideological shifts have occurred since 1973 and perhaps these changes can account for the bulk of the changes in attitudes that Smith finds.

Alan S. Yang, using data from 1973 to 1996, finds that attitudes toward the morality of homosexuality remained steady until the 1990s, but liberalized thereafter. Willingness to restrict the civil liberties of homosexuals has declined steadily since 1973. Yang did not consider how changes in demographics or other attitudes may have contributed to these attitudinal shifts. It is unclear, then, to what extent these changes in attitudes are independent of, or are a product of, the changing demographics or cultural ideological beliefs.

## Changing Demographics

Research on attitudes toward homosexuality typically has focused on characteristics that differentiate people with positive and negative attitudes. The literature generally concludes that older, less educated people, African Americans, people living in the South or Midwest, males, people residing in small communities, and religious fundamentalists are more negative toward homosexuality than are younger, more educated people, whites, those living on the Pacific Coast, females, residents of big cities or big city suburbs, and religious liberals.

The last quarter century has seen important demographic shifts that may have had countervailing effects on attitudes toward homosexuality. Research has failed to take these shifts into account, even though research indicates that these factors can influence reports of attitudes toward homosexuality. Specifically, several changes in U.S. demographics should lead to more positive attitudes toward homosexuality. The most pronounced change is the increase in those with a college degree. Between 1970 and 1997, the percentage of adults with at least a college degree more than doubled, while the percentage with less than a high school degree decreased. The GSS data indicate that those who lived on a farm when they were 16 years old decreased by half between 1973 and 1998, while those who lived in a big city suburb nearly doubled. GSS data also indicate that the number of liberal Protestants and those with no religion increased from 1973 to 1998. Fundamentalist Protestantism peaked in the mid-1980s and has been on the decline since. Research suggests that those with more education, who live in urban areas, or are religious liberals tend to hold more positive attitudes toward homosexuality, and thus the increase in these segments of the population should indicate a positive shift in attitudes.

Other population shifts might indicate a negative shift in attitudes toward homosexuality. The most pronounced shift in this direction is the aging of the population; the median age steadily increased between 1974 and 1997. The percentage of whites and percentage of females in the population have slightly decreased. Because those who are older, nonwhite, or male tend to hold more negative attitudes concerning homosexuality, these changes might lead to negative shifts in attitudes.

A shift in the regional location of the population might have countervailing consequences on attitudes toward homosexuality. Research suggests that those living in the Midwest and the South have the most negative attitudes, and those on the Pacific Coast have the most positive attitudes. While the proportion of the population living in the Midwest has declined, it has increased in the South and the Pacific, suggesting countervailing effects on attitudes toward homosexuality.

Demographic changes, then, may explain a significant amount of the change in attitudes toward homosexuality in the last quarter century. However, the population shifts that have occurred should lead to both negative and positive changes in attitudes.

## Changing Attitudes in the American Population

Shifts in public opinion have occurred among the population over the last quarter century. Smith, studying attitudes from World War II to the late 1980s, finds increasing liberalism, particularly concerning race relations, women's rights, equal rights, abortion, civil liberties, and sexual morality. However, during the mid-1970s, this liberalizing trend slowed in some areas or was even slightly reversed. Benjamin I. Page and Robert Y. Shapiro find a similar pattern: Attitudes became increasingly liberal through the 1960s and 1970s, but hit a plateau in the 1980s. This research suggests that attitudes toward homosexuality would become slightly more liberal during the 1970s and then level off. However, because their data end in the late 1980s, these studies do not indicate what changes might have occurred in attitudes toward homosexuality after that time period.

General Social Survey (GSS) data indicate that general attitudes have changed over the time period. Americans have become increasingly supportive of premarital sex, but decreasingly supportive of extramarital sex. Americans are decreasingly likely to restrict the civil liberties of atheists, but slightly more willing to restrict the civil liberties of Communists. A cyclical pattern is evident in political views, with liberals ranging from 24 percent to 31 percent of the population, and conservatives ranging from 30 percent to 39 percent. From the 1970s through the mid-1980s, Americans held increasingly traditional religious beliefs, with more people supporting prayer in school, and believing the Bible was the literal word of God. These beliefs declined in the early 1990s, and then increased again in the late 1990s.

If attitudes toward homosexuality are embedded within larger cultural ideological changes, I would expect to see either an overall positive shift in attitudes toward homosexuality, or that attitudes become more negative through the early 1980s, more positive until the early 1990s, and then more negative again in the late 1990s. If, however, changing demographics accounts for the change in attitudes, then I might expect to see a more positive shift in attitudes toward homosexuality. Although changing demographics lead to countervailing effects, the shift toward a better-educated population is the most pronounced shift over the last 25 years. . . .

## Attitudes Have Changed

[By examining data from the General Social Survey—a national area probability study—between 1973 and 1998, I have concluded that] attitudes toward the morality of homosexuality and the willingness to restrict the civil liberties of homosexuals have changed in the last quarter century. Americans' attitudes regarding the morality of homosexuality became slightly more liberal from 1973 to 1976, became increasingly conservative through 1990, and have become more liberal since 1990. Over the same 25-year period, willingness to restrict the civil liberties of homosexuals declined steadily, the only departure being a brief increase in negative attitudes in the late 1980s. Changes in the demographics of the population account for about one-third of the change in attitudes toward homosexuality, specifically, increasing levels of education. The shifts in attitudes toward the morality of homosexuality hold up even with controls for beliefs about the morality of sex outside of marriage, political views, and traditional religious beliefs. Shifts in attitudes toward civil liberties of homosexuals hold up apart from trends in attitudes toward greater civil libertarianism, political views, and traditional religious beliefs. About half of the pattern of change in attitudes toward homosexuality can be accounted for by demographic and cultural ideological shifts in the United States. Thus, change in attitudes is partially independent of other changes in the population, as measured here.

> *"The liberalization of public opinion on homosexuality . . . can be attributed at least in part to the political activism and visibility of [homosexual] communities."*

Two points still need to be addressed: (1) Why are the trend lines different for the judgment of the morality of homosexuality and the willingness to restrict the civil liberties of homosexuals? (2) What accounts for the change in attitudes that cannot be explained by the changing demographics or cultural ideological beliefs in the United States?

The American public clearly makes a distinction between whether homosexuality is morally wrong and whether homosexuals should be allowed certain civil rights. While the public still overwhelmingly views homosexuality as wrong, the majority is unwilling to restrict the civil liberties of homosexuals. Two possibilities help explain this distinction.

## Morality Versus Civil Liberties

First, the "morality" question of the GSS concerns homosexuality as a practice, while the "civil liberties" questions concern gays and lesbians as a group. Thus, the morality question focuses directly on homosexual behavior, particularly sexual behavior, while the civil liberties questions focus on issues of minority group status. The morality question may be picking up Americans' puritanical attitudes concerning sexuality, and gay sexuality in particular, while the civil liberties questions do not call up these puritanical attitudes.

Strategies to evoke or avoid this sexual image of gays have been used by both sides of the debate on homosexuality. How political arguments are framed has a profound impact on their reception in the public. Gay activists often have found it easier to gain public support by focusing political campaigns on their rights as a minority group. By likening themselves to other disadvantaged groups, they encourage the public to think of gays and lesbians as disadvantaged and discriminated against. Those on the religious right often try to vilify gays and lesbians by calling forth images of gay sexuality and portraying them as hyper-sexualized, predatory, and deviant. This frame separates gays and lesbians from other minority groups, portraying them as somehow morally suspect.

Questions about morality also call forth images of "free will" and "choice" with regard to homosexuality. Research indicates that people who believe that homosexuality is a choice are more likely to condemn it than do those who believe that gays and lesbians are born that way. The religious right argues that gays and lesbians are not like other minority groups because they have chosen their lifestyles, therefore other groups genuinely deserve civil rights protections while gays and lesbians do not. The religious right has profiled a number of "ex-gays"—individuals who have chosen to become straight—as a way of re-asserting that homosexuality is a freely chosen, and sinful, behavior.

Second, examining the distinction made by Americans between the morality of homosexuality and civil liberties for homosexuals, it is useful to compare the situation of homosexuals with that of other minority groups. Since World War II, an increasing number of Americans have supported equal opportunity for African Americans; however, although in 1990 the majority of white Americans believed that African Americans should have equal opportunity, whites still held many negative stereotypes about African Americans. This suggests that the distinction between morality and civil liberties is not unique to the situation of gays and lesbians. This distinction emphasizes the definition of "tolerance" in political sociology, whereby an individual grants rights to a particular group even though he or she dislikes that group.

## Reasons for Change

What caused the change in attitudes toward homosexuality that cannot be accounted for by the changing demographics and cultural ideological beliefs of the population? There are several possibilities. Epstein (1999) writes that the liberalization of public opinion on homosexuality in the United States can be attributed at least in part to the political activism and visibility of the lesbian/gay/ bisexual/transgender communities. In 1960, no cities or states protected the rights of gays and lesbians, sodomy was outlawed in every state, and no openly gay or lesbian individuals held elected office. By 1997, 11 states and many cities and counties had passed legislation protecting the rights of gays and lesbians, 30 states and the District of Columbia had abolished their sodomy laws, and a number of gays and lesbians held elected office.

Although the gay movement is said to have begun in the early 1950s, it received a jump-start in June of 1969 with the riots at the Stonewall Inn in Greenwich Village. Since then, the gay liberation movement has been visible throughout the United States. The movement made significant gains in the 1970s, but the emergence of AIDS, the rise of the religious right, and the election of a social conservative as president in the 1980s set the movement back. This may be reflected in the increasingly negative attitudes toward the morality of homosexuality and the temporary reversal in the long-term trend of increasing civil libertarianism in this time period. As the public began to disassociate AIDS and gay men in the early 1990s, and as the liberation movement made some public moves, such as the National March on Washington and the 25th anniversary of the Stonewall Riots, attitudes toward homosexuality began to become more positive again. The gay liberation movement has been publicly active in gaining rights and access for gays and lesbians, and its activism appears to have led to more positive attitudes toward homosexuality.

> *"Americans appear to be gradually becoming more accepting of homosexuality."*

Still other possibilities exist as causes of the change in attitudes toward homosexuality. The concern in the United States for the distinction between private morality and public control could affect attitudes toward homosexuality. Individuals may feel it is wrong to be homosexual, but may not want the government to legislate morality, and therefore they do not support restricting the civil liberties of homosexuals. The success of radical elements of the religious right during the 1980s may have caused a backlash in the 1990s, producing more liberal attitudes. Other liberal movements such as the civil rights and women's movements may have influenced attitudes toward homosexuality by making people aware of the discrimination against other disenfranchised groups. Perhaps the shift in attitudes occurred because of greater media attention to gay and lesbian issues, apart from the activism of the gay and lesbian liberation movements. . . .

Previous research has not systematically examined the change in attitudes Americans hold toward the morality of homosexuality and the civil liberties of homosexuals. I examined how demographic changes and cultural ideological shifts in the American public have impacted changes in attitudes toward homosexuality. These factors account for some, but not all, of the change in attitudes observed over time. An increasing number of individuals are unwilling to restrict the civil liberties of homosexuals, and a decreasing number of individuals believe that homosexuality is always wrong. Americans appear to be gradually becoming more accepting of homosexuality, independent of shifts in demographics and cultural ideological beliefs in the population. It is possible that these changes in attitudes are due largely to the gay and lesbian liberation movements.

# Gays and Lesbians Should Not Be Given Special Rights

**by Justin Raimondo**

**About the author:** *Justin Raimondo is a San Francisco writer.*

The gay activists of yesteryear asked government to leave them alone. Their political program centered on decriminalizing homosexual relations between consenting adults. But today, as tolerance of homosexuality grows, gay activists are increasingly turning to government to impose their agenda on society. Though state power has been used as a bludgeon against gay people since at least the Middle Ages, suddenly today's gay leaders seem to be picking up the club themselves, saying, "Now it's our turn." This is a great irony—and a potential cause of trouble for homosexuals and turmoil for America.

## Rebelling Against Government

The birth of the gay liberation movement in America can be dated to the evening of June 27, 1969, when patrons of the Stonewall Inn, a homosexual bar in Manhattan, resisted a police attempt to close the place down. For three days a neighborhood rebellion effectively kept the police from carrying on the ancient tradition of shaking down gay bars and busting the ones that didn't pay up. In the official complaint, the operators of the Stonewall were cited for not having a liquor license. But even if they had applied, it is doubtful their request would have been granted: the state licensing bureau was notoriously hostile to gay establishments. The first modern gay protesters, then, were rebelling against regulation. Indeed, liberation from government generally was a central idea of gay liberation.

But something happened to divert the gay movement from this original goal. Today, the so-called gay rights movement sees government as the agency, not the enemy, of liberty. From socialized medicine to anti-discrimination legislation to mandatory "tolerance" lessons in the schools, there is no scheme to increase the power of government these alleged freedom fighters do not endorse.

As long as homosexual acts between consenting adults are illegal in some states, I believe organizations dedicated to their repeal have a legitimate place in the constellation of human rights causes. Beyond this strictly limited goal, however, a political movement based on sexual orientation is a grotesque aberration. The fact that the gay rights movement has taken on an increasingly authoritarian style is the inevitable result of basing political allegiances on clan loyalties instead of philosophical principles.

## Only Individual Rights

In a free society there are no gay rights, only individual rights. For homosexuals and heterosexuals alike, these rights boil down to a single principle: the right to be let alone. Politically, the gay rights movement must return to its early libertarian roots. This would begin the vital process of de-politicizing homosexuality and defusing a dangerous culture war the gay minority can never win.

Even the state "neutrality" that gay "centrists" like contributing writer at the *New York Times* Andrew Sullivan advocate would force government treatment of homosexuality as on a par with heterosexuality, as seen in Sullivan's demands for gay pseudo-"marriage" and open gays in the military. True neutrality, however, would involve not recognition but indifference, inattention, inaction. A neutral state would neither penalize nor reward homosexual behavior. It would neither forbid nor would it grant legal status to homosexual marriage. In a military setting, a neutral state would subject all sexuality to the same rigorous regulation.

Gays must reject the nonsensical idea that they're oppressed by "heterosexism," a vile ideology that subordinates and denigrates homosexuals by insisting on the centrality of heterosexuality in human culture. There is no escaping human biology, however much such a project entrances cloistered academics who imagine that human sexuality is a "social construction" to be altered at will. Homosexuals are and always will be a rarity, a tiny minority necessarily outside of the traditional family. The heterosexual "bias" of social institutions is not something that needs to be imposed on a reluctant society by an oppressive state, but a predilection that comes quite naturally and inevitably. If this is "homophobia," then nature is a bigot. If gays use the power of

> *"In a free society there are no gay rights, only individual rights."*

the state to correct this historic "injustice," they are engaged in an act of belligerence which will rightly be seen as a challenge to the primacy of the traditional family.

Even many gay liberals recognize that the gay rights model has outlived whatever usefulness it may once have had. The idea of gay people, particularly gay men, as a victim group is so contrary to reality it is no longer sustainable. In economic, political, and cultural clout, gays wield influence way out of proportion to their numbers, a fact which has spawned numerous conspiracy theories. . . . The idea of a powerful homosexual cabal is a persistent theme in conspiracy literature, one that mimics the form and style of anti-Semitic lore.

Overlaid with the victim propaganda of the past 20 years, this image of hidden homosexual power combines to produce a quite unappealing character: a creature of privilege constantly whining about his plight. If the gay political leadership is so concerned about the alleged rise of anti-gay bigotry, perhaps they will take care to project a less bash-able image.

As a specialized contingent of an army dedicated to ramming "multicultural" socialism down the throats of the American people, the gay lobby capitalizes on the worst insecurities of its constituents. Holding up the bogeyman of the "Religious Right" to keep the troops in line, the gay politicos point to Senator Jesse Helms [who has been charged with being homophobic] and say, "Without us, you wouldn't have a chance against him."

But in fact no major religious conservative has called for legal measures against homosexuals. The Christian Coalition, the Eagle Forum, and other grassroots conservative activists only involved themselves in supposedly "anti-gay" political activities defensively, in working to overturn gay rights legislation that attacked their most deeply held beliefs.

> *"The volatility of the issues [that gay rights activists] are raising . . . risks a social explosion for which they must be held accountable."*

The leadership of the gay movement is playing with fire. The great tragedy is that they will not be the only ones burned. The volatility of the issues they are raising—which involve religion, family, and the most basic assumptions of what it is to be human—risks a social explosion for which they must be held accountable. The boldness of the attempt to introduce a "gay positive" curriculum into the public schools, the militant victim stance that brooks no questioning, the blunt intolerance once they gain power in urban ghettos like San Francisco—all this, combined with the fact that the gay rights paradigm itself represents an intolerable invasion of liberty, is bound to produce a reaction from the majority.

## Gay Rights Fiction

It's time to challenge the fiction that the "gay rights" movement speaks for all or even most gay people. It does not. Gay rights legislation violates the principles of authentic liberalism, and homosexuals should speak out against it—to distance themselves from the excesses of a militantly destructive movement, to help avert societal damage, and to right some grave wrongs. Those wrongs are the political assault being waged on the heterosexual family by the theoreticians of the gay rights revolution; the endless ridicule of religion that suffuses the gay press; and the limitless contempt for all tradition and "bourgeois values" that permeates the homosexual subculture.

And the search for a gay "ethnicity" is as much a dead-end as the effort to forge a gay political movement. In no sense is homosexuality comparable to being, say, Armenian. There is no gay culture separate from the culture in general, and in spite of pseudoscientific claims to the contrary, there is no genetically encoded gay race. There is only behavior engaged in by a diverse range of individuals, each acting from his or her own motives and predispositions.

Efforts to sanctify such behavior, or to explain it in such a way that it has no moral content, are counterproductive as well as unconvincing. Attempting to somehow reconcile homosexuality with the customs and religious beliefs of the majority is to concede the one right that people, gay and straight, really do have—the right not to have to justify one's existence.

The obsession with "coming out," and the essentially feminine self-centeredness such a ritual implies, is surely another aspect of the gay movement that has to go. Do we really need to know the sexual proclivities of our neighbors and co-workers, or even our brothers and sisters, aunts and uncles?

To expect approval or official sanction for so personal a matter as sexuality is a sign of weak character. To unblushingly ask (nay, demand) such approval in the form of some act of government is an act of unparalleled bad taste. It is also a confession of such a devastating lack of self-esteem, of inner emptiness, that its public expression is hard to fathom. Self-esteem is not a quality to be sought from others, nor can it be legislated into existence.

The history of the gay movement reveals that ideology and Eros are antipodes. Politics, said writer George Orwell, is "sex gone sour," and sour certainly describes the worldview of gay rights dogmatists. This is evident just by looking at them: Beleaguered on every side by a "heterosexist" society, and usually too homely to get a date, these poor souls have so politicized their sexuality it can hardly be said to exist.

Instead of the preening moralism of gay "visibility," a sensible resolution of the Gay Question would call for a return to the joys of private life, the rediscovery of discretion and even anonymity. The politicization of everyday life—of sex and the core institutions of the culture—is a trend to be fiercely resisted, not just by gay people but by lovers of liberty in every sphere of human endeavor.

# Gays and Lesbians Are Treated Fairly by the Military

**by Charles Moskos**

**About the author:** *Charles Moskos is a professor of sociology at Northwestern University.*

President Bill Clinton has joined the bandwagon against his own "don't ask, don't tell" policy on homosexuals in the military. In a radio interview, Mr. Clinton cited the brutal murder of Pfc. Barry Winchell at Fort Campbell, Ky., as evidence that the policy doesn't work. Earlier Hillary Clinton pointed to the increase in the number of people discharged for homosexuality to make the same point.

The claim that the policy isn't working does not stand up to scrutiny. Consider the Winchell case. Pvt. Calvin Glover was convicted in a court-martial last week of bludgeoning Winchell to death; other soldiers testified that Winchell had been the target of vicious taunts by his fellow servicemen. But how does this implicate "don't ask, don't tell"? Had Winchell been openly gay, would his fellow soldiers have been more restrained? Indeed, opponents of homosexuals in the military could easily use the murder to argue that the military should return to its traditional policy of asking one's sexual orientation and discharging anyone even suspected of being homosexual.

## Command Was Deficient

In any case, Defense Department regulations specifically state that "hostile treatment or violence against a service member based on a perception of his or her sexual orientation will not be tolerated." Clearly, it was the command in Winchell's unit, not the policy, that was deficient.

The increase in homosexual discharges since "don't ask, don't tell" also requires examination. The number of discharges for homosexuality *has* almost doubled since the implementation of the policy—to 1,145 in 1998 (still less than 0.1% of the force) from 617 in 1994. More than 80% of such discharges in recent years are for "statements," purportedly voluntarily given by the service numbers. The number of discharges for homosexual "acts" have actually declined since 1994.

Gay-rights advocates argue, of course, that the growth in discharges for "statements" is largely the result of commanders improperly seeking out homosexuals. Undoubtedly that sometimes happens. Yet commanders now report being worried that they might be accused of conducting "witch hunts," and thus will process an alleged homosexual only when a blatant case of "telling" is dumped in their lap.

Let me offer an alternative hypothesis on the increase in "statements." Whether you're gay or not, saying you are is now the quickest way to leave the military with an honorable discharge. That almost all discharges for homosexuality occur in the first term of enlistment, and more than half in the first year, gives some credence to this interpretation.

Furthermore, identifying oneself as homosexual carries less stigma than it once did. Consider that white male soldiers are twice as likely to be discharged as black men. White women are four times as likely to be discharged as black women. Are commanders singling out whites and investigating their sexual orientation? It's much more likely the stigma against homosexuality is stronger in the black community than among whites generally, and thus blacks are less willing to declare that they are gay.

> *"Whether you're gay or not, saying you are is now the quickest way to leave the military with an honorable discharge."*

The policy toward homosexuals in the military must be appraised in terms of the fundamental principles that underlie the ban. "Don't ask, don't tell," which I helped design, was a compromise between those, such as Mr. Clinton, who favored allowing homosexuals to serve openly and those, including a majority in Congress, who believe that "homosexuality is incompatible with military service," in the words of the 1993 law that authorized the policy. The Pentagon policies are, in fact, somewhat more lenient than the language of the statute.

No one can seriously argue that homosexuals across the board are ineffective soldiers, sailors, airmen or Marines. Many homosexuals have served with distinction. What is at issue is allowing those who are *openly* homosexual into the military. Proponents of lifting the ban are quick to draw an analogy between the exclusion of homosexuals and racial segregation in the military. But the proper analogy is not black and white but male and female.

Sex between service members undermines order, discipline and morale. So does invasion of sexual privacy. That is why the military separates the living quarters of men and women. If members of the armed forces were able to go their own way off duty, as those in most civilian occupations can, there would be no serious argument against allowing open homosexuals in the armed forces. But the military is an institution that requires enforced intimacy and lack of privacy.

## Stripped of Privacy

Nowhere in our society are the sexes forced to undress in front of each other. Most women—and many men—dislike being stripped of privacy before the opposite sex. Similarly, most heterosexual men and women dislike being exposed to homosexuals of their own sex. If we respect women's need for privacy from men, then we ought respect those of heterosexuals with regard to homosexuals.

Of course, there are concealed homosexuals in the military who function just fine. But that is the point. Closeted homosexuals do not cause feelings of invasion of privacy precisely because they are covert. One could argue that homosexuals could be accommodated in today's military by rearranging living areas as is already done for men and women. But it boggles the mind to think of the characterizations that would accrue to all-homosexual military groups. In any event, gay-rights advocates have never seriously pushed for this option.

Sure, there are foolish reasons for excluding homosexuals from the armed forces. But that doesn't mean we should ignore the good ones. Any policy that involves large numbers of people will be applied imperfectly. But "don't ask, don't tell" brings to mind what [former British prime minister] Winston Churchill once said about democracy: It is the worst system possible, except for any other.

# Hate Crime Laws Are Unnecessary

## by Robert H. Knight

**About the author:** *Robert H. Knight is the director of cultural studies at the Family Research Council, a research and educational organization that promotes the traditional family.*

The Family Research Council, which I represent, deplores criminal violence in any form, and believe it should be punished to the full extent of the law. We also believe that Americans should continue to work diligently toward racial reconciliation.

## Hate Crime Laws Are Seriously Flawed

However, we strongly oppose the 1999 Hate Crimes Prevention Act (HCPA), which is fundamentally flawed on numerous counts.[1]

It sets up special classes of victims, who are afforded a higher level of government protection than others victimized by similar crimes, violating the concept of equal protection.

It would politicize criminal prosecutions, pressuring local agencies to devote more of their limited resources to cases that the federal government deems important.

It would add nothing to the prosecution of real crimes of violence, vandalism, or property destruction, which are already covered by statutes in every state, and which should be punished to the full extent of the law.

It would vastly expand the power and jurisdiction of the federal government to intervene in local law enforcement matters.

It would have a chilling effect on free speech by making unpopular ideas a basis for harsher treatment in criminal proceedings. Over half of the so-called "hate crimes" in the last Justice Department report were categorized, by the department, as intimidation or simple assault, which do not necessarily involve

---

1. Congress did not pass the Hate Crimes Prevention Act.

From Robert H. Knight's testimony before the Senate Committee on the Judiciary Regarding the Hate Crimes Prevention Act of 1999, May 11, 1999.

anything more than words. This makes name-calling literally a federal case.

The definition of what constitutes a "hate crime," while clear in some instances, is very unclear in others.

In recent weeks we have seen even the mildest statement of traditional sexual morality attacked as "bigotry," "hatred," "gay-bashing," "intolerance," "prejudice," and "ignorance." Homosexual activists have even suggested that statements opposing homosexuality amount to inciting violence. Incitement, as you know, is not constitutionally protected speech. The aim seems to be to silence all opposition to acceptance of homosexuality.

## Overestimating the Extent of Hate Crime

According to FBI statistics, "hate crimes" comprised less than 1/10 of 1% of total violent and property crimes in 1997. In 1997, police agencies in 48 states and the District of Columbia reported "hate crimes" at a rate of less than one case per law enforcement agency, the vast majority of which are already covered under existing federal law. The most frequently reported—nearly half—of those incidents (or crimes) not covered, involve verbal intimidation, some of them no more than name-calling. But the backers of this Act want to give the federal government massive new powers based on the incidence of about a dozen incidents per state in a nation of 270 million citizens.

Leah Farish, an attorney specializing in civil rights issues, points out that "hate crime" statistics vary widely. She notes, "Advocacy groups consistently overestimate—for their own political purposes—the numbers of hate crime that are reported by law enforcement."

One such organization, the National Institute Against Prejudice and Violence, estimates the victims of what it terms "ethnoviolence" to be between 800,000 and one million students annually. However, the FBI's own statistics on bias incidents on school campuses show 555 in 1992 and 799 in 1996.

The New York City Gay and Lesbian Anti-Violence Project claims that in 1996 there were 18 anti-gay incidents in Cleveland, 176 in El Paso, and 96 in Chicago. However, FBI statistics reported only 2 in Cleveland, 1 in El Paso, and 6 in Chicago.

At a press conference in January of 1998, Attorney General Janet Reno said, "I see more anti-bias training and conflict resolution programs than ever before in our schools, in our communities, and I see them working." Miss Reno also admitted that in most cases, local and state agencies already have the authority to act on the problem—and are doing so.

## Explaining Federal Power

Still, she backs the HCPA, which grants the federal government far-reaching new powers under the Interstate Commerce Clause. If someone calls a homosexual a name while making use of the facilities of interstate commerce, this bill could cover it. It is no wonder that the federal government has grown by leaps and bounds in recent years when the agents of centralized power employ such logic.

The *Washington Post* has warned of the dangers of focusing on motivation rather than criminal acts. In a December 1, 1997, editorial, the *Post* contended, "[T]he proposal would be largely redundant of state laws, getting federal prosecutors and agents involved in crimes that have only limited interstate dimensions." The *Post* further noted that "[e]xpanding the federal ability to differentiate what are called hate-crime acts from analogous acts committed for other reasons is a mistake that Congress should refrain from making."

The *Post*'s views are echoed by such liberal commentators as William Raspberry, Clarence Page, Michael Kelly and Nat Hentoff, as well as conservative columnists Jeff Jacoby, Maggie Gallagher, Tony Snow, Paul Craig Roberts and others.

Michael Kelly writes, "Of all the violence that has been done in this great expansion of state authority over, and criminalization of, the private behavior and thoughts of citizens, none is more serious than that perpetuated by the hate-crime laws. Here, we are truly in the realm of thought crimes. Hate-crime laws require the state to treat one physical assault differently from the way it would treat another—solely because the state has decided that one motive for assaulting a person is more heinous than another."

> *"[Hate crime laws] would have a chilling effect on free speech by making unpopular ideas a basis for harsher treatment in criminal proceedings."*

Clarence Page writes, "As an African-American, I belong to one of the groups currently protected by hate crime legislation. Yet, hate crime laws have not made me sleep better at night. I am more likely to lay awake wondering how I can justify the noble intent of such laws with the violence they inflict on the principles of free speech and equal protection of the law."

## Thought Crime

In effect, the HCPA creates thought crime, because the criminal acts themselves are already prosecutable. The Family Research Council believes that maintaining good order through swift prosecution and consistent, strict punishment of real crime is imperative. But justice must be impartial, without favored classes of victims or specially censured perpetrators. Creating special classes is inconsistent with the Constitution's 14th Amendment guarantee of equal protection under the law.

Furthermore, some in the media and in government have begun to interpret public opposition to normalizing homosexuality as "hate." Homosexual activists have characterized even mild formulations of opposing views as a proximate cause of violence. As football great Reggie White and Senate Majority Leader Trent Lott learned in 1998, expressing the biblical view that homosexual activity is sinful is scarcely tolerated among some activists and media members, who equate it with yelling "fire" in a crowded theater.

The 1998 Truth in Love advertising campaign, in which former homosexuals gave the good news that all people are loved by God and have the hope of salvation and that homosexual behavior can be changed, was blamed for gay student Matthew Shepard's murder in Wyoming in 1998, despite zero evidence that the perpetrators had ever seen the ads or been influenced by them in any way. The San Francisco City Supervisors went on record as directly blaming pro-family groups for Mr. Shepard's death. If an undiluted message of love is considered grounds for charges of complicity in a murder, then we have moved far down the road toward silencing anyone who holds to traditional morality. In Canada, it is already a federal offense to criticize homosexuality over the airwaves. The hate crimes bill paves the way in America for similar throttling of opinion.

> *"The Hate Crime Prevention Act creates thought crime, because the criminal acts themselves are already prosecutable."*

## Creating Special Categories of Victims

Homosexuals, like other citizens, should be protected to the full extent of the law. But that is not what this bill is about. Rather, the HCPA is the centerpiece of an effort to place homosexual behavior above criticism by portraying those who practice it as victims in need of special protections not afforded to other Americans. There simply is no credible evidence that the police and courts are allowing criminals to prey on homosexuals more than on any other citizens.

America has nearly 20,000 homicides each year. In 1997, three of 18,209 homicides were associated with "sexual orientation—less than two-hundredths of 1 percent of total homicides. And this does not count the "gay-on-gay" killings that occur much more frequently.

Family Research Council unequivocally condemns all violent crime, committed for any reason, including the fatal attack on Mr. Shepard in Wyoming. We believe that Matthew Shepard is as important and deserving of attention as any of the thousands of other Americans who are murdered every year. Wyoming does not have a "hate crimes" law, yet one of Mr. Shepard's killers had to cut a deal with state prosecutors to escape the death penalty in exchange for two life terms without the possibility of parole, while the other man charged faces the death penalty in his upcoming trial.

African American James Byrd's racially motivated dragging death in Texas in 1998 is another case frequently cited to justify the need for "hate crimes" laws. Texas does not have a "hate crimes" statute, but the man who has been convicted has been sentenced to death, and the other suspect, if convicted, could receive the death penalty as well. And Mr. Byrd's case is already covered under the federal hate crimes law. The fact remains that state laws, police forces and judicial systems are adequate to handle such crimes and that federal intervention via the Hate Crimes Act is not needed.

## Unequal Enforcement

There is evidence that "hate crimes" laws are not enforced equitably. In Madison, Wisconsin, Ralph Ovadal, a pastor and founder of Wisconsin Christians United, was physically attacked in 1996 while protesting a pro-homosexuality photo display at a public school. Ovadal and another man held two large signs— one read, "Homosexuality Is Wrong" and the other, "Homosexuals: Repent or Perish." Another man grabbed one of the signs and hurried away. When Ovadal confronted the man about taking the signs, he punched Ovadal, knocking him to the ground. According to a medical report, the assault caused "abrasions, contusions and an injured ankle." The assailant was never charged with a "hate crime," despite the existence of a strong "hate crime" law on the books of Madison, a liberal college town. The attacker eventually bargained down a misdemeanor battery charge to an ordinance violation, comparable to a traffic ticket.

In San Francisco in 1993, Pastor Chuck McIlhenny, whose home had been firebombed in 1990, called the city hate crimes unit when homosexual activists attacked a church. He was told that the Christians had their point of view, and the homosexual activists had theirs, and that they "cancel each other out." Despite the destruction of property, physical assault of parishioners, and the disruption of a worship service, the police would not come to their aid. Apparently, some hate-crime victims are more important than others.

Back to the national picture: If anti-bias programs are working, and offenses are already being handled adequately at the local and state levels, what real purpose does the Hate Crimes Prevention Act serve? Miss Reno revealed it when she announced that the Justice and Education Departments will distribute manuals to "help teachers get young people to understand that they should celebrate their differences and not fight over them." With the emphasis on sexual "orientation," this means that Jewish, Christian and Muslim children will be taught to "celebrate" homosexuality. President Clinton announced a new nationwide school program as part of his support for the Hate Crimes Prevention Act. This amounts to federal officials interfering in local schools to "re-educate" children that their families' most deeply held beliefs amount to hateful bigotry. Already, in schools across the country, young children—even first graders—are being subjected to homosexual propaganda in the names of "tolerance" education and AIDS education.

If we are to continue as free men and women, able to form opinions and speak our minds without fear, we cannot make attitudes or thoughts the subject of federal intervention and criminal prosecution. The "Hate Crimes Prevention Act of 1999" may be well-intentioned, but its practical outcome is a step toward thought control, expanded governmental power, and tyranny masquerading as tolerance. We respectfully urge senators not to support this bill.

# Chapter 3

# Should Society Encourage Increased Acceptance of Homosexuality?

# Chapter Preface

In 1974, the American Psychiatric Association (APA) voted to delete homosexuality from its official list of mental disorders. In an official statement, the association declared, "Whereas, homosexuality per se implies no impairment in judgement, stability, reliability, or general social or vocational capabilities, therefore, be it resolved that the American Psychiatric Association deplores all public and private discrimination against homosexuals." Many within the association believed that the statement would lead to improvements in the way homosexual patients were being treated. Gay rights activists—who had pressured the APA to change its official stance—heralded the change as a means of helping society accept gays and lesbians.

The majority of APA members believed that the organization's new stance was supported by scientific evidence. The studies that the association had examined consistently showed that most gays and lesbians accepted their sexual orientation and were not impaired by it. Furthermore, many within the mental health profession began to believe that the problems experienced by their homosexual patients were the result of society's negative views about homosexuality, not homosexuality itself.

The move to alter the association's official stance on homosexuality was not embraced by all APA members, however. In fact, 42 percent of the membership opposed the decision. Moreover, many mental health experts not affiliated with the APA were even more reluctant to change their views. Some psychoanalysts—therapists who follow the practices of Sigmund Freud—rejected the claim that homosexuality was normal. In fact, the American Psychoanalytic Association rejected efforts to endorse the APA's 1974 position on homosexuality. Diana Miller, a child and adult psychiatrist and psychoanalyst, reports that psychoanalysts in training during the 1980s "could not help noticing hostility toward gay men and lesbian women, and stereotyped and pathologizing views." Finally, in 1991, the association passed a resolution opposing public and private discrimination against homosexuals. Most psychoanalysts now believe that their profession has finally aligned itself with Freud, who said in 1921, "Homosexuality . . . is nothing to be ashamed of, no vice, no degradation. It cannot be classified as an illness."

Conflict between members of the mental health community regarding the normalcy of homosexuality still exists. While the vast majority of therapists today view homosexuality as normal, a small minority continues to believe that homosexuality is a symptom of "developmental arrest"—a derailment of natural sexual development. These experts claim that homosexuality is a disease that should be treated. They contend that organizations such as the APA have buckled under pressure of gay rights and other liberal groups. Some members of this minority, such as Charles Socarides, practice reparative therapy, which is intended to help homosexuals become heterosexual. Psychoanalyst Houston MacIntosh says Socarides' practice "provides a counterbalance to the current rush to embrace the gay political agenda by the leadership of the American Psychoanalytic Association."

Despite the lack of anonymity within mental health organizations about how to treat homosexual patients, the profession overall has been instrumental in helping to encourage acceptance of gays and lesbians. Removing homosexuality from what a gay newspaper called the "psychiatric sicklist" has prompted many members of society to view homosexuality in a more positive light. In the following chapter, experts debate whether increased acceptance of homosexuality is desirable and what the stance of therapists, churches, teachers, and private organizations should be.

# Christians Should Accept Homosexuality

## by Bruce J. Simpson

*About the author: Bruce J. Simpson is archbishop of the Independent Western Rite Orthodox Catholic Church.*

One of the most difficult and contentious conflicts in Christianity has been, and continues to be, the homosexual and the Church. All one has to do is turn on the television and listen to any of the televangelists, or for that fact the local Sunday pulpit, and one can find a constant, impassioned theme on the evil and sinfulness of the gay and lesbian population. These messengers of God's love are quite content to put the homosexual in the same category as murderers, adulterers, child molesters and worse. Why? What motivates not only right-wing fundamentalists but some mainline churches such as Roman Catholicism? From where does this vicious, self-righteous homophobia stem?

### Using the Bible to Justify Persecution

The Bible, of course, is the answer given by these pious holy men and women of God. Sacred scripture, both old and new, is the authority cited as justification for the persecution, discrimination and murder of homosexuals. An examination of the scripture passages most often used is required.

Using the New American Bible, I draw from Genesis, chapter 19. This passage, which describes the destruction of the cities Sodom and Gomorrah, is the main example from the Bible given by those who damn homosexuality. In this version, they interpret the key phrase as "intimacies," as in "Bring them out to us that we may have intimacies with them." The term in the original Hebrew is "yadha," or "yada," meaning "to know." This term can be found in ancient Hebrew scripture 943 times and is used to signify sexual activity only about 10 to 12 times. Many scholars question the exact meaning of "yada" in this context. Did they wish to assault them? Or rob them? Or did they want to rape them? For if sex is what they wanted, it would not have been consensual sex but rather gang rape. Additionally, the fact that Lot would offer his two daughters to appease the mob tells us that these were not gay men but probably hetero-sexual men who used rape as a vehicle for domination, much as one does in prison. Throughout Western civilization, evidence indicates that by raping a man, emasculation occurs, putting him in the same category as women—which is the ultimate shame for a man. Fre-quently, soldiers not only raped the women on the losing side of a battle but the soldiers as well, completing the defeat.

> *"Sacred scripture . . . is the authority cited as justification for the persecution, discrimination and murder of homosexuals."*

One must also keep in mind the laws of hospitality to strangers that was very important in those nomadic days. Many believe that the sin that destroyed Sodom was not homosexuality but the way in which the city's inhabitants treated strangers. But since hospital-ity dictates that you offer welcome to all strangers you encounter, the Church finds itself in an awkward position. Many churches are far too busy condemn-ing gay people and driving them from the Lord's house, so they can hardly ad-mit that inhospitality, abuse and offense to visitors were the grievous sins of the residents of Sodom.

In Judges 19:15–29, one finds an extremely close parallel to the story of Sodom. Once again, the people of the town demonstrate a lack of hospitality, and most important, gang rape occurs. This time, a woman was raped and abused all night when the intended male victim was not brought out and handed over to the mob. When is the last time a story appeared in the media regarding a group of homosexual men raping a woman all night?

If one looks to the New Testament, Matthew 11:23–24, it is obvious to the most ardent homophobe that the sin of Sodom was failure to give protection, comfort and shelter, as in Luke 10:5–12. In Mark 7:10–11, Jesus talks again about hospitality. Further adding to the difficulty of this passage are the fears, prejudices and contemporary moral codes of those who translated the Bible through the ages. Scholars also note that it was not until the 12th century that the story of Sodom was interpreted to mean homosexuality.

## Problems with Translation

Finally, scholars tell us that the Hebrew word used to connote homosexual or bestial sex is "shakhabh." This term does not appear in the passage. In Leviticus 18:22, we find "You shall not lie with a male as with a woman; such a thing is an abomination." In Hebrew, the word for abomination is "to'ebah," which is usually reserved for condemnation of idolatry, not sexual acts. Scholars believe that what was being condemned here with "to'ebah" was temple prostitution, which was common, and not gay relationships. Many people in those days took great pains to condemn and eliminate temple prostitutes, who were both male and female. Another example would be the word "arsenokoitai." In 1 Corinthians 6:9–10

(1952 Revised Standard Version translation), "arsenokoitai" means "homosexuals." The 1977 Revised Standard Version translates this word as "sexual perverts." The 1989 Revised Standard Version translates the word as "sodomites." A review of other translations reveals the word to have meant "homosexuals," "sodomites," "child molesters," "perverts" or "people of infamous habits."

Finally, the New American Bible translates "arsenokoitai" as "practicing homosexuals"! A 1st century text now reflects 20th century Roman teaching—i.e., to be a homosexual is not a sin, but to be a "practicing homosexual" . . . well, now, that is condemned!

Another of the important words is the Greek "malakoi," which has been translated through the ages to mean "catamites," "the effeminate," "boy prostitutes" and "sissies." But until the 20th century, in Roman Catholicism the word meant "masturbators." As prejudices changed, so has the biblical translation.

Many of the passages are tied to the Jewish Holiness Code, which forbade many things and has been abandoned by the 20th century Church with one exception: homosexuality.

For New Testament authority, St. Paul is brought out like a new fire truck on the 4th of July. Paul is a premier founding father of the Christian Church, and as such, his words hold great weight; but as Bishop Spong, Episcopal bishop of New Jersey, says, "They are Paul's words, not God's."

> *"It was not until the 12th century that the story of Sodom was interpreted to mean homosexuality."*

In Romans 1:26–27, God is seen to have given men and women "up" to disgraceful passions. This act was in reprisal for idolatry and failure to recognize God as who He is. So we have God as the causal connection to acts, which they then condemn! This does not make sense. Why would God cause men and women to engage in acts that were not of their nature as a punishment for ignoring His goodness?

## Considering Context

All of the passages that refer to homosexuality must be considered in the context in which they were written. Spong and others hint that St. Paul himself may have been gay and acted out in a self-hating way, which he could not accept in scripture, so no homosexual could be accepted. I'm not sure I believe this.

For nowhere does Jesus say anything about gay people. His only comments on sexual morals are the ones He spoke to the prostitute and the adulteress. If homosexuality were such a sin, does it not make sense that Jesus would have talked about it at least once? Nevertheless, Jesus makes no reference at all to homosexuality.

One reason that the 12 tribes of Israel might have condemned homosexual activity was that it was sexual activity that failed to produce more Israelites. In a time when war was always a possibility—which really has not changed much—

a constant supply of new warriors was needed.

Truly, then, the Bible is subject to interpretation by those who study it. I believe the Bible to be the word of God in its very essence. Nevertheless, the imperfect hands and minds of men have filtered this essence down through the ages.

## Created in the Image of God

As to the nature of gay men and women, I believe that homosexuals are created in the image of God. In Genesis 1:26–27, God says, "Let us make man in our image, after our likeness." God is an all-loving God, and therefore He would not allow His children to "choose" homosexuality and then become victims their whole lives. God's likeness includes black, white and every hue of color in between—male and female—so why not gay and straight? Would we limit God in His capacity to create his children to only what man believes to be correct? I believe it is now, and always has been, a naturally occurring phenomenon. St. Thomas Aquinas, writing on whether man has free will, states: "For the sheep seeing the wolf, judges it a thing to be shunned, from a natural and not a free judgment, because it judges, not from reason, but from natural instinct." So also do I believe that gay people are attracted to one another by natural instinct. The capacity to love and worship and build lives together is not limited to just heterosexuals.

I find it to be a moral imperative that the gay and lesbian community be ministered to. How can it be righteous to withhold the love and acceptance of the Lord from those who may be different from the majority? Certainly, the ancient Jews saw Jesus as a radical and as someone who was different. Did not Jesus walk among those who were the despised of his time, spreading the good news and accepting them in love?

If there is no foundation for excluding gay people from the Church, how can it be tolerated? How much pain and sorrow must be caused in the name of the "perfect love" before we shout, "Enough!"? Why must the self-righteous among us rant and rave about that which they know nothing?

How can these "moral leaders" of the Church be so certain that gay people should be condemned for being who they are and have this condemnation be virtuous? How can the Roman Catholic Church condemn the use of condoms when the birth rate has exploded in Third World countries, adding to an already overburdened population? How can the Vatican condemn the use of condoms in an age when AIDS threatens the entire human race? It is not birth control that they should condemn; it is the sin of birthing children who cannot be fed, educated and given a decent life that should be condemned.

> *"If homosexuality were such a sin, does it not make sense that Jesus would have talked about it at least once?"*

I continue to be amazed at how hung up we are as a Church on the issue of sexuality in general, let alone homosexuality. We find pious, prayerful men through the ages castigating the homosexual and preaching with a believed certain knowledge that they are right. I reject these teachings. One has to be gay to truly understand what it is to be gay and to live life as a gay person.

Not all gay sexual relationships are naturally good; neither are all heterosexual relationships. Both bodies of sexual activity can be abused. But for many, sexual maturation leads one to a life mate who is the ideal that all should strive toward.

If we accept the basic premise that we are of God, then our basic nature is good. I refuse to believe that our Lord rejects loving, caring gay relationships—both sexual and nonsexual, for it is possible to love a friend deeply without sex being part of that relationship.

## Exclude No One

Some pastors will counsel their homosexual parishioners to be asexual—not have sex, that's the answer! I reject that notion also. The joy of sex and the intimacy it brings within a relationship can be a most fulfilling aspect of that relationship. Surely, God would not want to deny us the joy that this gift can bring simply because we are gay. This would be like putting a child in a candy factory and telling him not to touch the candy! Likewise to have two people in a loving relationship and not allow them to give of themselves that which is most personal is silly. Only a lifelong celibate could urge such a thing and not realize what he or she is asking.

I believe that gay people are entitled to the same access to the Lord's house and the sacraments as heterosexuals. A truly gospel-based parish would exclude no one. It should be a broad spectrum of the community, where all of the sacraments are made available to the gay community.

The current debate over gay marriage both saddens and amuses me. For years, heterosexual society has condemned gay people for being promiscuous. Now they are fighting like hell to prevent two gay men or women from committing to each other for life. In an ideal society, gay marriage should be allowed. But since we are not an ideal society, I support union ceremonies and take great joy in performing them.

The Church through the ages has hurt hundreds of thousands of gay and lesbian people. It must stop! It is reported that 30 percent of youth who commit suicide do so due to their sexual orientation. This must stop!

The love and acceptance of God must be brought to *all* people. The prejudice and hatred of the Christian right must be rejected and fought. Those who act out of ignorance must be educated.

Finally, I find comfort when I read Matthew 5:10—"Blest are those persecuted for holiness sake; the reign of God is theirs." I call upon all churches to accept and love their gay and lesbian members and stop denying them the love of God, which is not theirs to deny.

# Therapists Should Not Try to Change Gay People's Sexual Orientation

**by Laura Markowitz**

**About the author:** *Laura Markowitz is editor of* In the Family, *a magazine for gay people and their families, and a senior editor for the* Family Therapy Networker.

Just after Chris turned 16, in 1982, his mother began to worry about his withdrawal from friends and activities. When she pressed him to talk about his feelings, he told her he was upset because he thought he was probably gay. Worried and confused, his parents spoke to the school guidance counselor, who referred them to a therapist in their small New England city who advertised himself as a specialist in "conversion therapy" (CT). For the next year, Chris went once a week to Dr. L., a licensed clinical psychologist, who told Chris and his parents during the first session that he "didn't believe the gay-rights people who said gays couldn't be changed," and that he had a 95-percent success rate "converting" gays to "normal life."

Chris remembers feeling relieved when Dr. L. told him he was sure he could "fix" the "problem." It's not uncommon for clients to be distressed about being gay when they first come out, but two camps of therapists diverge on what to do during this emotional crisis, and this difference of opinion has lately flared into a battleground. A minority of therapists believe, like Dr. L., that sexual orientation is not fixed and that therapy can "repair" or "convert" unhappy gay and lesbian clients to heterosexuality. They say it's the therapist's responsibility to listen to what the client wants and not be swayed by the "gay agenda" in the therapy room. They believe it's no different than a client saying, "I have a drinking problem and want to change."

This camp of therapist is far outnumbered by the majority of mental health practitioners from all the fields who say it is not only faulty thinking, but it is dangerous practice to try to "convert" anyone to another sexuality. "Just because a client comes in and says 'fix this' doesn't mean therapists should jump in without understanding," says Dorothy Cantor, a clinical psychologist in private practice in Westfield, New Jersey. "If a client comes to me and says 'I want you to help me find the courage to end my life,' I obviously wouldn't take that at face value and try to help her kill herself." Cantor says it's the same thing with clients who want not to be gay. "Good therapy means helping them explore why they are unhappy being gay, not teaching them to hate themselves even more." These clinicians view gay clients' self-loathing and shame as normal occurrences during the early stages of coming out in a homophobic and heterosexist society. "CT is terrible science," says Doug Haldeman, an openly gay counseling psychologist in Seattle who has worked with hundreds of survivors of CT. "It's based on long-debunked ideas that homosexuality is the result of developmental arrest or family dynamic. Those therapists believe queer people are incapable of living happy or fulfilling lives and see themselves on a mission to save people who feel that the gay lifestyle is incompatible with their life goals. Its basically a kinder, gentler version of the burn-in-hell variety of homophobia, but just as damaging."

The good news is that CT has been officially denounced by most of the major mental health associations—psychiatrists, social workers, psychologists and others—who have taken unequivocal positions saying there is no scientific evidence whatsoever to support the claims that therapy can change anyone's sexual orientation. The American Psychological Association (APA) passed a resolution—

> *"Conversion therapy has been officially denounced by most of the major mental health associations."*

which Haldeman was instrumental in writing—in August 1998 during its annual convention, with little outward dissension. "It's important to note that this resolution comes out of a 98-percent heterosexual council of representatives," says Cantor, a past-president of the APA, "made up of 125 people elected from our state associations or divisions. So this very broad spectrum of psychologists from all over the country and from every sector of the profession—practitioners and scientists—concurred that CT is not valid."

## Conversion Therapists

The bad news is that many therapists have been quietly ignoring the standards of practice set forth by their professions and continue to practice CT. When homosexuality was depathologized 26 years ago, it was not a unanimous decision. The American Psychiatric Association's 10,000 members only passed the referendum by 58 percent of the vote. But while the majority trumpeted the decision as a significant advance against homophobia—and it was—what were the other 42 percent thinking, and, even more important, what were they doing in the privacy of their own clinical practices? As the other professions followed suit and began, albeit slowly, to stop teaching that homosexuality was an abnormality or the result of some developmental or family problem, there continued to be those who believed in CT. Some even accused the "gay agenda" of silencing them, and claim to have a proven track record of success with CT.

This small band of CT practitioners might have stayed in obscurity if not for the 1998 anti-gay campaign started by a coalition of fundamentalist Christian groups, who took out full-page advertisements in major newspapers around the country encouraging homosexuals to change their sexual orientation. While the ads were mainly touting religious interventions—faith, prayer and fellowship communities—to help turn homosexuals from their "sinful" path, these ads sowed confusion in the public. Could homosexuals really be "cured"? While the major professional associations quickly voted on resolutions to reaffirm that homosexuality isn't a mental disorder and doesn't need treatment, one small association of CT therapists was finding an eager audience for its message.

> *"There is no empirical data to support the validity of sexual orientation change counseling."*

The National Association for Research and Therapy of Homosexuality (NARTH), formed in 1992, and purported to have about 500 therapist members, claims to have had great success changing clients' homosexual orientation, although their studies are dismissed by critics as being improperly done and overly biased. With an international service of licensed therapists offering "sexual reorientation treatment," and a nonprofit association that solicits and accepts donations, NARTH seeks to "educate the public about the truth of homosexuality." They hold an annual meeting in the same locations as the American Psychoanalytic Association's annual conference, maintain an elaborate web site and publish a newsletter three times a year, all devoted to the "science" and practice of converting unhappy homosexuals.

On their web site (www.narth.com), NARTH responded to the APA's resolution, writing that while they oppose the irrational fear and hatred of homosexuals, "and the social stigmatization and obstruction of the civil rights of homosexuals," they see "another group whose civil rights are at stake in this issue: the many dissatisfied homosexuals whose freedom to choose the direction of their treatment is now being threatened" by the APAs Office of Gay and Lesbian Affairs. They accuse their colleagues of being swayed by politically correct bias to encourage clients to embrace their homosexuality, even if the client doesn't want to. But critics of NARTH say the same thing about CT therapists. "Gay and lesbian therapists are allowing clients the freedom and safe space to explore their true feelings," says Laura M.I. Saunders, a clinical psychologist in Hartford, Connecticut, who works with adolescents. Dorothy Cantor agrees: "Good therapy is helping people become more true to themselves," she says. "I believe NARTH exploits homophobia to promote their own dangerous bias against homosexuality."

## Faulty Logic

Although NARTH literature is careful to say that their group "oppose[s] the social stigmatization and obstruction of the civil rights of homosexuals," those words ring empty in the face of statements such as this one by co-founder Benjamin Kaufman, M.D., who writes on the web site, "It remains very politically incorrect—very marginalizing—to even make the suggestion of a dialogue that opens up the question of the normality of homosexuality." Elsewhere, NARTH states, "Scientific research supports age-old cultural norms that homosexuality is not a healthy natural alternative to heterosexuality." They are alarmed that teenagers are being taught that homosexuality is a lifestyle alternative equal to heterosexuality. "It does far more harm than good to tell a teenager that his attraction toward members of the same sex are normal and desirable," alluding to the fact that teens are being "pushed in the direction" of a gay lifestyle.

The problem with NARTH logic, says Cantor, is the faulty premise that homosexuality is a choice. "It reminds me of a client I once worked with, a man in a state hospital who believed he was a vampire," remembers Cantor. "If you accepted his premise, everything he did was logical, including his jumping out a hospital window because he believed he could fly. He had a whole elaborate system to explain how he had become a vampire after being bitten on the neck by an African bat. But his scenario was based on a schizophrenic premise. We know this in research: if you start with an erroneous premise, you build an erroneous case." If you start with the premise that sexual orientation is a matter of choice, you will believe you can change it. Preliminary findings from a nationwide study of gay and lesbian people who have been through counseling to change their sexual orientation, led by researchers Ariel Shidlo and Michael Schroeder, confirm what the APA and other associations have been saying for years: there is no empirical data to support the validity of sexual orientation change counseling.

> *"Many more therapists than anyone previously suspected nurture some belief that conversion therapy works."*

## A Growing Threat

A small group of renegade therapists doesn't sound like much of a threat to the well-institutionalized belief that homosexuality is not a mental illness, except that CT has been eagerly adopted by the fundamentalist groups who are promoting religious conversion therapy. "In recent years, religious groups have been the only organizations which have had the courage to undertake this kind of discussion," writes Kaufman, "but they have not been assisted in any way by psychiatric professionals. And so NARTH was founded; it became clear that we must have a credible secular organization which could move beyond the strife and misinformation." There are a growing number of these religious groups who are very interested in whatever methods—prayer, faith, therapy—that might help unhappy homosexuals go straight. Some of the major players in the movement to change gays to straight include the Exodus Movement, made up of 75 ministries in the United States, Asia and Europe; Courage, a Roman Catholic group with about 15 centers in North America; Evergreen International Inc., a Mormon treatment center with 13 branches in the United States, Australia and Canada; Homosexuals Anonymous, with chapters throughout the country, offering a 14-step "recovery" program; and the recently created Parents and Friends of Ex-Gays (P-FOX), supporting the family and friends of ex-gays (a kind of *doppelganger* of Parents and Friends of Lesbians and Gays).

> *"[One conversion therapist] instructed his young client to imagine his friend covered in feces and vomit because . . . 'that's what a guy kissing a guy is like—disgusting.'"*

"NARTH people are benefited by a relationship with the religious right," says Doug Haldeman, "because of an inexhaustible supply of clients, and NARTH gives this Christian fundamentalist movement 'experts' to hold up and point to." There are a lot of clients out there looking for CT, he says, but that doesn't make CT any more legitimate—it just proves how entrenched homophobia and heterosexism are in our society.

It would be comforting to think we could write CT off as an inconsequential phenomenon, but alarming new research suggests that many more therapists than anyone previously suspected nurture some belief that CT works. Two years ago, the Gay and Lesbian Task Force of the Connecticut Psychological Association sent out a survey to all Connecticut psychologists asking about their practice with gay and lesbian clients, and then they expanded the survey to include Maine and Maryland. Of the 400 respondents, an average of 4 percent across all states are practicing CT. Almost twice that number still believe in its efficacy. "The respondents have been in practice for an average of 16 years," says Ozlem Camli, the head researcher and a clinical psychologist in Hartford, "so we're not talking about beginning therapists. They have seen an average of 4 gay or lesbian clients in the past 12 months, and 27 gay or lesbian clients in their careers." Camli, and her partner and co-researcher, Laura Saunders, were even more alarmed about the inordinately high nonresponse rate to that question: 23 percent of the Maryland respondents, and 21 percent of the Maine respondents were not willing to say whether or not they believed CT works, even though the survey was completely anonymous. "We think they were either uncomfortable with their response or afraid to say what they really believed," says Saunders. The researchers conclude that there are even more therapists who believe CT works but who don't want to say so, and this worries them. "People who believe in conversion therapy need to come out about it," says Camli. "Otherwise, it stays dangerous. We have heard a lot of horror stories from people who were pushed by therapists to be someone they were not meant to be, and were told how they need to be, and that is not ethical treatment. When teens are brought to therapy and their parents want us to change them, we should be clear about what therapy can and can't do. Our research shows that 15 percent of clients who come for conversion therapy are adolescents brought by a parent."

## What CT Therapists Do

What is it that CT therapists do? According to NARTH, they "explore the conscious and unconscious conflicts from which the condition originated." Chris, now an artist in his thirties, spent a year with Dr. L. doing just that, and also going through Dr. L.'s brand of behavior modification and desensitization. Dr. L. would sit on the couch next to the youth and show him heterosexual pornography magazines, asking every few minutes what Chris felt about this picture or that one, trying to create a profile for Chris of the kind of woman he could be attracted to and the kind of heterosexual fantasies he could nurture. Chris tried to feel interested in the photographs and occasional X-rated movie Dr. L. would show during their sessions, but felt like a failure when he didn't feel stimulated by them. Dr. L. encouraged him to "try harder" and assigned Chris homework—to take the magazine home and masturbate between sessions. When Chris reported truthfully that none of it turned him on in the least—in fact, much of the pornography disgusted him—Dr. L. emotionally withdrew and became cold, aloof and disapproving, which made Chris feel ashamed and humiliated. After a few experiences of his therapist turning away from him, Chris says, he learned to lie about his "progress."

Almost four months into the treatment, Dr. L. finally asked Chris about his homoerotic feelings, and when Chris described his favorite fantasy of being kissed by his best friend, Glenn, Dr. L. told him confidently that Chris could be saved because he hadn't turned the corner on "truly sick fantasies" by imagining more than the kiss. Chris felt relieved that he wasn't truly sick, but he was still confused about the nature of his fantasies, which were not only sexual, but also romantic and loving. "I was in love with my best friend, but Dr. L. thought of homosexuality as a sexual perversion," says Chris. "Love never crossed his mind." Dr. L. did tell Chris to guard against "further polluting yourself" by making sure he would never be alone with his friend, and if possible to try to avoid him altogether. When Chris was unable to stay away from his friend, Dr. L. taught him an imagery exercise to try to help Chris develop aversion to the idea of homosexual contact with Glenn. He instructed his young client to imagine his friend covered in feces and vomit because "no one wants to kiss that, right? And that's what a guy kissing a guy is like—disgusting," Dr L. assured him. This nightly exercise, which Chris says he earnestly tried to do, left him feeling even more confused because he somehow couldn't help editing the fantasy to include him lovingly showering off his soiled friend and then passionately embracing him.

The third component to Dr. L.'s conversion therapy was "educating" Chris about the realities of homosexuality. He assured Chris that the stereotype of gays as sexual predators was accurate, and that if he did allow himself to give in to his homosexual feelings, he would end up alone, persecuted and unloved, and could possibly turn into a sexual molester. "You don't want to grow up to be a dirty old man in some park, preying on young boys, do you?" Dr. L. once asked a terrified Chris. Dr. L. also expounded on his theory that homosexuality was caused by dysfunctional family dynamics. The therapist surmised that Chris's mother had been over-involved in his life while his father had been pushed out of the dyad. Chris became distant and private around his mother, hoping that would cure him. Chris's father was told to spend more time doing boy things with Chris, and so they went to football games. Chris was ashamed—but didn't confess to Dr. L.— that he had been turned on watching the football players. Chris says that to this day, Dr. L. probably considers him a success story for CT, because when Chris left therapy, he had a date with a girl to his senior prom and had fabricated a web of lies for his therapist about having heterosexual fantasies. At the end of the last session, Dr. L. assured Chris's relieved parents that their son had been "temporarily confused" but that he was now "cured" and would lead a "normal" life.

> *"Gays and lesbians [who] live with opposite-sex partners . . . haven't been converted, they have simply volunteered to move into the closet."*

Four months later, Chris attempted suicide and checked himself into a psychiatric hospital. There, he met with a therapist who had radically different views about homosexuality. She helped Chris begin his healing by saying, "There's nothing wrong with being gay."

## Counter-Brainwashing

Helping clients who have been harmed by CT is Doug Haldeman's specialty. The former president of Division 44 [the Society for the Psychological Study of Lesbian, Gay, and Bisexual Issues] initially had a hard time understanding why clients would voluntarily seek CT. "I learned to imagine the world of the client," he says, "how it would feel to believe you were damned to hell, that you would never have children, that your family would cut you off and that you would be a pervert for the rest of your life." The rigors of CT seemed a small price to pay for the promised joy and social approval that awaited them if they could do this one little thing. "I imagined the pressure brought to bear on them. I imagined myself trying to change something as profound as my sexual orientation, and then I developed compassion and sensitivity," says Haldeman.

One of his earliest cases so upset him that as a result he became involved in policy work. Brad was a Mormon in his late twenties who came to Haldeman after having been through electroshock therapy (ECT) to cure him of his homosexuality. He had gone willingly—even gladly—for the treatments suggested by his therapist because Brad felt his afterlife was in jeopardy, and not only would he not get into heaven, but the rest of his family would also suffer for eternity because he wouldn't be there and they would miss him. The ECT left him unable to function sexually, and he became depressed, isolated and suicidal. It took many years of psychotherapy to help him repair his self-esteem, but the physiological damage was never fully healed. Haldeman helped him with cognitive restructuring—understanding how his beliefs and the beliefs of the people around him had created his self-loathing—and talking about how wanting to please others so much made it difficult for him to live his own life. Haldeman helped Brad come to terms with his strong desire to have a spouse and children and live according to his religion, and the consequences he might face if he decided to conform to heterosexuality even though he still had homosexual attraction. Most of all, he assured Brad that it wasn't his fault for being gay and it wasn't his fault for not being able to change his sexual orientation. Brad was enormously relieved to know he wasn't still gay because he hadn't tried hard enough—a hidden shame commonly felt by ex-CT clients. After several years of difficult work, Brad left therapy and had found a husband and was making a life for himself in the gay community.

Haldeman sees his work as a kind of counter-brainwashing. "They probably think gay-affirmative therapy is brainwashing," he says, "but the significant difference is that I don't see the clients as broken and needing to be fixed. My job is to help them explore who they are and to offer them alternative ways to think about themselves. But it's neither my job, nor anyone else's job, to change them. It's just wrong for therapists to advertise that it can be done. It can't," he says. Bisexuals may have more success foregoing their homosexuality and choosing to conform to heterosexuality. Gays and lesbians may live with opposite-sex partners and create heterosexual-looking lives, but inside themselves they know who they are. They haven't been converted, they have simply volunteered to move into the closet.

The bottom line about NARTH and CT is that it is bad therapy because it is wrong to support and to feed clients' self-hate about being homosexual or bisexual. It does a deep, soul-twisting kind of damage that is the polar opposite of what therapy is supposed to be about, which is helping clients accept the incontrovertible truth they already know about themselves. Consider these words by lesbian writer Daphne Scholinski, who describes her teenage years in a mental hospital in *The Last Time I Wore a Dress:* "The staff was under orders to scrutinize my femininity: the way I walked, the way I sat with my ankle on my knee, the clothes I wore, the way I kept my hair. Trivial matters, one might say. But trivial matters in which the soul reveals itself. Try changing these things. Try it. . . . See how far you can contradict your nature. Feel how your soul rebels."

# Schools Should Teach Acceptance of Homosexuality

**by Beth Reis**

**About the author:** *Beth Reis is a public health educator for the Safe Schools Coalition of Washington, which is based in Seattle.*

We really don't have a choice when it comes to teaching about sexual orientation in public schools. Children are already learning about it. The problem is they are often receiving inaccurate, destructive messages.

## Learning the Code

Author Katherine Whitlock said in her book *Bridges of Respect: Creating Support for Gay and Lesbian Youth* that:

> In schools across the country, even very young children learn the codes, passed on in jokes and whispers: "Don't wear certain colors to school on a particular day, or you're queer." Lessons are learned each time a child discovers that one of the surest ways to deliver an insult is to accuse another of being a *lezzy*, a *faggot*, a *sissy*. Children may not always know what these words mean, but they know the pejorative power of this language. Lessons are learned each time adults speak and act as if everyone in the world is heterosexual, or should be. Adult acquiescence in homophobia places lesbian and gay youth at great emotional and sometimes physical risk.

All students, regardless of their sexual orientation, learn mythology and hatred in school. All are hurt by it. Teachers can educate *actively*, replacing mythology with knowledge and hatred with respect, or they can educate *passively* as they have in the past. Those are the only alternatives. Either way, they communicate important messages.

There are a number of important reasons why teachers should teach *actively:*

• Because it is personally important to many children. Between 2 and 9 percent of Americans are homosexual or bisexual. This means a high school with a student body of 1,000 probably has 20 to 90 gay, lesbian, and bisexual students (plus a few who are transgender). In addition, some students also have a brother, sister, mother, or father who is a sexual minority. At least six million children in the United States have a gay or lesbian parent. Every child deserves accurate information and respectful messages about himself or herself or about loved ones.

• Because it can build self-esteem and resiliency. Teachers need to tell gay, lesbian, and bisexual youth that they are good people and that they have faith in them. This would help reduce the likelihood that they will, as a disproportionate number of sexual minority youth do, engage in such self-destructive behaviors as dropping out of school, abusing alcohol and other drugs, becoming homeless (by choice or not), experiencing sexual abuse and exploitation, or considering suicide.

• Because it can help support and enhance relationships in all families. Sexual minority youth are sometimes embraced and cherished by their families. More often, however, they fear rejection and hide their feelings from their families. Teachers can provide information to parents and put them in touch with other parents. They can help some students to feel confident and strong enough to confide in their families.

Not all families, of course, can accept their gay and lesbian children. Some teens who come out to their families are assaulted and/or kicked out of their homes. One study found that 8 percent of gay and 11 percent of lesbian youth were physically abused by parents or siblings because of their sexual orientation. In Seattle, 40 percent of homeless youth are gay, lesbian, or bisexual. Teachers can provide supportive resources for these youth. They can also help heterosexual students become allies for family members who are gay, lesbian, or bisexual.

> *"Every child deserves accurate information and respectful messages about himself or herself."*

• Because it can counteract stereotypes and prejudice as well as reduce the likelihood of violence. In the poignant words of one seventh grader, "God made all of us so we're all special in our own way. So stop the names because if you don't think I'm special, you're wrong. . . ."

The U.S. Department of Justice reports that homosexuals are probably the most frequent victims of hate-motivated violence in the nation. Schools are actually one of the least safe places for openly gay and gender role nonconforming youth and for those who voice support for gay and lesbian civil rights. Students are sometimes publicly humiliated, threatened, chased, followed, spit on, assaulted, and raped.

Gay, lesbian, and bisexual youth who witness harassment of gay peers often react by hiding their orientation even more vigorously out of fear or self-hate.

Some protect themselves by joining in the bullying. Heterosexuals who observe the persecution may experience guilt about their silent complicity and a sense of powerlessness similar to that experienced by their homosexual, bisexual, and transgendered peers.

Students learn early on to rigidly comply with gender roles. Students fear becoming targets of harassment . . . regardless of their sexual orientation. Young men may have sexual relations with girls as a way of proving their maleness. Similarly, young women may get pregnant to try to prove their femaleness.

• Because it can provide accurate information. Only accurate information can replace the ignorance and stereotypes that hurt all children.

• Because it can provide answers to questions that kids are asking. Young people ask questions about homosexuality during general lessons on family life and sexual health. They are surrounded by news such as the gay/lesbian marriage debate and the ongoing struggle of gays in the military. They are not oblivious to these issues. But they do need guidance and direction. Here are some questions from young people from the fifth through the eighth grade (ages 10 to 15) in Seattle, Washington:

• *"What does being gay mean?"*
• *"How do you know a gay man from a regular man?"*
• *"Do teenagers always think they're gay?"*
• *"What if people say you're gay?"*
• *"What do you do if you think a teacher is gay?"*
• *"If you're a gay boy, can you have wet dreams?"*
• *"Do homosexuals have sex?"*
• *"How could you tell if I'm gay?* [signed] *Lonely."*
• *"Why do guys like guys and girls like girls?"*
• *"Why do you become gay?"*
• *"Is it true that AIDS is mostly in the homosexual community?"*
• *"Can you get babies if you're gay?"*
• *"What should you do if people call your friend lezzy?"*

A teacher who refuses to respond to these kinds of earnest questions communicates values just as loudly as if she or he responded. Which values would teachers rather help a student build: that "ignorance, intolerance, and hate are acceptable" or that "people should respect one another and care about one another's feelings, regardless of differences?"

*\*The spelling of students' comments was corrected for this article.*
*The author would like to thank Linnea Nicoulin for her assistance in updating and adapting this article from a presentation made for the Association for Sexuality Education and Training (ASSET) serving the Northwest United States and neighboring Canada.*

# The Boy Scouts Should Accept Homosexuals

## by Linda Hills

**About the author:** *Linda Hills is executive director of the American Civil Liberties Union of San Diego and Imperial counties in California.*

The California Supreme Court stood both justice and Boy Scout Law on their heads in March 1998. Its ruling that the Scouts may exclude those who are gay or who do not share the Scouts' view of God ignored the court's own record of banning discrimination by essentially public organizations.

This is also not a victory the Scouts should be proud of. It allows the Scouts to continue to contradict the beliefs they claim to represent as expressed in the Boy Scout Law.

## A Public Organization

California's Unruh Civil Rights Act prohibits discrimination by "all business establishments of every kind whatsoever." The California Supreme Court has said that only truly private clubs which do not transact business with the general public are exempt from the act. On this basis, the court has required The Boys Club to admit girls and the Jaycees and Rotary Clubs to admit women.

The Boy Scouts is a truly massive organization which operates in the public marketplace. It has more than 4.5 million members recruited from the general public; hundreds of paid staff; many facilities, such as camps, which are available for use by nonmembers; and substantial income derived from a variety of sources, including sales of goods and services to the public at its many retail outlets and events. The Boy Scouts of America have an annual income in excess of $50 million. Much smaller organizations have been determined to be "businesses" by the court.

Moreover, the Boy Scouts receive significant support from government. This support ranges from below-market rent for space on public land—such as the San Diego Boy Scouts receive for their office in Balboa Park—to troops sponsored by police and fire departments. They also receive substantial funding from the United Way, which raises most of its money from payroll deduction programs, including those for government employees. If the Boy Scouts is truly a religious organization—one of their justifications for excluding nonbelievers—then a serious question of separation of church and state arises.

## Violating Their Own Code of Conduct

But public or private, the Boy Scouts cannot discriminate without violating their own code of conduct. The Boy Scout Law directs a Scout to "seek to understand others [and] respect those with ideas and customs other than his own," to "treat others as he wants to be treated," and to "respect the beliefs of others." Intolerance is foursquare against these principles and a group that helps shape boys into men should not teach it. As one of the attorneys in California's 1998 case noted, "'A Scout is prejudiced' should not be the 13th point of Scout Law."

In the past, the Boy Scouts segregated troops on a racial basis, excluded Japanese-American children during World War II and barred women from troop leadership. All of these practices were voluntarily reversed by the Scouts and no harm came to their mission to "serve others by helping to instill values in young people and in other ways prepare them to make ethical choices over their lifetime in achieving their full potential." Requiring ethical sexual conduct and respectful behavior toward religious activities is all that would be required to accommodate everyone into scouting.

Unfortunately, this wrong-headed decision by the Supreme Court prevents Californians from invoking the protection of the law should the social climate change and the Boy Scouts revert back to their old practices. And would-be Scouts who are gay or religious nonbelievers are left out in the cold by two venerable American institutions—the legal system and the Scouts.

> *"The Boy Scouts cannot discriminate without violating their own code of conduct."*

Luckily, courts in other states have come down on the side of nondiscrimination, and the issue may ultimately go to the U.S. Supreme Court. In the meantime, the Boy Scouts should take the next step in practicing what they preach.[1]

If they do not, the American Civil Liberties Union (ACLU) will continue to seek ways to change the Boy Scouts' discriminatory policy. Scout Law says a Boy Scout should have "the courage to stand for what he thinks is right even if others laugh at or threaten him." Scouts who follow that law would be welcome members of the ACLU.

---

1. In 2000, the U.S. Supreme Court ruled that the Boy Scouts of America had the right to discriminate against openly homosexual scoutmasters.

# Christians Should Not Accept Homosexuality

## by Fabian Bruskewitz

**About the author:** *Fabian Bruskewitz is the bishop of Lincoln, Nebraska.*

The official doctrine of the Catholic Church on the morality of homosexual acts is set out with brevity and clarity in the *Catechism of the Catholic Church:*

> Homosexuality refers to relations between men or between women who experience an exclusive or predominant sexual attraction toward persons of the same sex. It has taken a great variety of forms throughout the centuries and in different cultures. Its psychological genesis remains largely unexplained. Basing itself on Sacred Scripture, which presents homosexual acts as acts of grave depravity, tradition has always declared that homosexual acts are intrinsically disordered. They are contrary to the natural law. They close the sexual act to the gift of life. They do not proceed from a genuine affective and sexual complementarity. Under no circumstances can they be approved.

> The number of men and women who have deep seated homosexual tendencies is not negligible. This inclination, which is objectively disordered, constitutes for most of them a trial. They must be accepted with respect, compassion, and sensitivity. Every sign of unjust discrimination in their regard should be avoided. These persons are called to fulfill God's will in their lives and, if they are Christians, to unite to the sacrifice of the Lord's Cross the difficulties they may encounter from their condition.

> Homosexual persons are called to chastity. By the virtues of self-mastery that teach them inner freedom, at times by the support of disinterested friendship, by prayer and sacramental grace, they can and should gradually and resolutely approach Christian perfection.

## The Church's Position on Homosexuality

In an earlier document, issued in 1986, the Holy See had also spoken officially about the Catholic position in regard to homosexual acts. This document, concerned with the pastoral care of homosexual persons, was the successor of a previous and even more important document issued in 1975, which was entitled "A Declaration on Certain Questions Concerning Sexual Ethics." The 1975 document, which has validity for Catholic moral theology, stressed the duty of trying to understand the homosexual condition and noted that culpability for homosexual acts should be judged with prudence. At the same time, there should be a distinction drawn between a homosexual condition or tendency and individual homosexual acts. These acts, of course, are deprived of their essential and indispensable finality and are intrinsically disordered and in no way can be approved.

Catholics, and many Christians with them, believe that the discussion of homosexuality should be based on a theology of creation, particularly that which is found in the first book of the Bible, Genesis, in which God is seen in His infinite wisdom and love bringing into existence all of reality as a reflection of His own goodness. He fashions the human race, male and female, in His likeness. Therefore, human beings are nothing less than the work of God Himself, and this includes the complementarity of the sexes, which are called to reflect the inner unity of the Creator. They do this in the most striking way in the transmission of life by the mutual self-giving to each other in the institution of marriage. We find further in Genesis that the truth about human beings as God's image has been obscured and smeared by original sin, with a concomitant loss of awareness of the covenantal character of the union of man with God. As Pope John Paul II says, the human body thus retains its "spousal significance," but now this is clouded by sin. Further, in Genesis 19, the deterioration due to sin is brought to a certain climax in the story of the men of Sodom. Although there may be other components to the sin of the Sodomites, it is quite clear that their sin consisted in their homosexual relations, not simply the abuse of hospitality. This is further corroborated by the legislation set down in Leviticus 18:20, which describes the conditions necessary for belonging to the Chosen People, and excludes from God's family those who behave in a homosexual way. In the New Testament this perspective is developed by St. Paul in 1 Corinthians 6, where he proposes that those who behave in a homosexual fashion will not enter the kingdom of God. He also, in Romans 1, uses homosexual behavior as an example of the blindness which has overtaken all of the human race. And, finally, in 1 Timothy 1:10, St. Paul explicitly names as sinners those who engage in homosexual acts.

> *"Those who behave in a homosexual fashion will not enter the kingdom of God."*

In 1997 a series of monographs was published by the Vatican's semi-official newspaper, *L'Osservatore Romano*, under the general title "Christian Anthropology and Homosexuality." These 14 studies by various authorities in psychology, psychiatry, family life, and moral theology are a treasure for those who seek to understand and deal with problems involving this phenomenon of homosexuality.

# The Sexual Function

The moral tradition of the Catholic Church on this issue is based on u.
of Divine Revelation and also on the light of natural reason. Under the glow v.
these two lights, the Church has always stressed univocally that the use of the
sexual function has its true meaning and moral rectitude only within a legitimate marriage. Through the symbolism of the sexual difference which marks
their bodily nature, man and woman are called to achieve two closely connected values: first, the gift of self and the acceptance of the other in an indis-
soluble union of one flesh, and second, an openness to the transmission of life.
Only in the context of legitimate marriage are these values proper to sexuality
adequately respected and achieved.

As Livio Melina, a professor of moral theology at the Pontifical Lateran University in Rome, says very well:

> In the homosexual act, true reciprocity, which makes the gift of self and the
> acceptance of the other possible, cannot take place. By lacking complemen-
> tarity, each one of the partners remains locked in himself and experiences
> contact with the other's body, merely as an opportunity for selfish enjoyment.
> At the same time, homosexual activity also involves the illusion of a false in-
> timacy that is obsessively sought and constantly lacking. The other is not
> really other. He is like the self; in reality, he is only the mirror of the self
> which confirms it in its own solitude exactly when the encounter is sought.
> This pathological narcissism has been identified in the homosexual personal-
> ity by the studies of many psychologists. Hence, great instability and promis-
> cuity prevail in the most widespread model of homosexual life, which is why
> the view advanced by some, of encouraging stable and institutionalized
> unions, seems completely unrealistic.

# Not Open to Procreation

Melina goes on to note that it is obvious that the homosexual act lacks openness to the procreative meaning of human sexuality. In the sexual relationship
of husband and wife, their bodily act of mutual self-giving and acceptance is
ordered to a further good, which transcends both of them: the good of that new
life which can be born from their union, and to which they are called to dedi-
cate themselves. It is the logic of love itself which requires this further dimen-
sion and transcendence, without which the sexual act risks turning in on itself
by concentrating on the search for pleasure alone, and literally sterilizing itself.
Through its openness to procreation, the intimate act of the spouses becomes
part of time and history and is woven into the fabric of society. The homosexual
act, on the contrary, has no roots in the past and does not extend to any future.
It is not grafted into the community or the succession of generations. It remains
locked in an unreal moment outside time and social responsibility. To speak of
the spiritual fruitfulness of homosexuality is unduly to ascribe the positive aspect which is always involved in true friendship and of which homosexual per-

sons are also capable, to homosexual practices which are psychologically marked by a frustrating sterility. In fact, psychologists with broad clinical experience state that often when an authentic personal friendship forms between male homosexuals, it frequently happens that they are then unable to continue having these homosexual relations. Because the unitive and procreative aspects of sexual activity which give a legitimacy to its prac-

> *"Pathological narcissism has been identified in the homosexual personality."*

tice can only be found in marriage, a loving and life-giving union of man and woman, the Catholic Church has always taught, and continues to teach, that a person engaging in homosexual behavior acts immorally. As the Congregation for the Doctrine of the Faith puts it:

> To choose someone of the same sex for one's sexual activity, is to annul the rich symbolism and meaning, not to mention the goals, of the Creator's sexual design. Homosexual activity is not a complementary union able to transmit life. So it thwarts the call to a life of that form of self-giving which the Gospel says is the essence of Christian living. This does not mean that homosexual persons are not often generous in giving of themselves, but when they engage in homosexual activity they confirm within themselves a disordered sexual inclination which is essentially self-indulgent. As in every moral disorder, homosexual activity prevents one's own fulfillment and happiness by acting contrary to the creative wisdom of God. The Church in rejecting erroneous opinions regarding homosexuality, does not limit, but rather defends personal freedom and dignity, realistically and authentically understood.

## Free Will and Homosexuality

The Catholic Church teaches that morality is a morality of human acts. To be fully human, an act first has to be done volitionally, that is, out of free will and without external coercion. Second, it must be done with due deliberation, that is, an understanding of what is happening and what is being done. The morality of an act is determined in the objective order by its conformity to law, the natural law, which God writes on the heart of every human being, as well as divinely revealed law. Law can also require obedience when it is enacted by lawful authority in the Church and, sometimes, even in the state. The supreme subjective norm of morality is conscience, which is reason judging the rightness and wrongness of an individual act. For conscience, however, to be followed, as it must be, it is necessary for conscience to be properly formed. As Pope John Paul II puts it in his encyclical *The Splendor of Truth*, "Acting is morally good when the choices of freedom are in conformity with man's true good, corresponding to the wise design of God, indicated by His commandments which are a path leading to life." The Second Vatican Council, speaking of the norms of conjugal morality, justified their value precisely as being directed to keeping the exercise of sexual acts within the context of true love by safeguarding the total meaning of mutual self-giving and human procreation. The fundamental moral requirement is simply this: to do good and to avoid evil. It is our duty as human beings, then, using reason and divine revelation, to discover what doing good is and what evil is.

The Church has through almost 2,000 years of her history consistently made a distinction between the sin and the sinner. There must always be inflexible and flint-hard hatred of sin, while at the same time there must be compassion, understanding, and concern for the one who commits the sin, that is to say, the sinner. This theoretically is quite possible, but in practice it frequently is quite difficult to distinguish the sin from the sinner, since, as has been pointed out many times, we in a certain sense become what we do. In other words, if we lie, we become liars. If we fornicate, we become fornicators. If we do homosexual acts, we become homosexuals. Nonetheless, the door to mercy and forgiveness must never be closed. It should be pointed out, however, that in Christian theology, the conditions for mercy and forgiveness are repentance and recognition of sinfulness. It is not possible for God, even in His infinite mercy, to pardon one who refuses to accept His pardon or even refuses to recognize a need for such pardon.

## The Nature of Sin

This, of course, leads to another important aspect of the moral evaluation of homosexuality from the ecclesiastical point of view, which is to say, the distinction between the homosexual condition or inclination and actual homosexual acts. Homosexual acts are intrinsically disordered. In Catholic terminology, when they are done with free will and deliberation, they are mortal and lethal sins which terminate one's friendship and relationship with the Creator. They are intrinsically disordered because they lack an essential and indispensable goal.

The Catholic Church has not made any official pronouncement about the problem of homosexual orientation, that is to say, whether it can be or is acquired, or whether it is congenital and may have some basis in psychosomatic or even physical factors. If this orientation is not the result of morally negative choice, then, obviously, it cannot be called a sin. Nevertheless, even in that instance, that is, even when it is present without being desired, or willed, or deliberated upon, and therefore is not a sin, it is intrinsically disordered. It must be seen as a more or less strong inclination to intrinsically evil behavior from the moral viewpoint, and therefore, cannot be thought of as neutral or good. In Catholic tradition, this corresponds to what the Council of Trent calls the meaning of concupiscence, which is not sin in the true and proper sense but is an effect of original sin, and can be called sin insofar as it

> *"Homosexual activity is not a complementary union able to transmit life."*

comes from sin and inclines toward sin. There are many aspects of the human condition that are represented by such concupiscence, things such as excessive desire for power, selfishness, greed, and those kinds of perversions which we call kleptomania, sadism, and pyromania. Such disordered inclinations are not in themselves sins but are objectively disordered and lead to objective evil. And insofar as the acts that proceed from such inclinations are under the dominance of free will and have received due deliberation, they are sinful and culpable on the part of those who commit them.

Compassion for, and pastoral concern and care for, those people who have these kinds of orientations should never be confused with the approval of any acts that may derive from these inclinations. At the same time, Christian charity, which is not an option but an obligation for those who follow the teachings of Jesus Christ, requires that there be constantly exercised compassion, mercy, concern, and care for all people, even those who are inclined toward evil actions, and this is particularly the case if these inclinations have not been caused by their own incorrect use of free will.

## Two Kinds of Discrimination

A word should also be spoken about the word "discrimination." There are two kinds of discrimination, unjust discrimination and just discrimination. Unfortunately, the discussion about this issue in our present American society leads to a great deal of confusion and ambiguity, which sometimes result in apparent contradictions in Catholic approaches to anti-discriminatory legislation in various state legislatures and various municipalities. Certainly there is such a thing as unjust discrimination. And to deprive someone unjustly of work or housing or other arrangements simply on the basis of past actions, or on the basis of announced inclination, could and would be unjust. At the same time there are certain measures of just discrimination which are not only morally neutral but are sometimes morally necessary. For instance, it would be a case of just discrimination to prevent a pyromaniac from having a job as a custodian in a gasoline storage facility. It would certainly be just discrimination to disallow employment as a bank teller to a person given to kleptomania. There are certain kinds of activities which, I believe one can say, should not be engaged in by homosexuals, particularly if the homosexuality has certain other phenomena associated with it, such as pedophilia. It would be morally reprehensible to hire a pedophile to take care of a children's daycare center. Because of the simplistic use of particular political slogans in our time, this kind of just discrimination is frequently lumped together under a general title of discrimination and declared unacceptable in modern American culture, which exalts tolerance at any cost as the supreme virtue.

> *"The Church has . . . consistently made a distinction between the sin and the sinner."*

Moreover, Christians have not only a right but a duty to avoid placing people in occasions of sin. Housing discrimination, for example, with regard to homosexual couples is, in my view, a very just and rightful form of discrimination which *Christians* not only can, but should, exercise. They should refuse, for instance, to rent apartments or rooms to persons (heterosexual or homosexual) who are obviously in an intrinsically disordered arrangement in regard to their sexual lives.

## Opposing "Gay Culture"

It is also a right and perhaps a duty of Christians to see that the civil laws of the country in which they live recognize that the promotion and defense of families, founded on monogamous heterosexual marriage, is an essential part of the common good. The state should not be allowed, with their acquiescence, to deprive itself of the healthy social fabric that marriage alone can make possible and which is necessary for harmonious society and the continuation of human civilization. In my view, as well, a Christian, and certainly a Catholic, has a right and a duty to oppose "gay culture," which does not simply mean a tragically homosexually-oriented person but rather signifies a collection of persons who publicly adopt a homosexual lifestyle and are committed to having such a lifestyle accepted by society as fully legitimate in civil law. Melina states quite correctly that "justifiable opposition to offenses and discrimination which violate a person's rights cannot be confused with this demand [of "gay culture"]. In fact a systematic plan for the public justification and glorification of homosexuality is taking place, starting with the attempt to make it fully accepted in the minds of society. It aims through increasing pressure at a change in legislation so that homosexual unions may enjoy the same rights as marriage including that of adoption."

Jesus promised, "You shall know the truth, and the truth shall set you free" (Jn. 8:32). We are also told in Sacred Scripture that we are to "speak the truth in love" (Eph. 4:15). So God, who is at once truth and love, calls us to minister in the Church to all people, including those people with homosexual inclinations or homosexual acts in their past. It does not serve the cause of either truth or love, however, if they do not infuse one another. Truth is not truth unless it is accompanied by love, just as love is not genuine love unless it is accompanied by truth.

Obviously, there is much more that could be said about this issue, particularly in refutation of various and serious misinterpretations of Sacred

> *"Homosexual acts are intrinsically disordered."*

Scripture, such as the relationship of David and Jonathan, or even more blasphemously, those who would misunderstand or misinterpret the relationship of Jesus Christ and the "disciple whom He loved," which from the Greek text tells us very clearly is a disinterested, pure, and dispassionate love and has absolutely nothing to do with any homosexual relationship or inclination. The Fathers of the Church have always considered with undeviating consistency homosexuality as an intolerable sin for Christians. And although it was a cultural fact in ancient times, just as it is in our own, the general norms of Christian ethics, from the first days of the Catholic Church's existence to the present, have been unvarying in their understanding that human sexual activity is permissible only in the context of Christian marriage.

I would like to conclude this very brief presentation of the teaching of the Catholic Church on homosexuality with a paraphrase from the poet John Donne, who said quite eloquently: Human beings are never really free unless they are chained by God's commandments, just as they are never really pure until they are ravished by God's love.

# Therapists Should Help People Overcome Homosexuality

## by Mary Meehan

**About the author:** *Mary Meehan is a Maryland writer who has been published in many periodicals ranging from the* Human Life Review *to the* Washington Post.

Many people want to change the homosexual condition in themselves or to avoid the condition in their children. They may have religious convictions that homosexual activity is wrong, or they may simply believe that it leads to much unhappiness. They want to avoid dying from AIDS or suffering from other serious disease. And they want to avoid passing early death or deep suffering on to someone else.

They should know that there is genuine hope about both change and prevention. Neither is easy, but both are possible.

Discussion should begin with an understanding of what the homosexual condition is and what causes it. It involves sexual attraction toward persons of the same sex as oneself, as evidenced by sexual fantasies or by sexual activities that persist into adulthood. Homosexuals, like heterosexuals, have "crushes" or infatuations, and they fall in love with particular persons.

### Male and Female Homosexuals

Male homosexuality, though, often involves promiscuous sex; sometimes one male has hundreds of sexual partners over a lifetime. Male homosexual practices include mutual masturbation, oral sex, and anal intercourse. The last-named practice, in particular, leads to a high rate of AIDS and to other diseases, including hepatitis, gonorrhea, syphilis, herpes, shigellosis, acute rectal trauma, rectal incontinence, and anal cancer—a true catalog of horrors.

Female homosexuals, or lesbians, tend to be less promiscuous than males.

They are more likely to have long-term or mutually faithful unions, although many have a series of lovers over a lifetime. Their sexual practices include mutual masturbation, oral sex, and sometimes intercourse with a dildo. Medically speaking, their sexual practices are less dangerous than those of male homosexuals, especially where AIDS is concerned.

How does a homosexual tendency begin? There are theories aplenty, each with its partisans. Much of the literature suggests many causes, with one often reinforcing another.

## Causes of Homosexuality

In 1993 National Institutes of Health scientist Dean Hamer and colleagues caused a stir with a report suggesting a genetic contribution to homosexuality. They indicated a linkage between an area of the X chromosome (Xq28) and sexual orientation, based on a study of 40 families each of which included two homosexual brothers. Media reports led many to believe that Hamer's group had found a "gay gene," or that someone soon would. But Hamer makes clear in his book, *The Science of Desire* (New York: Simon & Schuster, 1994, coauthored by Peter Copeland) that his median estimate was merely that the Xq28 area "plays some role in about 5 to 30 percent of gay men."

Others challenged even this limited conclusion. Dr. Jeffrey Satinover, a psychiatrist, is critical of Hamer's work and contends that most such studies "have many flaws." Satinover suggests that a genetic contribution may operate, but in an indirect way, just as genes for great height may provide a capability for basketball-playing, but do not cause someone to become a basketball player.

In *Homosexuality and the Politics of Truth* (Grand Rapids, Mich.: Baker Books, 1996), Satinover notes that some innate traits result at least partly from intrauterine influences on the unborn child. "Hormones, infections, exercise, general health, the ingestion of licit or illicit drugs, and many other variables," he writes, "influence this environment." Sometimes, he notes, the normal "chemical signals get crossed" so that a baby who is *genetically* male appears to be a female but is infertile, or a baby has both male and female sexual features and is a true hermaphrodite. These cases, although rare, suggest the importance of considering intrauterine influences.

> *"A child develops a homosexual disposition because the same-sex parent has been emotionally distant, cold, or hostile."*

One of the oldest psychological theories still makes sense: that a child develops a homosexual disposition because the same-sex parent has been emotionally distant, cold, or hostile. Dr. Elizabeth R. Moberly, in *Homosexuality: A New Christian Ethic* (Cambridge, England: James Clarke & Co., 1983), writes that the child has a normal need for love from the same-sex parent and attachment to that parent. When love and attachment are missing or defective, the child suffers emotionally and has a "defensive detachment" from the same-sex parent. That is, to avoid more emotional pain, the child rejects the parent and the masculinity (or femininity) the parent represents. But the child still needs the same-sex love he or she *should* have received from the parent, and later homosexual tendencies are essentially an effort to make up for the missing love.

Psychologist Joseph Nicolosi, whose therapeutic approach is based partly on Moberly's insights, has said that male homosexual behavior is a "search for the lost masculine self." In *Reparative Therapy of Male Homosexuality* (Northvale, N.J.: Jason Aronson, 1997, rev.), Nicolosi describes defensive detachment as a "self-protective stance" in which a boy expresses his anger by ignoring his father and denying that the father "has any importance in the family" and by "conspiring with mother in collusion against father."

When the boy is roughly between the ages of five and twelve, Nicolosi writes,

> He is typically fearful and cautious toward other boys his age, staying close to his mother and perhaps grandmother, aunts, or older sisters. He becomes the "kitchen window boy," who looks out at his peers playing aggressively and, what appears to him, dangerously. He is attracted to the other boys at the same time he is frightened by what they are doing. Defensive detachment emotionally isolates him from other males, and from his own masculinity. Females are familiar, while males are mysterious.

> Then when sexual needs begin to seek expression in early adolescence, it is understandable that the direction of such a young man's sexual interests will be away from the familiar and toward the unapproachable. We do not sexualize what we are familiar with. We are drawn to the "other-than-me."

Some experts emphasize poor relations with playmates in early childhood. Dr. Richard Fitzgibbons, a psychiatrist who has worked with many homosexuals, believes that a little boy's lack of hand-eye coordination and athletic ability causes peer rejection so strong that it can lead to homosexuality. "It's hard for many people to believe," Fitzgibbons said in an interview, "how important it is in the development of masculine identity to be good in sports. It's *essential* in this culture. It shouldn't be, but it is."

He believes that boys are rejected by their peers as early as three or four years of age if they are not good in sports. If a little boy lacks athletic ability and is rejected by other boys, he may play mainly with girls and may adopt their mannerisms in exaggerated form. Other boys may then reject him even more definitively as "sissy" and "queer" and "fag," so he stays with the girls and becomes convinced that he is very different from other boys—which eventually he is. He may also develop a deep, although possibly unconscious, anger at boys who have tormented him. Fitzgibbons says that some men with this background would like to kill those who treated them so badly.

Many homosexuals were molested by male family members or strangers when they were young. Although this can be terrifying and repulsive to them initially, it can also lead to sexual arousal and to a habit of homosexual behavior. It often leads to their typing themselves as innately homosexual; males would not be attracted to them and molest them, they reason, if they were normal.

Dr. Moberly believes that defensive detachment from mothers plays a major role in lesbianism, and some case studies support this. But sexual abuse by a male—a relative, neighborhood boys, or a stranger—may be a larger factor; it certainly appears with depressing regularity in the literature. So do poor relations with a father. Often several negative factors combine to produce the condition, as described by ex-lesbian Jane Boyer:

> I was raised by two alcoholic parents. My father was a violent and rageful man. I developed an intense hatred for men, and determined in my heart I would never let a man get close to me. I was also sexually abused as a child—which only reinforced my feelings of hatred. Because my mother was a victim of my father's violence, I became her protector and caretaker. "Mom," I vowed, "I hate it that you are weak, clingy, and powerless. I will have nothing to do with womanhood." (Jane Boyer, "Married—and Trapped in Lesbianism," Exodus International *Update*, June 1996.)

Other factors contributing to male or female homosexuality may include:

• a father who, having wanted but failed to get a son, treats his daughter as a boy

• a mother who favors a "more feminine" daughter over one who is "tomboyish" or a father who favors a "more masculine" son over one he perceives as too sensitive

• a mother who over-protects or "smothers" her son, possibly competing with the father for the son's love

• the combination of a weak father, who does not draw his son into the world of men and masculinity, and a domineering mother who draws the son into her world

• the work-addicted or television-addicted parent who is just "too busy" to spend time with a child

• parents who are hostile to each other and constantly fighting, so that their children learn to fear marriage and the heterosexual patterns leading to it

Parents are not always at fault. Sometimes, for example, a father's rejection of his son is *perceived* rather than real. If the father is working overseas while the son is very young, the little boy may have no male role model and may be smothered by female relatives. Sometimes simple bad luck plays a role, bringing together several unfavorable circumstances.

## Prevention

How can the homosexual condition be prevented? A child is likely to have a normal sexual disposition when the parents have a happy marriage and when they give much love to all of their children, never favoring one over another but recognizing and encouraging the special gifts of each. In a large family, it is important to avoid neglecting older children as younger, cuter, and more demanding ones come along.

The father should spend some time just with his sons in "guy things" such as sports or car repair. A boy who is fearful or clumsy in sports should receive extra help from the father, who should praise each little success but not expect an athletic star. A boy who doesn't care for football or basketball may do very well in quieter sports such as bowling, fishing, canoeing, or anything in the Boy Scout line. Some boys—like some dads—may never develop a great interest in sports, but can learn enough to get along with other boys.

> *"Many homosexuals were molested by male family members or strangers when they were young."*

When a father is absent because of death or divorce, an uncle or a much older brother should step in as a father figure. When there is no other male in the family, a "mentor" program such as Big Brothers may provide a volunteer to fill the role.

A mother, of course, should spend time with her daughters in clothes shopping, decorating, cooking, and such. Rigidity should be avoided, though; these are by no means the only things that girls are interested in or that can be of practical value to them. If your daughter shows an occasional interest in "guy things"—such as changing the oil in the family car—don't panic!

Parents should not normally worry about young girls' "tomboy" interests, for they may simply indicate an attraction to outdoor fun. Don't be fixated on the mantra, "Girls can't . . . Girls don't." Of course, there is cause for concern if a girl is determinedly mannish, but this is highly unlikely in a happy family where the mother is a good model. If the mother is absent through death or divorce, the father should ask an older female relative to be a mentor to his daughters.

Good parents are concerned about their children's playmates. This should include being sure that each child has friends of the same sex. Parents should not tolerate children's taunting of playmates with name-calling such as "sissy," "queer," or "fag," or, for that matter, "fatty" or "retard." Not only is such name-calling cruel, but it may cut so deeply that the victim never feels accepted by other children. The names can be self-fulfilling prophecies. Parents should teach their children to help other kids instead of making fun of them.

Good parents can also prevent much trouble by teaching their children modesty and by telling them that no one should touch them "in an unholy way"—to quote one ex-gay who was himself molested as a child. Experts on child sexual abuse recommend telling children in a matter-of-fact way that they should protest in a loud voice if anyone tries to molest them. They should move away quickly and tell a parent or other trusted adult about the incident right away. Child-molesting depends on secrecy, and secrecy can result in a child's suffering for many years. A quick and loud response—by the child and the parents—can prevent more abuse and warn others about the offender.

## Changing Sexual Orientations

Families with a member who is struggling with homosexuality should be aware of the National Association for Research and Therapy of Homosexuality (NARTH). This group refers people who want to overcome their homosexual condition to psychotherapists around the country. (NARTH can be reached at: 16633 Ventura Blvd., Suite 1340, Encino, CA 91436; (818) 789-4440; www.narth.com.)

Dr. Fitzgibbons claims a high recovery rate among teenagers he works with, especially "those who really are willing to work" and who "have not become sexually addicted." He emphasizes healing the emotional pain his patients have suffered. "As that emotional pain is healed," he says, homosexual attractions usually "diminish and resolve completely." Fitzgibbons stresses a spiritual approach and one that encourages patients to forgive those who have harmed them in the past, including playmates who taunted and rejected them.

Nicolosi believes it is essential for a male homosexual to develop nonsexual friendships with other men, which will "demystify" other males and help the client resume the process—interrupted when he was a child—of developing his own male identity. Nicolosi often gives his clients practical advice about developing masculine identity and self-confidence. He believes that his reparative therapy can work for teens, but only when "the teenager himself is motivated." He also believes that religious faith "furthers the therapy."

Lesbians who want to change their orientation might want to read Jeanette Howard's *Out of Egypt* (Crowborough, England: Monarch Publications, 1991). Howard, a counselor and ex-lesbian who appears to be writing from an evangelical Protestant perspective, offers useful suggestions about overcoming emotional dependence and loneliness and about developing healthy woman-to-woman friendships.

> *"A child is likely to have a normal sexual disposition when the parents have a happy marriage."*

The process of change, especially for people who have been homosexually active for years, can be quite difficult. As Jane Boyer once remarked, changing is "not for wimps." But it can be very rewarding.

Success in counseling or therapy means a great reduction in homosexual feelings. Many people find that, as their homosexual feelings decrease, they become attracted to members of the opposite sex. Some eventually marry and have children. Other remain single but celibate. This does not mean they will never again have homosexual feelings or attractions, but these are likely to be relatively fleeting and manageable as time goes by.

They may not find perfection, just as the rest of us do not, but they find peace.

# Schools Should Not Teach Acceptance of Homosexuality

**by Camille Paglia**

**About the author:** *Camille Paglia is a professor of humanities at the University of the Arts in Philadelphia.*

Spin the gay bottle! Pin the tail on the gay donkey! Welcome to the wild and wonderful world of American public education.

## The Newton Gay Hit Parade

The prestigious Oak Hill Middle School of Newton, Massachusetts, has posted, for the edification of its 11- to 13-year-old students, the photos of 14 major gay figures of the ancient and modern world.

The purpose? To show that "it's OK to be gay" and that "gay is good," school officials told the *Boston Globe*. The female art teacher who created the bulletin-board exhibit declared, "Kids commit suicide over their sexuality; it's up to us to take this issue from under the covers, and say, 'It's OK, it's normal.'"

Who made the Newton gay hit parade? Not just professed gays like Marcel Proust, Andy Warhol, James Baldwin and Newton's own Congressman Barney Frank, but Alexander the Great, Michelangelo, Leonardo da Vinci, William Shakespeare, Walt Whitman—and Eleanor Roosevelt. "If kids question how the wife of a president could be gay, good," declared the teacher, who defined her professional goal as "teaching tolerance and respect."

But wouldn't students be better off if their teachers fed them facts rather than propaganda? Proclaiming Eleanor Roosevelt gay is not only goofy but malicious. It reduces a bold, dynamic woman whose entire achievement was in the public realm to gossip and speculation about her most guarded private life.

Only in puritanical Anglo-American culture could kisses and hugs (the acts with which Mrs. Roosevelt is charged) be transformed into salacious evidence for prosecution and conviction. False accusations in 17th-century Salem got you hanged as a witch. False accusations in 20th-century Newton get you hoisted as a gay saint.

## The Political Distortion of Art

As a specialist in the history of the arts, I am outraged at the coarse political exploitation and distortion of art, a trend that began 25 years ago on our college campuses. That Michelangelo, Leonardo and Walt Whitman were attracted to young men, I have no doubt. But those phenomenally productive geniuses were obsessively solitary characters who may have diverted their sexual energies into art. In the absence of hard information, to call them "gay" is ethically wrong. And to introduce major artists to schoolchildren via sexual scandal rather than through the art itself is a perversion of education.

> *"The intrusion of militant gay activism into primary school does more harm than good."*

Those who promote Shakespeare's homosexuality for their own ideological agenda conveniently overlook the fact that none of his 37 plays address homosexuality, or allude to it except in negative terms. (Is Iago, with his evil fixation on Othello, now to be a gay role model?) On the contrary, Shakespeare is world-famous for his celebration of heterosexual love, as in the eternally popular "Romeo and Juliet."

There are two romantic objects of Shakespeare's sonnets, conventionally called the Dark Lady and the Fair Youth, but it is not at all clear that physical consummation occurred with the latter. In fact, in Sonnet 20 Shakespeare remarks that his friend's penis is an obstruction to their union and elsewhere explicitly urges him to marry.

Sexual orientation is fluid and ambiguous, and homosexuality has multiple causes. It certainly is not inborn, as was claimed by several small, flawed studies of the early 1990s. The intrusion of militant gay activism into primary school does more harm than good by encouraging adolescents to define themselves prematurely as gay, when in fact most teens are wracked by instability, insecurity and doubt.

Questionable and overblown statistics about teen suicide (like those about rape few years ago) are being rankly abused. In most cases, the suicide attempts are probably due not to homophobic persecution but to troubled family relations—which may be the source of the social maladjustment and homosexual impulses in the first place. Trumpeting gayness in adolescence short-circuits their psychological inquiry and growth.

Many pressing civil-liberties issues remain to be resolved for gays—the right to serve with honor in the military, for example, or the extension of equal benefit to domestic partners. But the kind of arrogant cultural imperialism shown in Newton—where "tolerance and respect would clearly not be accorded to a fundamentalist Christian or Hindu who declared homosexuality immoral"—can only create a backlash empowering the religious far right.

Preachers of the left and preachers of the right must stay out of our public schools. "Self-esteem" is not the purpose of education. Teachers should stop posing as therapists and do-gooders and get back to introducing the huge expanse of art, literature, history and science to American students, who desperately need cultural enrichment and intellectual development.

# The Boy Scouts Should Not Be Forced to Accept Homosexuals

## by Melanie Kirkpatrick

**About the author:** *Melanie Kirkpatrick is the assistant editor of the* Wall Street Journal*'s editorial page.*

The U.S. Supreme Court did a good turn the day it accepted the case of the gay Boy Scout. That case will be argued in April 2000, and the court will do another good turn—for the Constitution and for all of us, gays included—if it decides in favor of the Scouts.[1]

## Freedom of Association

For the *Boy Scouts of America v. James Dale* is about every American's First Amendment freedom of association. If the Boy Scouts lose, so will the thousands of other private, voluntary associations that organize themselves on the basis of race, religion, ethnicity, gender or sexual orientation.

By now the Boy Scouts have nearly two decades of hard experience battling legal challenges to their right to join together under a common moral code. "Three G" cases, as they are known, have been brought by gays, girls and atheists (the "godless") demanding admission. The Scouts have won most Three-G cases, with the supreme courts of California, Kansas, Connecticut and Oregon all finding for them.

But not New Jersey. The state Supreme Court ruled in the summer of 1999 that Mr. Dale, an avowed homosexual who says he wants to be a gay role model, must be permitted to serve as an assistant scoutmaster. The state court gave three reasons, which in and of themselves provide an instructive look at just how far judicial reasoning can stray from common sense.

---

1. The U.S. Supreme Court ruled in 2000 that the Boy Scouts of America had the right to discriminate against openly homosexual scoutmasters.

First, it held that scouting isn't the kind of "intimate association" protected by the First Amendment. That will come as news to the boys who are members of Cub Scout packs and Boy Scout troops, which typically number 15 to 30 members each. An essential part of scouting is that it is small-scale and personal. A scoutmaster is supposed to be a "wise friend" to his small group of Scouts.

Second, the court took it upon itself to decide that the leaders of the Boy Scouts don't really understand their own values. The Scouts maintain that the Scout Law's exhortation to be "clean" and the Scout Oath's promise to be "morally straight" are inconsistent with homosexual conduct. Not so, replied the New Jersey jurists. Rather, they substituted a view of their own, declaring that a gay assistant scoutmaster was perfectly in keeping with the mission and values of the organization. The Scouts are now in the preposterous position of having to prove to the Supreme Court that they actually mean what they say.

And third, the New Jersey court declared that requiring the Scouts to appoint a homosexual scoutmaster isn't an infringement on their right of free speech. The Scouts say a message they abhor is being forced upon them. How else may an organization communicate its message other than through its leaders? What is a boy supposed to think when he sees Mr. Dale in his Scout uniform?

## Friends of the Court

The New Jersey court also ruled that New Jersey's antidiscrimination law applies to the Boy Scouts, which it determined are a "public accommodation" rather than a private association. The court has plenty of company in this view. A look at the arguments in several of the many friend-of-the-court briefs filed in support of Mr. Dale show the ludicrous lengths to which some will go to convert the Scouts' private convictions into impermissible public policies. A number of the briefs make

> *"Some will go to [ludicrous lengths to] convert the Scouts' private convictions into impermissible public policies."*

much of the fact that Boy Scouts sometimes use government facilities, such as parks and public schools, just, of course, as many other private organizations do:

• The American Bar Association points out that scouting is an "important training ground for leaders in commerce, politics and society." It therefore supports the New Jersey court's view that scouting is a public accommodation in part because Scouts can benefit from close ties with Congressmen, presidents, generals and astronauts.

• The American Association of School Administrators maintains that the Boy Scouts are in effect a government organization because they help the government by picking up trash in national parks. (If only Scouts learned to litter, perhaps their views would be considered private.)

• But the argument that takes the Alice-in-Wonderland prize comes from the state of New Jersey's brief. This purports to prove scouting's close association with government by pointing to its merit badge for citizenship, which teaches Scouts about the Declaration of Independence, Constitution and Bill of Rights. According to this logic, since the Boy Scouts study the First Amendment, they are condemned to forfeiting their rights under that amendment.

Many familiar liberal groups have submitted briefs in favor of Mr. Dale, just as a number of familiar conservative and libertarian organizations support the Scouts. In the end, though, the case is about something much more important than Scouts or gays. It's about a core value of American society: the right to associate, and not associate, with whomever we please.

The 1999 edition of the *Encyclopedia of Associations* lists 22,049 national organizations, including hundreds whose membership is limited to a single sex, ethnicity, race or religion. State and local associations add up to tens of thousands more. These organizations—black big brothers, Jewish singles, gay lawyers, women police officers, Hispanic accountants—are an intrinsic part of American civic life.

Without such associations, our society would be fundamentally altered. Do gays, for example, want their organizations flooded by fundamentalists trying to "convert" them? A much-quoted line from the Boy Scouts' Supreme Court brief says it best: "A society in which every organization must be equally diverse is a society which has destroyed diversity."

> *"A society in which every organization must be equally diverse is a society which has destroyed diversity."*

Yes, the Boy Scouts discriminate on a number of levels—no girls, no gays, no atheists. If critics are concerned about diversity, they might look at one important measure—religion—by which scouting may well be the most diverse organization in America. Some 66% of Boy Scout troops and Cub Scout packs are sponsored by religious organizations—1,200 different nominations in all, including Zoroastrians, Moravians, Quakers and Sikhs as well as the more ubiquitous Methodists, Mormons and Catholics. Every troop is open to boys of any religion.

Many good people will differ over whether the Boy Scouts ought to admit Mr. Dale and other open homosexuals. Those who believe they should have every right to work to change the Scouts' minds—and to be respected for their views. But the Boy Scouts and other private associations have a right too—to be free to pursue their own convictions without government interference.

# Chapter 4

# Should Society Sanction Gay and Lesbian Families?

# Chapter Preface

In 1972, Jeanne and Jules Manford watched their television in horror as their gay son was physically assaulted during televised coverage of a gay rights protest while police stood by and did nothing. Later, Jeanne marched with her son in their city's Gay Pride March, carrying a sign that identified herself as the proud mother of a gay child. Lesbians and gay men attending the parade rushed up to Jeanne and asked if she could help their parents become as accepting as she was. A year later, the Manfords organized a group of about twenty people whose goal was to offer support to the families of gays and lesbians. By 1979, grassroots groups identifying themselves as PFLAG—Parents and Friends of Lesbians and Gays—had sprung up all across the United States. Twenty PFLAG groups formed a national association in 1981, and today, the confederation has local chapters in more than four hundred communities in the United States and other countries.

Today, while most of the public debate about gay families focuses on whether or not gays and lesbians should be allowed to marry and raise or adopt children, privately, gays and lesbians are often most concerned with whether or not their own families accept them. Some gay men and lesbians say it would be difficult to start their own families without the support of their parents and siblings. Others are encouraged to start families because they do not feel accepted by their own family members and long for familial closeness. In debating whether gays and lesbians should be allowed to raise children of their own, many commentators say it is important to remember that gays and lesbians are themselves grown children, already part of a family. Many therapists point out that the healthier the relationship is between a gay person and his or her family, the healthier the gay person will be and the more successful he or she will be as a parent.

PFLAG has been instrumental in helping the families of gays and lesbians accept them, and in consequence, making it easier for gay children to establish successful families of their own. PFLAG chapters offer monthly meetings where straight family members can come to learn how to accept their gay loved ones. During these meetings, people share their concerns with others in the group and receive support and guidance. Parents report feeling accepted by the group, an acceptance that is often lacking in their relationships with other people, who often disapprove of homosexuality and blame them for raising a gay child. One PFLAG parent says of the organization, "This is a family that has left behind the hate and embraced love."

PFLAG chapters such as the one established by founders Jeanne and Jules Manford have helped thousands of families accept their gay sons and daughters,

aunts and uncles, parents, siblings, and friends in the face of often virulent social disapproval of homosexuality. The authors in the following chapter debate
whether society should sanction gay and lesbian families. To be sure, many gay
people are pushing for the right to marry and legally adopt and raise children of
their own, but for most gays and lesbians, the first family where acceptance becomes an issue is the one they were born into.

# Society Should Allow Same-Sex Marriage

**by Alec Walen**

**About the author:** *Alec Walen is a professor of legal, ethical, and historical studies at the University of Baltimore.*

It was a foregone conclusion that the 1996 Defense of Marriage Act (DOMA) would become law. A majority in this country believe that gay marriage is wrong and demeaning to the institution of marriage, and our politicians do a reasonably good job of representing the interests of their constituents, at least on nontechnical matters like this. Rare indeed was the member of Congress who expressed concern over the fact that the DOMA's sole aim is to perpetuate the unequal treatment of homosexuals by defining marriage for the purposes of federal law as "a legal union between one man and one woman."

## Constitutional and Moral Arguments

There are both constitutional and moral problems with this inequality. Because of the constitutional problems, we may yet be saved from the law by the Supreme Court.[1] But that is not my concern here. I want to argue that denying homosexuals the right to marry whom they love is morally unjustifiable.

As Representative Patrick Kennedy (D-RI) said, the debate over the bill "is really about a simple question, a question of equal rights. Marriage is a basic right. . . . Love and commitment are essential pillars of marriage. They are qualities that do not discriminate on account of gender. . . . Love and commitment can exist between a man and a woman and it can and does exist between men and between women." Unless it can be shown that love and commitment are not the only pillars of marriage, and that the other pillars cannot exist between men or between women, or unless there is some social need pressing enough to deny homosexuals a basic right, the DOMA stands as an unjust obstacle to equality.

1. The Defense of Marriage Act has not been overturned.

Justifying the DOMA arguments is a moral burden that none of its supporters ought to slough off lightly. What follows is an examination of the best arguments made by congressional supporters of the DOMA. Focusing on the congressional debate may seem to mistake political grandstanding for serious argument. But even if most congressional supporters of the DOMA do not really believe what they say, politicians are professional weather vanes—their words are a telling indicator of what people want to hear, and thus of what the people who elect them (theoretically, the majority of us) think.

## Arguments

After examining the arguments given by congressional supporters of the DOMA and showing that none of them carries the necessary moral burden, I will try to answer the following question: if there is no way the DOMA can be morally justified, why all the righteous talk in favor of it? One answer is that our culture is permeated by a current of authoritarian moral thinking. By this I mean that many Americans think that if the state does not enforce their values, disaster will follow. They see no virtue in a state that is neutral in the face of competing moral conceptions—and this shows why paying attention to the passage of the DOMA is important. For the new law symbolizes the extent to which we as a culture have yet to come to terms with the ideals of liberty and equality that we espouse.

In the following, all quotations are taken from the *Congressional Record* for the debates over the DOMA; House Debate, July 11–12, 1996; Senate Debate, September 10, 1996.

## (1) Majority Rule

*Representative Charles Canady (R-FL):* "Those of us who support this bill reject the view that [choice of a partner of the opposite sex or the same sex is] a matter of indifference. In doing so, we have the overwhelming support of the American people." Moreover, "Seventy percent of the American people are not bigots. Seventy percent of the American people are not prejudiced. Seventy percent of the American people are not mean-spirited, cruel, and hateful."

*Response:* Painting the opposition as insulting the people who elect you is good politics, but bad history. For most of our two hundred year history, the clear majority of people in this country thought it was immoral for

> *"Many Americans think that if the state does not enforce their values, disaster will follow."*

whites and blacks to marry. Yet this sentiment was an expression of bigotry. What makes the majority in America today suddenly immune from bigotry? Is it the fact that we now tolerate interracial marriage? Good start, but that doesn't show that we're all better now. Given their aim of perpetuating unequal treatment of homosexual couples, one can assert that the DOMA's supporters are not bigots (or unduly tolerant of and deferential to bigots) only if they give the new law a substantive moral justification. Appeals to majority consensus do nothing to establish the justice of that consensus.

## (2) The Essence or Definition of Marriage

*Senator Daniel Coats (R-IN):* "The definition of marriage is not created by politicians and judges, and it cannot be changed by them. . . . It is the union of one man and one woman. This fact can be respected, or it can be resented, but it cannot be altered."

*Response:* Coats's concept of marriage is implausibly narrow. No one can reasonably deny that polygamous marriages are marriages. Moreover, since many people think that same-sex couples can marry, nothing is gained by insisting that the definition of marriage does not allow for that. Concepts do what people want them to do, and insisting that one has insight into the pure essence of a concept is only a way of obscuring the background presumptions and purposes one brings to a debate. Since there is no obvious absurdity in same-sex marriage, the argument against it must appeal to more substantive reasons.

## (3) Universal Exclusion of Anything but Traditional Marriage

*Senator Phil Gramm (R-TX):* "[T]he traditional family has stood for 5,000 years. . . . In every major religion in history, from the early Greek myths of the 'Iliad' and the 'Odyssey' [written by the Greek poet Homer] to the oldest writings of the Bible to the oldest teachings of civilization, governments have recognized the traditional family as the foundation of prosperity and happiness. . . . Human beings have always given traditional marriage a special sanction. . . . Are we so wise today that we are ready to reject 5,000 years of recorded history? I do not think so."

*Response:* If this argument for humility were at all grounded in history, it would be worth taking seriously. But it is simply not true that societies throughout history have always given "special sanction" to marriage defined as a legal union between one man and one woman.

(a) Polygamy has very strong biblical historical credentials. Jacob, son of Isaac, married two wives, Leah and Rachel, and had children through them and their handmaids. Solomon had seven hundred wives and three hundred concubines (granted this was considered a sin, but because the wives were foreign, not because they were so many). Muslims from the time of Mohammed to the present allow men to marry more than one wife. And in Tibet, some women marry two or more men.

(b) Quoting from William Eskridge Jr.'s *The Case for Same-Sex Marriage:* "Same-sex unions were an integral part of the cultures of classical Greece and republican Rome, and imperial Rome recognized same-sex marriages. During the Middle Ages the Greek Orthodox and Roman Catholic Churches celebrated same-sex unions, as did imperial China. . . . Marriages in the so-called *berdache* tradition of gender-crossing effeminate men and 'amazon' women have been documented for dozens of other cultures in Africa, Australia, and Asia."

## (4) Jewish and Christian Traditions

*Representative Asa Hutchinson (R-AR):* "[M]arriage is a covenant established by God wherein one man and one woman are united for the purpose of founding and maintaining the family."

*Response:* There are at least three problems with this argument.

(a) One of the foundational commitments of this country is the separation of church and state. If a particular religion refuses to sanction same-sex marriages, the government should not force it to do so. Nor, however, should the government follow suit. It can only justify denying civil sanction to these marriages if there is a legitimate secular reason for doing so.

(b) As already noted, the Bible does not represent marriage as necessarily monogamous. Moreover, the Bible says not only "You must not lie with a male as with a woman" (Leviticus 18:22), but "You must not approach a woman while she is unclean from menstruation, to have intercourse with her" (Leviticus 18:19). Indeed, the Bible says, "If a man lies with a woman while she is menstruating, and has intercourse with her, . . . they must both be cut off from their people" (Leviticus 20:18). Where, then, are the calls for conditioning marriage on abstinence during menstruation?

> *"It is simply not true that societies throughout history have always given 'special sanction' to marriage . . . between one man and one woman."*

(c) Most religions in the West today accept the practice of picking and choosing which of the Bible's injunctions to follow, and many take as their guiding principle the ideal of love. Accordingly, again quoting Eskridge, "the Unitarian Universalist Association now affirms the growing practice of some of its ministers of conducting services of union of gay and lesbian couples and urges member societies to support their ministers in this practice. The Society of Friends leaves all issues to congregational decision, and thousands of same-sex marriages have been sanctified in Quaker ceremonies since the 1970s. . . . The General Assembly of the Union of American Hebrew Congregation (Reform Jewish synagogues) adopted a resolution in 1993 advocating legal recognition of same-sex unions." And same-sex marriages "have been sanctified by representatives of virtually all of America's leading religions."

## (5) Parenting of Children

*Senator Robert Byrd (D-WV):* "If same-sex marriage is accepted . . . America will have said that children do not need a mother and a father, two mothers or two fathers will be just as good. This would be a catastrophe."

*Response:* There are at least three problems with this argument. First, child rearing is not the only function of marriage. If it were, then we could deny heterosexual couples, one or both of whom is infertile, the right to marry.

Second, marriage for different-sex couples does not involve any testing of parenting skill. Surely a child abuser is more likely to do a bad job of parenting than a typical homosexual, yet heterosexual child abusers have a constitutional right to get married. If they have that right, then it makes no sense to deny it to same-sex couples.

> *"Gay and lesbian parents . . . can provide children with a nurturing relationship and a nurturing environment."*

Third, where is the evidence? According to Eskridge, "Studies have repeatedly shown that children raised in gay and (especially) lesbian households are as well socialized, as psychologically adjusted, and as capable of forming healthy peer relationships as children raised in different-sex or single-parent households." And in the recent case in Hawaii of *Baehr v. Miike,* the judge, after hearing a number of experts for both sides, similarly held, "Gay and lesbian parents and same-sex couples can provide children with a nurturing relationship and a nurturing environment which is conducive to the development of happy, healthy and well-adjusted children."

## (6) Homosexuals' Inability to Commit

*Representative Tom Coburn (R-OK):* "[T]here are studies to say that over 43 percent of all people who profess homosexuality have greater than 500 partners."

*Response:* Granting the premise that marriage involves a serious commitment, this argument carries no weight. First, many heterosexuals can't make serious commitments, yet they are not tested for their capacity to commit. Second, some homosexuals can commit; lesbian couples are in fact not known for their promiscuity. Third, presumably only those same-sex couples that really want to commit would seek to be married. Fourth, such statistical probabilities clearly could not be used to prohibit marriages between a man and a woman. Suppose, for example, it turned out that a significant percentage of professional athletes and movie stars have more than 500 partners. We still wouldn't dream of prohibiting athletes and movie stars from marrying. Finally, since marriage is the institution by which society recognizes and agrees to support a commitment, the problem gay couples may now have in committing should be an argument for, not against, gay marriage. . . .

## (8) The Destruction of Family and Society

*Representative Hutchinson:* "[O]ur Country can survive many things, but one thing it cannot survive is the destruction of the family unit which forms the foundation of society."

160

*Response:* How does disallowing same-sex marriage keep families stable? It does nothing to help married couples deal with the problems of violence or drug abuse; it provides no resources for education or counseling. It makes it more likely that same-sex couples will break up. It makes it more likely that homosexuals who want to partake of marriage will marry a different-sex person, thereby creating marriages that are highly susceptible to divorce or infidelity. What then is the argument?

Perhaps the underlying idea is that if marriage is not narrowly defined, then it will not be taken seriously, and the family will fall apart. Insofar as this has any plausibility, the relevant narrowness has to do with the seriousness of the commitment. But as we have seen, the idea that the commitment must be serious is in no way incompatible with extending the right to marry to same-sex couples.

The only other argument I can see is that licensing homosexual marriage is licensing homosexuality, licensing homosexuality is licensing licentiousness, and licentiousness will lead to the breakdown of the family, which will cause the breakdown of society. Thus it is to the moral status of homosexuality that we must turn.

### (9) The Immorality of Homosexuality

*Representative Bob Barr (R-GA):* "The flames of hedonism, the flames of narcissism, the flames of self-centered morality are licking at the very foundations of our society: the family unit." *Representative Coburn:* "I come from a district in Oklahoma who [sic] has very profound beliefs that homosexuality is wrong. . . . They base that belief on what they believe God says about homosexuality. . . . What they believe is, is [sic] that homosexuality is immoral, that it is based on perversion, that it is based on lust."

*Response:* Two reasons are given for why homosexuality is immoral: (1) religion says so, and (2) it is licentious. We have already looked at the religious argument and found it wanting. Not all religions agree, not even all mainstream religions. In addition, this country is based on a separation of church and state. That leaves the argument based on licentiousness.

> *"[Making same-sex marriage illegal] does nothing to help married couples deal with the problems of violence or drug abuse."*

I accept the premise that licentiousness is bad. If homosexuality were based on perversion or on lust, hedonism, or narcissism, it would be morally undesirable. The question is, what reason is there to think that homosexuality fits these descriptions?

Let's focus first on lust, hedonism, and narcissism. Some homosexuals act on the basis of lust, but so do some heterosexuals. Some homosexuals are hedonistic and narcissistic, but so are some heterosexuals. Even if these traits were more often found in homosexuals than heterosexuals, it is simply false that homosexuality is essentially based on any of them. The nature of the attraction and the reasons for forming relationships are essentially the same for homosexuals and heterosexuals. Sexual orientation determines the pool of people with whom one may form an intimate relationship, but it in no way determines the quality of the relationship one may form.

Perversion is a harder category to handle because it is unclear what is meant. It seems to convey the idea that homosexuality is in some way unnatural. But in what way? Like styrofoam, something not seen in nature? If that is what is meant, it is false. Other animals engage in homosexual behavior, as do members of all human societies. Is it that we were given a sex drive in order to reproduce? If that is the case, then all sexual intimacy that is not directed at reproduction is equally perverse. But who said the overriding purpose of our lives was to reproduce? This is a morality for rabbits, not humans. Yet anything more generous than this lapine morality, such as a morality that praised love and affection in their own right, would have another way to make sense of nonreproductive sexual activity—it can be a profound way of showing love and affection.

The question raised by the preceding review of the arguments in favor of the DOMA is, why do people think there is a deep connection between homosexuality and licentiousness? The underlying theory must be something like this: homosexuality is obviously wrong, and one would only engage in it if one were driven by lust or if one substituted some sort of hedonic principle for morality. This is so far from plausible, however, that one has to wonder why it has a grip on people.

> *"[Opponents of same-sex marriage] are so certain and dogmatic about their moral convictions that they cannot see other points of view as reasonable alternatives."*

My answer is that those who share this belief are moral authoritarians in the following sense. They are so certain and dogmatic about their moral convictions that they cannot see other points of view as reasonable alternatives. They cannot recognize as morally serious any position that values homosexual love as highly as heterosexual love. They have to dismiss it as a crude hedonic principle unworthy of the name of morality.

This analysis fits also with their belief that family and country are on the brink of disaster. If we, as a society, cease to endorse their principles, the result will be a moral free-for-all, chaos without norms. They cannot abide the thought that their moral view is merely one among many.

The same uncertainty and social instability that moral authoritarians cite as evidence that we are on the brink of chaos and social collapse, seem to me the growing pains of real moral progress: the growth of political equality. Among the most profound changes in this century is the extension of greater authority to women, blacks, and all those who had formerly been kept out of power. This change has necessarily been very disruptive to the norms of the old hierarchical order according to which women ruled over children, men over women, and white men over black people. In such a world everyone knew what was expected of him or her, and such knowledge was doubtless comforting (for most). But it was a world in which people were forced into roles regardless of how well they fit. And it was a world of unjustifiable privilege and authority for some, along with poverty and powerlessness for others. Breaking down the hierarchy that defined that world represents profound moral progress.

> *"Homosexual marriage, rather than being a threat, may actually provide a model."*

The demise of the old hierarchy has set a challenge for institutions such as marriage. Marriage will not again be stable until it can accommodate the equality of women. For this purpose, homosexual marriage, rather than being a threat, may actually provide a model. Same-sex partners will not be as tempted as different-sex partners to assume that each person should do one kind of work. Same-sex partners will be more likely to think about how to share responsibility in an equitable way, dividing it flexibly, aiming to accommodate the real rather than the stereotyped differences in their tastes and skills. Of course, same-sex marriages may mimic the sex roles of different-sex marriages, and may suffer from lack of broad social support, but they are more likely to model egalitarian relations.

I don't expect everyone to agree that homosexual marriages could be a model for heterosexual marriages. But the current state of the law, perpetuated by the DOMA, does not respect the view that they could be. Instead, it establishes the moral beliefs of the majority as official state doctrine. Ultimately, this is no different from the establishment of a state religion. It flies in the face of our core liberal commitment to the proposition that basic rights and liberties should only be restricted as far as necessary to preserve goods that everyone can agree are important.

Helping families provide stable homes for children is doubtless an important, generally recognized social goal. But the connection between the goal and the suppression of homosexual unions is so dubious that it cannot possibly support the sweeping restriction on all such unions. And although a majority in America is currently against same-sex marriage, that majority is nowhere near the general consensus on the importance of such values as love and commitment.

Moral authoritarians don't want to accept the moral burden of justifying restrictions on basic rights and liberties. They see society as either for them or against them. But if they think that allowing homosexuals to marry would give some advantage to homosexuals, they are wrong. By allowing same-sex marriage, the state would not thereby favor homosexual marriage or the views of those who support it. It would simply de-privilege different-sex marriage. Admittedly, neutrality may not have neutral effects. Some values will flourish more than others in a free environment, while some may need the state to prop them up if they are to survive or remain prominent. But that is not the state's business, at least not if it conflicts with basic rights and liberties. Those who embrace traditional values should be free to argue for them in the marketplace of ideas, but they have no just claim for protectionist measures.

It is tempting to say that the DOMA is simply a small setback for homosexual rights. But it represents more than that. At bottom, it represents a failure to live up to the liberal commitment to protect basic rights and liberties, a failure to advance the cause of political equality, and a retreat into moral authoritarianism.

# Family Courts Are Unfairly Biased Against Homosexual Parents

by Kathryn Kendell

**About the author:** *Kathryn Kendell is the executive director of the National Center for Lesbian Rights in San Francisco.*

Best estimates are that millions of children are being raised in homes headed by a lesbian or gay parent. The majority of these children are born into heterosexual marriages that end after a spouse "comes out" as lesbian or gay.

Each time a man or a woman in a heterosexual marriage with children is involved in a divorce in which his or her gay or lesbian sexual orientation is an issue, the potential for a custody battle looms. Each time an already divorced parent "comes out" as lesbian or gay, the threat of a custody modification based on sexual orientation is real.

## Children of Gays and Lesbians Do Fine

There is a substantial body of social science literature on the well-being of children raised in lesbian or gay households. This research consistently demonstrates no basis for any generalized concern about harm to children who are raised in lesbian or gay families.

Social science studies examining primarily the children of lesbian mothers, and to a lesser degree gay fathers, have focused on the children's gender identity, sexual orientation, self-esteem, and social adjustment. A review of the studies indicates no significant negative effect on children resulting from a parent's sexual orientation. In fact, researchers have found that on basic measures of well-being, children in lesbian and gay parent homes are generally indistinguishable from those in homes with heterosexual parents. Despite these findings, lesbian and gay parents continue to lose custody of their children in some courts in this country.

We live in a time when public discourse about lesbian and gay issues is prevalent. When positive depictions of lesbian or gay characters on television and in the movies are commonplace. When many Americans know someone who is gay or lesbian and when a substantial body of scientific data on sexual orientation and parenting is available. A time when a majority of state courts recognize that judicial deference to prejudice against lesbians and gays is as inappropriate as relying on prejudices against disabled persons, interracial couples, or religious minorities.

Given this landscape and the national trend, good parents continue to lose custody because they are openly gay. I suggest that a number of potent factors—ignorance about the reality of lesbian and gay parent families, long-standing antigay bias, ingrained stereotypes, and, in some cases, partisan religious convictions—combine to create a hostile judicial climate for lesbian and gay litigants in some regions of this country.

## The "Nexus" Test

The majority of state courts that have considered the impact of a parent's lesbian or gay identity in a contested custody or visitation case have adopted some variant of the "nexus" test. This standard, also called the direct adverse impact standard, requires a clear evidentiary connection, or nexus, between a parent's actions and harm to the child before the parent's sexual orientation assumes any relevance in a visitation or custody determination.

The nexus test is also used by most courts in custody disputes to evaluate the sexual conduct of a heterosexual parent. It is based on the general principle that like a parent's religious or political beliefs, a parent's sexual or moral behavior is relevant only if it adversely affects the child.

Under this standard, courts are to base their visitation or custody determinations on the evidentiary record. They must point to specific evidence that the child has been harmed by the parent's sexual orientation or living arrangements before having a custody determination on these factors.

The test is designed to provide a reliable, evenhanded, and child-focused approach, based on an individualized, fact-based assessment of all factors relevant to a child's welfare. In contrast, allowing a court to depart from the evidentiary record by substituting its own speculation for a factual finding of harm may result in a decision contrary to the best interests of the child.

> *"Despite [no evidence of harm], lesbian and gay parents continue to lose custody of their children."*

In presuming injury to a child solely as a result of a parent's orientation or relationship with a same-sex partner, a court may impute any degree of harm where none has been shown and may disregard characteristics of the heterosexual parent that are undesirable or harmful to the child. This could lead not only to the neglect of the child's best interests but also to inconsistent legal standards.

In theory, application of the nexus test should not result in a lesbian or gay parent losing custody based on sexual orientation alone. However, how the test is applied and what inferences the court draws from its review of the facts may result in loss of custody where other facts, standing alone, would not lead to this result.

Three recent cases serve to illuminate this point. In these rulings, in which courts ordered modifications of custody, the lesbian or gay parents lost although the courts denied the rulings were based on sexual orientation alone. Upon examination, however, it is clear that the parents would have retained custody or gained custody had they been less open about their sexual orientation.

### *J.B.F. v. J.M.F.*

The Alabama Supreme Court unanimously reversed a ruling by the court of civil appeals and granted a father's motion for modification of custody based on his ex-wife's "open lesbian relationship" and his own remarriage. The court acknowledged that J.B.F. loved her daughter and had provided her with "good care." Nonetheless, the court held that rather than hiding their relationship from her daughter (which presumably would have saved the mother from losing custody), J.B.F. and her partner "have established a two-parent home environment where their homosexual relationship is openly practiced and presented to the child as the social and moral equivalent of a heterosexual marriage."

> *"In presuming injury to a child solely as a result of a parent's orientation . . . , a court may impute . . . harm where none has been shown."*

What the court means by "openly practiced" is unclear. The court acknowledged that there was no evidence of any display of "sexual activity in the presence of the child, other than handholding and kissing that is not prolonged."

Rather than require the father to demonstrate that the mother's conduct had a "substantial detrimental effect" on the child—the usual burden in custody modification cases in Alabama—the court simply required the father to show that "a change in custody would materially promote the child's best interests and that the positive good brought by this change would more than offset the inherently disruptive effect of uprooting the child." This holding set the stage for the court to disturb the long-standing and successful custodial arrangement.

The court concluded in favor of the father, noting "the inestimable developmental benefit of a loving home environment that is anchored by a successful marriage is undisputed." Of course, the court found J.B.F. unable to provide this benefit, although her own relationship had been of longer duration than her ex-husband's new marriage. It is worth noting that the court cited no credible evidence of any harm or disruption to the child based on her mother's relationship.

## *Pulliam v. Smith*

The North Carolina Supreme Court, in a split decision, reversed the court of appeals and granted an order modifying custody against a gay father. Here, as in *J.B.F.,* the court went out of its way to note that the mother did not have to prove detriment to the children based on the father's sexual orientation. Rather, if the change in custody would "beneficially affect" the children, custody could be modified.

> *"Many courts still believe a child will . . . be compromised in some . . . way by living . . . with a gay or lesbian parent."*

The state supreme court, like the trial court, seemed riveted to the fact that the father and his partner shared a bedroom "directly across the hall and approximately three feet from the door of the children's bedroom." Several times the court noted that Smith's two sons had apparently seen him and his partner together in bed.

As in *J.B.F.,* however, there was no allegation that the children had observed any inappropriate sexual activity. Nevertheless, the court ruled:

> We conclude that activities such as the regular commission of sexual acts in the home by unmarried people, failing and refusing to counsel the children against such conduct while acknowledging this conduct to them, allowing the children to see unmarried persons known by the children to be sexual partners in bed together . . . support the trial court's findings of "improper influences" which are "detrimental to the best interest and welfare of the two minor children."

The court then made the rather extraordinary claim that Smith was not being denied custody because he was a "practicing homosexual" but rather because he "was regularly engaging in sexual acts with Mr. Tipton in the home while the children were present."

The court did credit trial court evidence that showed Smith's older son was "emotionally distraught" at being told by Smith that he was gay. From this "substantial evidence" the court concluded by favorably quoting the trial court: "The activity of the defendant will likely create emotional difficulties for the two minor children." The state supreme court agreed with this conclusion even though there was no evidence to support such conjecture.

Like J.B.F. in Alabama, it is arguable that had Smith lied to his children about his relationship and his sexual orientation, he might have retained custody.

## *Weigand v. Houghton*

In this case, the Mississippi Supreme Court affirmed a trial court's ruling denying a petition for modification brought by a gay father on behalf of his 14-year-old son. The father, now living in California, based his petition on incidents of domestic violence in the mother's home, the stepfather's abuse of alcohol, the mother's lack of time with the boy, and the stepfather's past convictions for felony assault.

The court found that there had been a change of circumstances that detrimentally affected the youth. The court noted that the boy had been "greatly disturbed" by the violence he witnessed in the home and that it had been the boy himself who had called 911 to report the assault of his mother. The court found that the father had a stable home in California and was well bonded with his son.

Despite these findings, the trial court held that custody should remain with the mother. The court's conclusion, affirmed by the state supreme court, rests primarily on its views about the father's sexual orientation. The trial court found that

> the natural father is an admitted homosexual who lives with and engages in sexual activities with another man on a day-to-day basis. . . . The fact that the plaintiff and his "life partner" engage in sexual activity which includes both oral and anal intercourse is repugnant to this court. . . . The conscience of this court is shocked by the audacity and brashness of an individual to come into court, openly and freely admit to engaging in felonious conduct on a regular basis and expect the court to find such conduct acceptable. . . .

The dissenting opinion pointed out that the Mississippi unnatural intercourse statute applies equally to heterosexuals and that in California, where the father lives, same-sex adult sexual conduct is not considered criminal.

In *Weigand*, as in the other two cases, there was no actual evidence of harm resuiting from the gay or lesbian parent's sexual orientation. Although the court found the boy to have suffered harm while in his mother's care, the father's motion for modification was denied based on speculation about supposed harm that might come to the boy should he live with his gay dad.

Fortunately, most courts have adopted and objectively apply some variant of the nexus test. In most courts, sexual orientation alone, without actual evidence of harm, is insufficient to deny a lesbian or gay parent custody or liberal visitation.

> *"As lesbian- and gay-headed households grow in visibility, societal exposure to these families will . . . erode longstanding ignorance and prejudice."*

But old habits die hard. Many courts still believe a child will fail to develop a healthy gender role, will grow up gay, or will be compromised in some other way by living or having regular visitation with a gay or lesbian parent. A wealth of research combats these myths, but ignorance about the real lives of lesbian and gay parents, coupled with persistent stereotypes, combine to produce outcomes like those in Alabama, North Carolina, and Mississippi.

Certainly, great progress has been made in assuring that lesbian and gay parents will not be subject to disparate treatment in custody or visitation disputes. Nevertheless, many examples of disparate treatment or outright bias persist. As lesbian- and gay-headed households grow in visibility, societal exposure to these families will continue to erode long-standing ignorance and prejudice.

# Gay Adoption Benefits Society

## by the American Civil Liberties Union

**About the author:** *The American Civil Liberties Union is the nation's oldest and largest civil liberties organization.*

The 1990s have seen a sharp rise in the number of lesbians and gay men forming their own families through adoption, foster care, artificial insemination and other means. Researchers estimate that the total number of children nationwide living with at least one gay parent ranges from six to 14 million.

At the same time, the United States is facing a critical shortage of adoptive and foster parents. As a result, hundreds of thousands of children in this country are without permanent homes. These children languish for months, even years, within state foster care systems that lack qualified foster parents and are frequently riddled with other problems. In Arkansas, for example, the foster care system does such a poor job of caring for children that it has been placed under court supervision.

### Legal and Policy Overview of Lesbian and Gay Parenting

Many states have moved to safeguard the interests of children with gay or lesbian parents. For example, at least 21 states have granted second-parent adoptions to lesbian and gay couples, ensuring that their children can enjoy the benefits of having two legal parents, especially if one of the parents dies or becomes incapacitated.

Recognizing that lesbians and gay men can be good parents, the vast majority of states no longer deny custody or visitation to a person based on sexual orientation. State agencies and courts now apply a "best interest of the child" standard to decide these cases. Under this approach, a person's sexual orientation cannot be the basis for ending or limiting parent-child relationships unless it is demonstrated that it causes harm to a child—a claim that has been routinely disproved by social science research. Using this standard, more than 22 states to date have allowed lesbians and gay men to adopt children either through state-run or private adoption agencies.

Nonetheless, a few states—relying on myths and stereotypes—have used a parent's sexual orientation to deny custody, adoption, visitation and foster care. For instance, two states (Florida and New Hampshire) have laws that expressly bar lesbians and gay men from ever adopting children. In a notorious 1993 decision, a court in Virginia took away Sharon Bottoms' 2-year-old son simply because of her sexual orientation, and transferred custody to the boy's maternal grandmother. And Arkansas has adopted a policy prohibiting lesbians, gay men, and those who live with them, from serving as foster parents.

## Research Overview of Lesbian and Gay Parenting

All of the research to date has reached the same unequivocal conclusion about gay parenting: the children of lesbian and gay parents grow up as successfully as the children of heterosexual parents. In fact, not a single study has found the children of lesbian or gay parents to be disadvantaged because of their parents' sexual orientation. Other key findings include:

- There is no evidence to suggest that lesbians and gay men are unfit to be parents.
- Home environments with lesbian and gay parents are as likely to successfully support a child's development as those with heterosexual parents.
- Good parenting is not influenced by sexual orientation. Rather, it is influenced most profoundly by a parent's ability to create a loving and nurturing home—an ability that does not depend on whether a parent is gay or straight.
- There is no evidence to suggest that the children of lesbian and gay parents are less intelligent, suffer from more problems, are less popular, or have lower self-esteem than children of heterosexual parents.
- The children of lesbian and gay parents grow up as happy, healthy and well-adjusted as the children of heterosexual parents.

## A Crisis in Adoption and Foster Care

Right now there is a critical shortage of adoptive and foster parents in the United States. As a result, many children have no permanent homes, while others are forced to survive in an endless series of substandard foster homes. It is estimated that there are 500,000 children in foster care nationally, and 100,000 need to be adopted. But last year there were qualified adoptive parents available for only 20,000 of these children. Many of these children have historically been viewed as "unadoptable" because they are not healthy white infants. Instead, they are often minority children and/or adolescents, many with significant health problems.

There is much evidence documenting the serious damage suffered by children without permanent homes who are placed in substandard foster homes. Children frequently become victims of the "foster care shuffle," in which they are moved from temporary home to temporary home. A child stuck in permanent foster care can live in 20 or more homes by the time she reaches 18. It is not surprising, therefore, that long-term foster care is associated with increased emotional problems, delinquency, substance abuse and academic problems.

In order to reach out and find more and better parents for children without homes, adoption and foster care policies have become increasingly inclusive over the past two decades. While adoption and foster care were once viewed as services offered to infertile, middle-class, largely white couples seeking healthy same-race infants, these policies have modernized. In the past two decades, child welfare agencies have changed their policies to make adoption and foster care possible for a much broader range of adults, including minority families, older individuals, families who already have children, single parents (male and female), individuals with physical disabilities, and families across a broad economic range. These changes have often been controversial at the outset. According to the Child Welfare League of America (CWLA), "at one time or another, the inclusion of each of these groups has caused controversy. Many well-intended individuals vigorously opposed including each new group as potential adopters and voiced concern that standards were being lowered in a way that could forever damage the field of adoption."

> *"The children of lesbian and gay parents grow up as happy, healthy and well-adjusted as the children of heterosexual parents."*

As a result of the increased inclusiveness of modern adoption and foster care policies, thousands of children now have homes with qualified parents.

## Myths vs. Facts

*Myth:* The only acceptable home for a child is one with a mother and father who are married to each other.

*Fact:* Children without homes do not have the option of choosing between a married mother and father or some other type of parent(s). These children have neither a mother nor a father, married or unmarried. There simply are not enough married mothers and fathers who are interested in adoption and foster care. Last year only 20,000 of the 100,000 foster children in need of adoption were adopted, including children adopted by single people as well as married couples. Our adoption and foster care policies must deal with reality, or these children will never have stable and loving homes.

*Myth:* Children need a mother and a father to have proper male and female role models.

*Fact:* Children without homes have neither a mother nor a father as role models. And children get their role models from many places besides their parents. These include grandparents, aunts and uncles, teachers, friends, and neighbors. In a case-by-case evaluation, trained professionals can ensure that the child to be adopted or placed in foster care is moving into an environment with adequate role models of all types.

*Myth:* Gays and lesbians don't have stable relationships and don't know how to be good parents.

*Fact:* Like other adults in this country, the majority of lesbians and gay men are in stable committed relationships. Of course some of these relationships have problems, as do some heterosexual relationships. The adoption and foster care screening process is very rigorous, including extensive home visits and interviews of prospective parents. It is designed to screen out those individuals who are not qualified to adopt or be foster parents, for whatever reason. All of the evidence shows that lesbians and gay men can and do make good parents. The American Psychological Association, in a recent report reviewing the research, observed that "not a single study has found children of gay or lesbian parents to be disadvantaged in any significant respect relative to children of heterosexual parents," and concluded that "home environments provided by gay and lesbian parents are as likely as those provided by heterosexual parents to support and enable children's psychosocial growth." That is why the Child Welfare League of America, the nation's oldest children's advocacy organization, and the North American Council on Adoptable Children say that gays and lesbians seeking to adopt should be evaluated just like other adoptive applicants.

> *"There simply are not enough married mothers and fathers who are interested in adoption and foster care."*

*Myth:* Children raised by gay or lesbian parents are more likely to grow up gay themselves.

*Fact:* All of the available evidence demonstrates that the sexual orientation of parents has no impact on the sexual orientation of their children and that children of lesbian and gay parents are no more likely than any other child to grow up to be gay. There is some evidence that children of gays and lesbians are more tolerant of diversity, but this is certainly not a disadvantage. Of course, some children of lesbians and gay men will grow up to be gay, as will some children of heterosexual parents. These children will have the added advantage of being raised by parents who are supportive and accepting in a world that can sometimes be hostile.

*Myth:* Children who are raised by lesbian or gay parents will be subjected to harassment and will be rejected by their peers.

*Fact:* Children make fun of other children for all kinds of reasons: for being too short or too tall, for being too thin or too fat, for being of a different race or religion or speaking a different language. Children show remarkable resiliency, especially if they are provided with a stable and loving home environment. Children in foster care can face tremendous abuse from their peers for being parentless. These children often internalize that abuse, and often feel unwanted.

Unfortunately, they do not have the emotional support of a loving permanent family to help them through these difficult times.

*Myth:* Lesbians and gay men are more likely to molest children.

*Fact:* There is no connection between homosexuality and pedophilia. All of the legitimate scientific evidence shows that. Sexual orientation, whether heterosexual or homosexual, is an adult sexual attraction to others. Pedophilia, on the other hand, is an adult sexual attraction to children. Ninety percent of child abuse is committed by heterosexual men. In one study of 269 cases of child sexual abuse, only two offenders were gay or lesbian. Of the cases studied involving molestation of a boy by a man, 74 percent of the men were or had been in a heterosexual relationship with the boy's mother or another female relative. The study concluded that "a child's risk of being molested by his or her relative's heterosexual partner is over 100 times greater than by someone who might be identifiable as being homosexual, lesbian, or bisexual."

*Myth:* Children raised by lesbians and gay men will be brought up in an "immoral" environment.

*Fact:* There are all kinds of disagreements in this country about what is moral and what is immoral. Some people may think raising children without religion is immoral, yet atheists are allowed to adopt and be foster parents. Some people think drinking and gambling are immoral, but these things don't disqualify someone from being evaluated as an adoptive or foster parent. If we eliminated all of the people who could possibly be considered "immoral," we would have almost no parents left to adopt and provide foster care. That can't be the right solution. What we can probably all agree on is that it is immoral to leave children without homes when there are qualified parents waiting to raise them. And that is what many gays and lesbians can do.

# Society Should Not Allow Same-Sex Marriage

## by Richard G. Wilkins

**About the author:** *Richard. G. Wilkins is a professor of constitutional law and managing director of the World Family Policy Center at Brigham Young University.*

Throughout the ages, marriage between man and woman has been essential to individual development, social progress, and communal prosperity. Because of the important roles it has played in the evolution of modern society, marriage has become a "highly preferred" legal relationship. This unique status is reflected in the numerous statutory and other legal preferences that have been created for the marital relationship, ranging from special tax and employment benefits to laws dealing with property ownership and intestacy.

## Marriage Is Under Attack

Today, however, the "highly preferred" status of marriage is under attack on several fronts. In the face of mounting divorce and abuse rates and the increasingly large number of children born out of wedlock, some question whether marriage has any continuing social value. Others (often building upon the increasingly low esteem in which modern marriage is held) question why the historic legal preferences conferred on husbands and wives should not be conferred upon alternative partnership arrangements such as two men and two women who wish to enjoy the benefits of a "marital" relationship. These advocates, in fact, often assert that federal and state constitutions mandate the conferral of marital benefits on such partnerships.

This paper seeks to answer the question: Must the various legal preferences conferred on traditional marriage be extended to alternative partnership arrangements? The answer is no. The legal lines that have been drawn to protect and encourage the marital union of a man and a woman are principled and essential to furthering society's compelling procreative interest. Indeed, once outside the union of a man and a woman, there is no principled constitutional basis for distinguishing between (or among) any form of consensual sexual behavior. Recognition of a constitutional right to same-sex marriage, therefore, would open the door to legally mandated conferral of all legislative preferences now reserved for marriage upon any form of consensual sexual coupling, no matter how idiosyncratic. Society should not encourage (nor perhaps could it endure) such an outcome.

## The Constitutional Framework

Before analyzing the most common constitutional claims made by proponents of same-sex marriage, I would like to address one oft-made but inapt assertion. Television and radio talk shows, along with newspaper opinion columns, are often filled with variants of the submission that laws preferring heterosexual marriage "impose the morals of some upon all, and the law has no business answering moral questions." This unfocused claim ignores the reality that any and all legal schemes enforce some moral code. Must we enjoin all provisions of state and federal criminal codes which reinforce the moral and religious precept that "[t]hou shalt not steal"? Of course not. As Justice Edward D. White wisely noted in disposing of the argument that sodomy laws reflect an unconstitutional moral judgment, "[t]he law . . . is constantly based on notions of morality, and if all laws representing essentially moral choices are to be invalidated . . . , the courts will be very busy indeed."

Once beyond the alleged impropriety of legislative actions reflecting a moral judgment, advocates for the judicial recognition of alternative marital partnerships generally focus upon two constitutional provisions: the due process and equal protection clauses of the Fourteenth Amendment to the United States Constitution. Under both clauses, the constitutional analysis of legislative action is quite similar. If legislative line-drawing intrudes upon a "fundamental right" or "suspect classification," the challenged regulation will be subjected to close judicial scrutiny. By contrast, if a "fundamental right" or "suspect classification" is not involved, the legislative judgment (in the vast majority of cases) will be sustained.

The on-going debate whether legislative and other legal preferences for heterosexual marriage pass constitutional muster has already consumed thousands of pages in the law reviews. Somewhat surprisingly, however, virtually all of the literature

> *"Any and all legal schemes enforce some moral code."*

concludes—on the basis of some variant of the due process or equal protection analyses explored above—that current statutory or legal preferences for heterosexual marriage are either irrational or subject to purportedly fatal strict scrutiny.

With due respect, and knowing that my opinion is in the decided academic minority, I submit that this consensus is seriously flawed. Laws preferring heterosexual marriage are *not* subject to strict scrutiny. This is because statutory and other legal preferences for heterosexual marriage are narrowly tailored to further the most imperative of all compelling governmental interests: "the very existence and survival of the race." Current widespread statutory and legal preferences for heterosexual marriage, therefore, are plainly constitutional.

## Reasonable Purpose, Not Strict Scrutiny

Far from suggesting that statutory preferences for heterosexual marriage should be subjected to strict scrutiny, a straightforward reading of the opinions of the United States Supreme Court establish that rational basis review is the relevant judicial benchmark. Legislative preferences for heterosexual marriage do not intrude upon any fundamental right, nor do they impermissibly harm any suspect class. Accordingly, statutory and other legal preferences for heterosexual marriage need only be reasonably related to a rational objective; a hurdle that is readily cleared.

Any claim that preferences for heterosexual marriage intrude upon a "fundamental right" necessarily rest upon some variation of an assertion made by a plurality of the Supreme Court in *Planned Parenthood of Southeastern Pennsylvania* v. *Casey.*

*"Current widespread statutory and legal preferences for heterosexual marriage . . . are plainly constitutional."*

In the course of reaffirming the right to abortion first announced in *Roe* v. *Wade,* Justices Sandra Day O'Connor, Anthony Kennedy and David Souter wrote that "[a]t the heart of liberty is the right to define one's own concept of existence, of meaning, of the universe, and of the mystery of human life." Advocates of same-sex marriage essentially submit that this broadly phrased notion of liberty guarantees them the right to demand that the label "marriage"—as well as all of the statutory and legal preferences which follow that label—be attached to their own idiosyncratically defined sexual couplings. While such arguments might get an "A" for rhetoric, they flunk the demands of established constitutional law.

Not every personal preference connected with "one's own concept of existence," "meaning" and "mystery" can (or ought to) be recognized as a "fundamental right." State policy makers, for example, can require policemen to adhere to dress and grooming standards—no matter how mysterious and meaningful a pony tail or beard might be to a particular law enforcement officer. Were it otherwise, our Constitution . . . would become a mere vessel into which a bare majority of the Supreme Court could pour their personal predilections at will. The Supreme Court has never adopted such a free-wheeling notion of review under the due process clause.

Accordingly, and far from protecting all notions of liberty that may be central to an individual's definition of "existence" and the "mystery of life," the due process clause protects only "those fundamental rights and liberties which are, objectively, 'deeply rooted in this Nation's history and tradition'" and "'implicit in the concept of ordered liberty,' such that 'neither liberty nor justice would exist if they were sacrificed.'" Moreover, the Court has required a "'careful description' of the asserted fundamental liberty interest" [as quoted in *Planned Parenthood of Southeastern Pennsylvania* v. *Casey*]. In short, even deeply held contemporary notions of "existence," "meaning" and "mystery" do not provide the judicial map for substantive due process excursions. Rather, "[o]ur Nation's history, legal traditions, and practices provide the crucial 'guideposts for responsible decision making'" [as stated in *Michael H.* v. *Gerald D.*].

> *"Marriage between a man and a woman provides the very foundation of society."*

Nothing in our nation's history, legal traditions, or practices supports the notion that "marriage" has been or should be expanded beyond the notion of a consensual coupling of a man and a woman. To the contrary, in the course of adjudicating marital rights or opining on the marital relationship, the Supreme Court has consistently linked its opinions to the traditional family structure of a man, a woman and their children by emphasizing the marital functions of conception, procreation, child rearing and education, and traditional family relationships in general.

This analysis forecloses, I believe, any serious assertion that statutory preferences for heterosexual marriage unconstitutionally impinge upon a fundamental right under the due process clause of the United States Constitution. Other scholars have persuasively shown that the same conclusion is warranted for the assertion that such preferences unconstitutionally target a "suspect class" under the equal protection clause. Legal preferences for heterosexual marriage, therefore, are not subject to strict (and generally fatal) judicial scrutiny.

## The Compelling Social Interests Tests

There are compelling reasons why heterosexual marriage is not subject to intrusive judicial review and its consequent judicial re-tooling. Marriage between a man and a woman provides the very foundation of society. The Supreme Court has had frequent opportunities to expound upon the fundamental importance of marriage to society. Over a century ago, the United States Supreme Court called marriage "the most important relation in life . . . having more to do with the morals and civilization of a people than any other institution. . . ." More recently, the Court described marriage as an "association that promotes a way of life, not causes; a harmony in living, not political faiths; a bilateral loyalty, not commercial or social projects. . . ." However ornate the rhetoric, the Supreme Court's discussions of marriage emphasize again and again a surpassingly important reality that (quite curiously) is often overlooked in the modern debates surrounding same-sex marriage: the unquestionable biological and historical relationship between marriage, procreation and child rearing.

As the Supreme Court noted in *Skinner* v. *Oklahoma,* "Marriage and procreation are fundamental to the very existence and survival of the race." The Court reemphasized this connection between marriage, procreation and child rearing in *Zablocki* v. *Redhail.* There, the Court placed the "decision to marry" on "the same level of importance as decisions relating to procreation, childbirth, child rearing, and family relationships" precisely because "[if the] right to procreate means anything at all, it must imply some right to enter" the marital relationship. The very concept of marriage, in sum, is indissolubly linked to the societal imperatives of procreation and child rearing.

As a result, organized society has a substantial interest in drawing legal lines that responsibly channel and encourage procreation. This theme has dominated Supreme Court decisions from the beginning. All of the family cases (from the earliest to the latest) recite that individuals have a unique interest in marriage because of its close connection to procreation and child rearing. Judicial recognition of this individual right to marriage and procreation, however, necessarily demands recognition of a correlative social interest held by the state: a substantial—indeed compelling—interest in channeling and promoting responsible procreative behavior. Only individuals marry and procreate. Society has a surpassing interest in the conduct and outcome of these individual behaviors, because these activities are fundamental to society's "very existence and survival."

## Sexuality and Procreation

These interests persist despite modern claimants for alternative marital unions who seek to sever sexuality completely from any relationship to procreation and child rearing. Such a severance of sexuality from reproduction has profound sociological, moral and philosophical consequences that have been discussed by, among others, Professors Robert George, Gerard Bradley and Hadley Arkes. According to these scholars, heterosexual relationships (and, in particular, marital relationships) differ significantly from other possible sexual acts: sexual relations between a man and a woman bound in marriage are described as an "intrinsic (or . . . 'basic') human good." This is due, in large part, to the fact that a heterosexual marital relationship has the biological potential for reproduction. Indeed, stripped of this reproductive potential, sexual relationships become nothing more than physically (and emotionally) agreeable genital stimulation.

*"Procreative power is the basis for society's compelling interest in preferring potentially procreative relationships over [others]."*

One need not dispute that mutually agreeable genital stimulation can have emotional, mental and physical overtones. Such stimulation may be the result of—or perhaps result in—intense attachments to a sexual partner. Nevertheless, absent any relation to procreation, the sexual act is reduced to a purely sensory experience (whether the sensation is physical, mental or emotional).

> *"Should courts depart from the . . . heterosexual definition of marriage, there will be little . . . ground upon which to deny marital status to any . . . sexual grouping."*

At this point, homosexual activists might argue that if marital law exists to further society's procreative imperative, why should legal protection be extended to infertile (whether by choice or otherwise) heterosexual unions? The argument, however, is wide of the mark. Traditional marriage, unlike any other sexual relationship, furthers society's profound interest in the only sexual relationship that has the biological potential for reproduction: union between a man and a woman.

Procreation requires a coupling between the two sexes. Sexual relations between a man and a woman, therefore, even if infertile, fundamentally differ from homosexual couplings. Homosexual couplings do not have the biological potential for reproduction: children are possible only by means of legal intervention (e.g., adoption) or medical technology (e.g., artificial insemination). Accordingly, and by their very nature, sexual relationships between a man and a woman (even if infertile) differ in kind from couplings between individuals of the same sex: heterosexual couplings in general have the biological potential for reproduction; homosexual couplings always do not.

This potential procreative power is the basis for society's compelling interest in preferring potentially procreative relationships over relationships founded primarily upon mutually agreeable genital stimulation.

## The Survival of Society

The institution of marriage furthers not mere sensory experience, but society's "very . . . survival." The law, moreover, has never been ignorant of the vital distinction between purely sensory experience and procreation. Constitutional law, for its part, *must* take cognizance of this biologically obvious distinction. Constitutional decision making, above all other forms of judicial decision making, must be grounded in both principle and reason. When it comes to the constitutional definition of marriage, the undeniable and well-grounded principle that has guided mankind for generations (including state legislatures and the Supreme Court since this country's founding) is straightforward: there is a fundamental difference between procreative sexuality and nonprocreative sexuality.

Reproduction is the only human act for which the two genders undisputably require the other. A woman can do everything in her life without a man, except reproduce. Vice versa for a man. Thus, the sexuality that unites a man and a woman is unique in kind. This uniqueness, in fact, is the very basis of the religious, historical and metaphysical notion that "marriage" indeed joins two flesh in one.

Furthermore, should constitutional law abandon the principle that reproductive sex has a unique role, we will be left with no basis upon which to draw principled constitutional distinctions between sexual relations that are harmful to individuals and/or society and relations that are beneficial. In fact, the same arguments that would seemingly require constitutional protection for same-sex marriage would also require constitutional protection for any consensual sexual practice or form of marriage. After all, once the principled line of procreation is abandoned, we are left with nothing more than sex as a purely sensory experience. The purely sensory experience cherished by any given sexual partnership will be no more or less precious than the purely sensory experience valued by another sexual partnership, no matter how socially repugnant. Should courts depart from the established heterosexual definition of marriage, there will be little (if any) principled ground upon which to deny marital status to any and all consensual sexual groupings. Bigamy, group marriage and—yes—even consensual incestuous coupling could all (and probably would all) accurately lay claim to the same legal entitlements.

### "Zone of Privacy"

Proponents of same-sex marriage, at this point, may nevertheless argue that they should be allowed to marry because a constitutional "zone of privacy" mandates that they be allowed to marry. This "zone of privacy," according to Justice Douglas, is a concept even "older than the Bill of Rights."

While it is true that a zone of privacy prevents society from policing certain bedroom behavior, the privacy argument—applied to same-sex marriage—proves too much. Privacy rights prevent governmental interference with relationships that are, indeed, private. Therefore, to the extent that homosexual relationships are private, they may properly be shielded (at least to some extent) by the "zone of privacy" from government intrusion. Transforming a privacy shield into a policy sword, however, turns the concept of "privacy" on its head: the assertion becomes not that homosexual conduct is private, but that it must be publicly acknowledged, condoned, recognized and normalized.

Same-sex advocates also assert that homosexual behavior harms no one, so the government has no interest in denying same-sex marriage. Nobody will be worse tomorrow, the argu-

*"The consequences of same-sex marriage may be severe."*

ment goes, because their homosexual neighbors are married today. While this contention may have some appeal, it is short sighted. No one knows what impact same-sex marriage will have on society. Moreover, it certainly has not been shown that society will be improved by same-sex marriage. For centuries, societies have been built upon the foundation of traditional families, and as the family is weakened, so is society. For instance, in the 1970s, one could argue that the loosening of divorce laws would inflict relatively minor pain on society. Thirty years later, the evidence tells a compelling story of the increased injury society endures every time the divorce rate rises and the traditional family is weakened.

Making divorce easier to obtain seemed progressive in the 70s, but today, when divorce has become a national norm and most households consist of unmarried individuals with no children, we begin to grasp that the divorce revolution has imposed high social costs indeed. It may, in fact, be impossible to show, now, that same-sex marriage will cause immediate harm to society or to individuals in society, but it is undeniable that same-sex marriage is not based on procreation and a commitment to new life and future generations. The assertion that any sexual relationship (no matter how idiosyncratic and no matter how far removed from the continuation of life) has the same benefit as traditional marriage is simply unproved. Same-sex marriage, moreover, may well have severe long-term social consequences that cannot be predicted or foreseen at this time. One thing, however, does seem clear: as society becomes increasingly focused on individual and immediate transitory desires, rather than on the perpetuation of life and a commitment to the future, the consequences of same-sex marriage may be severe indeed.

The judicial system should not be tempted to stray from the course marked by history and tradition, a course that is soundly built on society's interest in procreation. As Justice White astutely noted in rejecting the asserted constitutional right to consensual sodomy, "it would be difficult, except by fiat, to limit the claimed right to homosexual conduct while leaving exposed to prosecution adultery, incest, and other sexual crimes. . . . We are unwilling to start down that road." American courts, both at the state and federal levels, should be similarly unwilling to begin the task of judicially defining which sexual partnerships—among all the possibilities ranging beyond that of a man and a woman—must be legitimated with the long-honored title of "marriage."

## Furthering a National Objective

Because legislative preferences for heterosexual marriage do not infringe upon fundamental rights or target a suspect class, such preferences need only reasonably further a rational objective: a legal test that virtually answers itself. Society has an undeniable interest in preferring heterosexual marriage over alternative sexual relationships. Heterosexual marriage, unlike same-sex partnerships, has the biological potential for procreation. There is no gainsaying the importance of this societal interest. As the Supreme Court has recognized, procreation involves the "very existence and survival" of mankind. Laws protecting and preferring heterosexual marriage are a principled and necessary means of furthering this most imperative of all governmental objectives.

# Homosexual Parenting Should Not Be Legally Sanctioned

**by Lynn D. Wardle**

**About the author:** *Lynn D. Wardle is a professor of law at the J. Reuben Clark Law School at Brigham Young University.*

The proposed restructuring of the family to legitimate homosexual family relations may be among the most heavily advocated family law reforms to be discussed in recent years. For example, I reviewed as much of the law review literature as I could find on the subject of same-sex marriage that had been published between January 1990 and December 1995. I found seventy-two articles, notes, comments, and essays about same-sex marriage published in law reviews available in North America, a nine-fold increase over the eight law review pieces on the same subject published in a similar period two decades earlier, when the topic was first seriously raised in litigation in the United States. There has been a similar explosion in the law review literature advocating the legalization of what I will herein call homosexual parenting—that is, the exercise of unrestricted, unconditional parental relationship rights, fully equivalent to those enjoyed by heterosexual parents, by lesbian and gay couples, homosexual biological or adoptive parents, homosexual partners and ex-partners of biological parents, and homosexual prospective legal parents (homosexual individuals seeking to adopt children or become parents by means of assisted procreation). At least ninety different law review articles, comments, notes, or essay pieces primarily addressing custody, visitation, assisted procreation, and adoption issues involving gay or lesbian parents have been published since 1990, compared to only three pieces published in the same period twenty years earlier. . . .

## Legal Implications

The legalization of homosexual parenting, essentially rendering sexual conduct of a parent a presumably irrelevant factor for purposes of child custody, visitation, and other child welfare cases, would constitute a significant shift in the legal and social assumptions and legal model of parenting. Accordingly, the proposals to legalize same-sex marriage and homosexual parenting certainly should be thoroughly and carefully considered. Likewise, the legalization of same-sex marriage would represent profound alteration of the structure of marriage and the family. That, of course, is where the law review literature plays an important role. Historically, lawyers have distinguished themselves by their ability to take all sides in the debate of proposed legal reforms, and law reviews have excelled in providing a forum for the "free trade in ideas," the "robust debate of public issues" that is essential to our system of free government. The current generation of law review literature, however, fails to provide that important function with respect to the same-sex marriage and homosexual parenting issues. The current literature fails to provide almost any serious criticism, scrutiny, or even a modest exchange of opposing opinions. In the law reviews, the "broad dissemination of principles, ideas, and factual information . . . [and] robust public debate" that is needed to test and refine the proposal has not even begun. . . .

Most of the articles advocating homosexual parenting are filled with adult-rights talk. Although this certainly is a legitimate perspective, in this area of law (dealing with doctrines and policies protecting and promoting parent-child relations), it probably is not the most important focus. The focus on the welfare of children and the social interests in the parent-child relation ought to be central, and the adult-rights focus secondary. Yet much of the law review literature is clearly adult-advocacy literature attempting to vindicate a particular rule or principle for the benefit of a certain class of adults. The manipulation of child-oriented rules of law for the political purposes and benefits of adults is troubling. . . .

## Studies Are Flawed

The publication of studies of homosexual parenting in social science literature has dramatically increased in recent years. Like scientific reports purporting to find biological origins for homosexual behavior (gay genes, brain structures, etc.), most of the recently published social science studies about homosexual parenting are highly affirming of persons in homosexual relationships. They purport to show that childrearing by homosexual parents is equivalent to (as beneficial for children as), if not superior to, childrearing by heterosexual parents. Studies are cited in the law review literature as proof that the homosexual behavior or relationship of parents has no detrimental effect on parenting skills or on children raised by such parents. Likewise, the case law relies heavily, and often excessively, upon studies purporting to show that homosexual parenting is functionally equivalent to heterosexual parenting and not harmful to children. Because of substantial methodological and analytical flaws, however, the studies do not provide a reliable basis for such conclusions. . . .

The first methodological problem with many of the studies of the effect of parental homosexual behavior on children or childrearing is small sample size. In order to provide any conclusions that provide statistically reliable predictive data that would be valid for policy making, the samples must be of significant numerical size. For example, a recent study of the effect of certain "at risk" factors on the welfare of children involved a survey of 34,129 children from an initial sample of 250,000 surveys taken in 460 communities in thirty-two states. None of the studies of parenting by adults engaged in homosexual relationships is of comparable size or reliability. Most of the studies of childrearing by parents in homosexual relationships involve samples of a few dozen, frequently as few as ten to forty subjects—the studies of Charlotte Patterson, the most prominent producer and advocate of this literature, for example—and some studies use sample populations as small as five. The studies of such small sample populations do not provide reliable quantitative research conclusions about parenting or child development.

Another sampling flaw in many of the studies cited to show the lack of harm to children of gay or lesbian parenting is the reliance on the "sample of convenience." Many of the studies involve subjects who are self-selected, or at least not randomly selected, such as subjects "recruited through advertisements in homophile publications." Volunteers for such studies often have an interest in the outcome of the study that distorts the research. Thus, the sample population in these studies is not likely to fairly represent the whole group of homosexual parents that is

> *"The manipulation of child-oriented rules of law for the political purposes and benefits of adults is troubling."*

to be examined. The assertiveness and zeal of self-selected sample populations may not fairly represent the population sought to be sampled. . . .

Another sampling flaw concerns the control groups with which the homosexual parents and their children are compared. Seldom are married heterosexual families used as comparisons. Often the control groups consist of single heterosexual parents and their children. This results in comparison of a favorably composed group of homosexual parents and children with a control group drawn from the segment of the heterosexual parent-child population that is most disadvantaged. . . .

## Sexual Identity Concerns

Given the sympathetic orientation and methodological bias of the social science studies of the effects of homosexual parenting on children, it is remarkable that the data reported in some of these studies provides a basis for serious concerns about potential detrimental effects upon children raised by gay or lesbian parents. Because of the methodological flaws mentioned above (such as small sample size), the concerns cannot be called conclusive, but the data certainly raise questions that need to be examined. Until these concerns are conclusively dispelled, it would not be rational to adopt a public policy endorsing or legitimating homosexual parenting. The most obvious risk to children from their parents' homosexual behavior suggested by the current studies relates to the sexual development of the child. Both theory and empirical studies indicate the potential that disproportionate percentages of children raised by homosexual parents will develop homosexual interests and behaviors. . . .

One published case report suggests a link between a daughter's sexual behavior and fantasy and her mother's homosexual behavior: the daughter in the reported case study had experimented with homosexual practices and also indulged in heterosexual promiscuity, anxiously driven by her awareness of her mother's homosexual relations. Another study of New York children reared by lesbian mothers (mostly in couples) and those reared by divorced homosexual single mothers suggested that "[t]here is a possibility that rearing [by a homosexual parent] might influence [the child's] sexual partner choice, temporarily or permanently." Another researcher also observed that "a girl in a lesbian home could be more vulnerable [to developing homosexual attraction] because of an increased awareness of herself in relation to other women and a sensitivity to environmental prejudices such as 'the daughter of a gay woman could be gay herself'" and acknowledged that "the effect of an additional exposure to [the lesbian] subculture" might "promote internalized permission for homosexual behaviour." This researcher's study found that four of the twenty-six children raised by lesbian mothers were "asexual" compared to none of the twenty-eight children raised by heterosexual single mothers. Four of the children raised by lesbian mothers stated that they did not want to have children, compared to none of the children raised by heterosexual single mothers. Three of the thirteen lesbian mothers preferred for their daughters to become homosexual, compared to none of the fifteen heterosexual single mothers, and all of the heterosexual mothers (100%) hoped their children would marry and have children, but only nine of thirteen lesbian mothers (69%) wanted their children to have children. Although far from definitive and too small to provide reliable conclusions, this study clearly suggests that homosexual parenting may have some effect upon children in relation to the whole constellation of developmental issues surrounding their own sexuality. One critical report reviewed three reports that found homosexual orientation in approximately nine percent to twelve percent of children raised by homosexual parents and noted: "These three summaries of the literature—by three different teams of investigators—agree in stating that homosexual parents appear to produce a disproportionate percentage of bisexual and homosexual children." Indeed, one sympathetic review of the literature candidly acknowledged that "Clinical stud-

> *"Disproportionate percentages of children raised by homosexual parents will develop homosexual interests and behaviors."*

186

ies do suggest a number of possible areas in which the mother's sexual identity might be an issue for the children.". . .

## Anger, Hurt, and Confusion

Increased likelihood of homosexual interest is not the only potential risk for children raised by homosexual parents. Javaid's study also discovered "noticeable" concerns for both lesbian mothers and their sons regarding discipline, expectations, and general parent-child relations. Other studies have also reported that boys raised by homosexual mothers may have a lower self-image regarding masculinity. Children born to or adopted by lesbian mothers who were examined by Charlotte Patterson, for example, showed more symptoms of stress and were "more likely to report feeling angry, scared or upset." A study of children of lesbians by Karen Gail Lewis revealed a "defensiveness" on the part of the children of lesbian couples she studied, a pattern of denial—especially deep in the youngest child in the lesbian couples she studied, hostility from older boys, especially directed at the mother's lesbian lover, children's expressed concern for the welfare of siblings, children's concerns about their own sexuality, children's concerns about the integrity of their family, concerns about their mother's homosexual activities, evidence that one of the lesbian mothers expressly encouraged her daughters to make lesbian sexual choices, children forced to conceal one parent's secret sexual behaviors from the other parent, and "gross maladaptive behavior [by older teenagers that] occurred around the time of the mother's disclosure [of her lesbian relationship]." Likewise, the [1993 Philip A.] Belcastro study noted that studies biased in favor of homosexual parenting disclosed that children (especially daughters) of lesbians have increased levels of fantasized anxiety, increased tendencies toward inhibition, increased tendencies toward sadness (at least sons of lesbians), and disclosed increased cross-dressing among daughters, and less cooperative behavior. Sons of lesbians were reportedly more influenced by peers than children raised by heterosexual parents.

Finally, it is reasonable to be concerned that ongoing parental homosexual sexual behavior is harmful to children because that seems to be the lesson of the most relevant and analogous human experience—the experience of extramarital sexual relations generally. The standard and expectation that responsible sexual relations must occur within the heterosexual marriage relationship is deeply rooted in our society and legal system. Extramarital sexual behavior is associated with such harm to children as the breakup of their parents' marriage and the destabilizing, child-harming consequences of divorce. Parental extramarital relationships wound children, shaking, sometimes even destroying, their faith in marriage and in personal commitments of fidelity and intimacy. It hurts a child to learn that one parent has been unfaithful to the

> *"Boys raised by homosexual mothers may have a lower self-image regarding masculinity."*

other. That pain is very real and very wrenching. Parental extramarital relationships also provide a dangerous model for children, serving to pass intergenerational self-destructive behavior on to children. The message of intergender and intergenerational carelessness, and family-sacrificing selfishness not only hurts, but also may have a programming effect on children. The lesson of sexual self-gratification at the expense of familial fidelity conveys a tragic message about both family commitments and responsible sexual behavior in our society. In these days of so many harmful, even deadly, sexually transmitted diseases, the risks may be physical as well as emotional.

The potential harm to children from homosexual behavior of their parents, however, should not be exaggerated. First, many of the studies are not of large sample populations and have other methodological deficiencies. Moreover, the reasons that men and women turn to homosexual relationships are many and complex, and do not necessarily or always cancel or override their love for and commitment to their children. Some parents with homosexual orientation undoubtedly are very committed to the welfare of their children, and the kinds of potential risks that may be associated with homosexual parenting may not differ significantly from those associated with heterosexual parenting by adults who engage in heterosexual extramarital activity. Nevertheless, although the social science research is not conclusive, it does suggest that there are some particular and unique potential risks to children raised by active homosexual parents.

## The Advantages of Dual-Gender Parenting

Children raised by homosexual couples do not have both a father and a mother. If Heather is being raised by two mommies only, she is being deprived of the experience of being raised by a daddy. Both the common experience of humanity and recent research suggest that a daddy and a mommy together provide by far the best environment in which a child may be reared.

Among the most important reasons why heterosexual parenting is best for children is because there are gender-linked differences in child-rearing skills; men and women contribute different (gender-connected) strengths and attributes to their children's development. Although the critical contributions of mothers to the full and healthy development of children has long been recognized, recent research validates the common understanding that fathers, as well as mothers, are extremely important for child development.

Experts in many disciplines that have recently been studying fathering have reached "surprising unanimity" in their recognition that "[m]en nurture, interact with, and rear competently but differently from women: not worse, not better . . . differently." When fathers nurture and care for their children, they do so not quite as "substitute mothers" but differently, as fathers. For example, some studies show that fathers play with their infant children more than mothers, play more physical and tactile games than mothers, and use fewer toys when playing with their children. Mothers tend to talk and play more gently with infant children. Compared to mothers, fathers reportedly appear to "have more positive perceptions of the more irritable sons and less irritable daughters," and perceive their baby daughters to be more cuddly than mothers do. Mothers smile and verbalize more to the infant than fathers do, and generally rate their infant sons as cuddlier than fathers do. Moreover, "[m]en encouraged their children's curiosity in the solution of intellectual and physical challenges, supported the child's persistence in solving problems, and did not become overly solicitous with regard to their child's failures." One study found that six-month-old infants whose fathers were actively involved with them "had higher scores on the Bailey Test of Mental and Motor Development." Infants whose fathers spend more time with them are more socially responsive and better able to withstand stressful situations than infants relatively deprived of substantial interaction with their fathers. . . .

Parents are important as role models for their children of the same gender because "[c]hildren learn to be adults by watching adults." Children are generally more compliant with the parent of the same sex. The importance of the opposite-gendered parent for the complete emotional and social development of the child is now recognized as well: "Boys and girls build their notions of their sex roles from experience with both sexes." The loss of cross-gender parenting may have severe emotional consequences for the child. For example, the absence of a father in the home may result in a daughter having trouble relating to men throughout her adult life. . . .

## Instability and Poverty

Among the most profound advantage of marriage is basic economic security for children. Marital status is more closely associated with avoiding child poverty than any other factor. One study reported that more than half of the increase in child poverty in the United States between 1980 and 1988 "can be accounted for by changes in family structure during the 1980s." In addition, "[c]hanging family structure also accounted for 48 percent of the increase during the 1980s in deep poverty, and 59 percent of the rise in relative poverty among U.S. children." Many studies have shown that children in single-parent families are many times more likely to be living in poverty than children living with both a mother and father. William Galston, who served as a Domestic Policy Advisor to President Clinton, agreed that "[i]t is no exaggeration to say that a stable, two-parent family is an American child's best protection against poverty." Thus, "[a]s a matter of public policy, if not of morality, it pays for society to approve of marriage as the best setting for children."

Advocates of homosexual parenting may argue that two homosexuals could provide for a child economically better than a single parent. However, any overall economic benefit could be more than offset by the overall economic costs and chronic instability of homosexual liaisons, especially gay liaisons. Concerns about the welfare of children have caused the Scandinavian countries with legalized homosexual domestic partnerships to deny to same-sex couples all rights of adoption, including domestic adoptions and even stepparent adoptions, as well as rights of joint custody (in Denmark and Sweden) and assisted procreation. Homosexual parenting poses particular risks for the emotional and gender development of children. Children make the transition through developmental stages better, have stronger gender identity, are more confident of themselves, do better in school, have fewer emotional crises, and become functioning adults best when they are reared in two-parent, dual-gender families. . . .

## Putting the Needs of Children First

It is possible to justify legalization of some marriage-like status for same-sex couples without extending marriage-like benefits relating to childrearing. In the past eight years, four independent Scandinavian nations, Denmark, Norway, Sweden, and Iceland, have legalized same-sex domestic partnerships, extending to those registered relationships virtually all of the economic incidents of heterosexual marriage. However, those permissive laws are quite restrictive with regard to childrearing rights. The Icelandic law specifically excludes same-sex couples from adoption and artificial insemination. In Denmark, the same-sex couple may not adopt a child or exercise joint custody. The Swedish law excludes adoption, joint custody, and fertilization in vitro for registered same-sex domestic partnerships. In Norway, same-sex registered partnerships may not adopt.

> *"A daddy and a mommy together provide by far the best environment in which a child may be reared."*

All of these countries manifest a permissive policy concerning relations between two consenting adults, but all take a paternalistic posture when it comes to protecting children. The common theme is that adults can do what they want with regard to other consenting adults, but they are not free to do whatever they want with regard to children. These nations take great care to prevent adults from subjecting children to the potentially detrimental effects and consequences of adult sexual preferences. Although homosexual behavior may not bar a responsible biological parent from asserting parental rights—consistent, again, with the permissive nonjudgmental attitude about adult behavior—the Scandinavian states put the needs and interests of the children ahead of the autonomy rights of adults. Several years ago, Mary Ann Glendon demonstrated that in many ways in family law, European nations manifest a much greater care and protection for children than the laws of the United States. The Scandinavian laws extending legal benefits to same-sex domestic partnerships but restricting adoption, joint custody, and assisted procreation by those couples seem to manifest that distinctive concern for children. . . .

The social science literature that is cited in support of the claim that homosexual parenting is not significantly harmful to children is unreliable. Methodological defects and analytical flaws abound in the studies. The research is colored significantly by bias in favor of homosexual parenting. Despite the favorable gloss put on the data, some of the research suggests that there are some serious potential harms to children raised by homosexual parents. . . .

It would be premature and unwise to legalize homosexual parenting by extending full, unrestricted, parental relationship rights to homosexual parents equivalent to those of heterosexual parents. Legalization of same-sex marriage would be unwise for many of the same reasons. The impact upon children of such radical changes in the form and structure of the family and in the institution of marriage that is the basis of the family, and of society, have not been carefully considered.

Children are the innocent victims who suffer the most from choices their parents make to experiment for personal self-gratification with extramarital sexual relationships. We must be concerned that a parent who makes a calculated decision to deprive a child of a parent of the opposite gender may be making a decision that shows insufficient regard for the needs of children. As Dame Mary Warnock wrote in her committee's celebrated report on artificial conception technology: "[w]e believe that as a general rule it is better for children to be born into a two-parent family, with both father and mother, although we recognize that it is impossible to predict with any certainty how lasting such a relationship will be." In an important sense, the question whether homosexual parenting should be legitimated ultimately depends on what kind of society we want our children and grandchildren to grow up in. Parental fidelity to the relationship that generated a child, to the partnership that produced the child, is a powerfully positive influence in the life of the child. If we want to put children's needs first, we must preserve for them the basic social institution which has over the millennia been the most beneficial of all imperfect human institutions for children's welfare. Thus, we should think very carefully before accepting the invitation to legitimate the brave new world of homosexual parenting as a desirable environment in which to rear future generations.

# Gay Adoption Should Be Banned

**by Armstrong Williams**

**About the author:** *Armstrong Williams is a syndicated columnist, the host of a daily television show called* The Armstrong Williams Show, *and the host of two weekly online chat programs.*

The adoption system in this country is broken. Thousands of kids languish in substandard facilities that lack the resources to properly educate and nurture them, thus perpetuating the cycle of underachievement.

OK, so far I'm in agreement.

One possible solution is to open adoption up to homosexual couples.

## Maternal and Paternal Balance

The suggestion, currently being considered by several states, is remarkable on several levels. Not the least of which being its disregard for the unique characteristics of a loving union between husband and wife. That is to say, a loving union between man and woman provides a child with a maternal and paternal balance that helps a child navigate his own equal and opposite impulses. So that beyond love or finances, this sort of emotional stability is crucial to building a child's self-esteem. For this rather straightforward reason, a union between man and woman has always been central to our understanding of "family."

For an adoptive child, establishing an identity that meshes with social conventions is essential to constructing a healthy sense of self.

To abruptly break with social conventions, however, could saddle the adoptive child with severe identity confusion. An example: Data analyzed by Paul Cameron, psychologist and author of "The Truth About 'Gay Parents': An Analysis of the American Psychological Association/National Association of Social Workers' Brief in the Virginia Court of Appeals in the Pamela Bottoms Case," Family Research Institute, and published by the Family Research Institute revealed that "8.9 percent of children in homosexual households became homosexual while only 2.4 percent of the children raised in heterosexual households became homosexual." A 1989 survey of women previously married to men who practice homosexuality found a 12 percent incidence of homosexual behavior in their children, despite the fact that homosexuals account for only 2 percent of the general population.

Plainly, the social pressures associated with this sort of gender confusion are tremendous. That is the reality that confronts us. To subject adoptive children to this sort of emotional trauma by design is worst than misguided; it amounts to socially martyring a large segment of children, just to make a cultural statement about homosexual rights.

## Cultural Statements

Nonetheless, advocates for homosexual rights in this country continue to place themselves at the center of adoption law. Their justification: that the eroding nuclear family—through divorce and the general liberalization of the culture—has precipitated a change in traditional social structures. They have a point, they simply miss it: The crucial issue is not whether traditional social structures are changing, but whether embracing these changes is in the best interest of adoptive children.

Get it? Adoption law ought not to be about cultural statements in general or gay rights in the specific; it ought to be about the best interest of the children. While debate regarding homosexual rights has its place in the national dialogue, such issues are not central to the issue of adoption.

What is central to the debate is a proper understanding of cultural norms and how they influence our sense of self. Or, more to the point, how common law, common sense, history and science all tell us that the very nature of a homosexual relationship deprives a child of the emotionally stable environment that he or she requires.

While I am deeply sensible about the need to place adoptive children with families, this need does not justify placing them in any home.

Nor does it justify risking the emotional well-being of adoptive children just to make a political statement.

# Organizations to Contact

The editors have compiled the following list of organizations concerned with the issues debated in this book. The descriptions are derived from materials provided by the organizations. All have publications or information available for interested readers. The list was compiled on the date of publication of the present volume; the information provided here may change. Be aware that many organizations take several weeks or longer to respond to inquiries, so allow as much time as possible.

### American Civil Liberties Union (ACLU)
125 Broad St., 18th Floor, New York, NY 10004
(212) 944-9800 • fax: (212) 869-9065
website: www.aclu.org

The ACLU is the nation's oldest and largest civil liberties organization. Its Lesbian and Gay Rights/AIDS Project, started in 1986, handles litigation, education, and public-policy work on behalf of gays and lesbians. The union supports same-sex marriage. It publishes the monthly newsletter *Civil Liberties Alert*, the handbook *The Rights of Lesbians and Gay Men*, the briefing paper "Lesbian and Gay Rights," and the book *The Rights of Families: The ACLU Guide to the Rights of Today's Family Members*.

### Canadian Lesbian and Gay Archives
Box 639, Station A, Toronto, Ontario, Canada M5W 1G2
(416) 777-2755
website: www.clga.ca

The archives collect and maintain information and materials relating to the gay and lesbian rights movement in Canada and elsewhere. Its collection of records and other materials documenting the stories of lesbians and gay men and their organizations in Canada is available to the public for the purpose of education and research. It also publishes an annual newsletter, *Lesbian and Gay Archivist*.

### Coalition for Positive Sexuality (CPS)
PO Box 77212, Washington, DC 20013-7212
(713) 604-1654
website: http://positive.org

CPS is a grassroots direct-action group formed in 1992 by high-school students and activists. It endeavors to counteract the institutionalized misogyny, heterosexism, homophobia, racism, and ageism that students experience at school. It is dedicated to offering teens sex education that is pro-woman, pro-lesbian/gay/bisexual, pro–safe sex, and pro-choice. Numerous pamphlets and publications are available upon request.

### Concerned Women for America (CWA)
1015 15th St. NW, Suite 1100, Washington, DC 20005
(202) 488-7000 • fax: (202) 488-0806
website: www.cwfa.org

CWA works to strengthen the traditional family according to Judeo-Christian moral standards. It opposes gay marriage and the granting of additional civil rights protections to gays and lesbians. It publishes numerous brochures and policy papers as well as *Family Voice*, a monthly newsmagazine.

**Courage**
c/o Church of St. John the Baptist, 210 W. 31st St., New York, NY 10001
(212) 268-1010 • fax: (212) 268-7150
e-mail: NYCourage@aol.com • website: http://CourageRC.net

Courage is a network of spiritual support groups for gay and lesbian Catholics who wish to lead celibate lives in accordance with Roman Catholic teachings on homosexuality. It publishes listings of local groups, a newsletter, and an annotated bibliography of books on homosexuality.

**Dignity/USA**
1500 Massachusetts Ave. NW, Suite 11, Washington, DC 20005-1894
(800) 877-8797 • fax: (202) 429-9808
e-mail: dignity@aol.com • website: www.dignityusa.org

Dignity/USA is a Roman Catholic organization of gays, lesbians, bisexuals, and their families and friends. It believes that homosexuals and bisexuals can lead sexually active lives in a manner consonant with Christ's teachings. Through its national and local chapters, Dignity/ USA provides educational materials, AIDS crisis assistance, and spiritual support groups for members. It publishes the monthly *Dignity Journal* and a book, *Theological/Pastoral Resources: A Collection of Articles on Homosexuality from a Catholic Perspective*.

**Exodus International**
PO Box 77652, Seattle, WA 98177
(206) 784-7799
website: http://exodus.base.org

Exodus International is a referral network offering support to homosexual Christians desiring to become heterosexual. It publishes the monthly newsletter *Update*, lists of local ministries and programs, and bibliographies of books and tapes on homosexuality.

**Family Research Council**
801 G St. NW, Washington, DC 20001
(202) 393-2100 • fax: (202) 393-2134
website: www.frc.org

The council is a research and educational organization that promotes the traditional family, which the council defines as a group of people bound by marriage, blood, or adoption. The council opposes gay marriage and adoption rights. It publishes numerous reports from a conservative perspective on issues affecting the family, including *Free to Be Family*. Among its publications are the monthly newsletter *Washington Watch* and the bimonthly journal *Family Policy*.

**Howard Center for Family, Religion, and Society**
934 North Main St., Rockford, IL 61103
(815) 964-5819 • fax: (815) 965-1826
website: http://profam.org

The purpose of the Howard Center is to provide research and understanding that demonstrates and affirms family and religion as the foundation of a virtuous and free society. The center believes that the natural family is the fundamental unit of society. The primary mission of the Howard Center is to provide a clearinghouse of useful and relevant information to support families and their defenders throughout the world. The center publishes the monthly journal, *Family in America,* and the *Religion and Society Report.*

## Human Rights Campaign (HRC)
919 18th St. NW, Suite 800, Washington, DC 20006
(202) 628-4160 • fax: (202) 347-5323
website: www.hrc.org

The HRC provides information on national political issues affecting lesbian, gay, bisexual, and transgender Americans. It offers resources to educate congressional leaders and the public on critical issues such as ending workplace discrimination, combating hate crimes, fighting HIV/AIDS, protecting gay and lesbian families, and working for better lesbian health. HRC publishes the *HRC Quarterly* and *LAWbriefs.*

## Lambda Legal Defense and Education Fund
120 Wall St., Suite 1500, New York, NY 10005
(212) 809-8585 • fax: (212) 809-0055
website: www.lambdalegal.org

Lambda is a public-interest law firm committed to achieving full recognition of the civil rights of lesbians, gay men, and people with HIV/AIDS. The firm addresses a variety of topics, including equal marriage rights, parenting and relationship issues, and domestic-partner benefits. It publishes the quarterly *Lambda Update* as well as numerous pamphlets and position papers.

## Love in Action
PO Box 171444, Memphis, TN 38175-3307
(901) 767-6700 • fax: (901) 767-0024
website: www.loveinaction.org

Love in Action is a Christian ministry that believes that homosexuality is a learned behavior and that all homosexual conduct is wrong because it violates God's laws. It provides support to gays and lesbians to help them convert to heterosexuality. It also offers a residential twelve-step recovery program for individuals who have made the commitment to follow Christ and wish to leave their homosexuality behind. Current publications include a monthly newsletter.

## National Association for the Research and Therapy of Homosexuality (NARTH)
16633 Ventura Blvd., Suite 1340, Encino, CA 91436-1801
(818) 789-4440 • fax: (818) 789-6452
website: www.narth.com

NARTH is an information and referral network that believes the causes of homosexuality are primarily developmental and that it is usually responsive to psychotherapy. The association supports homosexual men and women who feel that homosexuality is contrary to their value systems and who voluntarily seek treatment. NARTH publishes the *NARTH Bulletin*, the book *Healing Homosexuality: Case Stories of Reparative Therapy*, and numerous conference papers and research articles.

## National Center for Lesbian Rights
870 Market St., Suite 570, San Francisco, CA 94102
(415) 392-6257 • fax: (415) 392-8442
e-mail: info@NCLRights.org • website: www.nclrights.org

Founded in 1977, the center is an advocacy organization that provides legal counseling and representation for victims of sexual-orientation discrimination. Primary areas of advice include custody and parenting, employment, housing, the military, and insurance. The center publishes the handbooks *Recognizing Lesbian and Gay Families: Strategies for Obtaining Domestic Partners Benefits* and *Lesbian and Gay Parenting: A Psychological and Legal Perspective* as well as other materials.

## Parents, Families, and Friends of Lesbians and Gays (PFLAG)
1726 M St. NW, Suite 400, Washington, DC 20036
(202) 467-8180 • fax: (202) 467-8194
e-mail: info@pflag.org • website: www.pflag.org

PFLAG is a national organization that provides support and educational services for gays, lesbians, bisexuals, and their families and friends. It works to end prejudice and discrimination against homosexual and bisexual persons. It publishes and distributes booklets and papers, including "About Our Children," "Coming Out to My Parents," and "Why Is My Child Gay?"

## Reconciling Ministries Network (RMN)
3801 N. Keeler Ave., Chicago, IL 60641
(773) 736-5526 • fax: (773) 736-5475
website: www.rmnetwork.org

RCP is a network of United Methodist churches, ministries, and individuals that welcomes and supports lesbians and gay men and seeks to end homophobia and prejudice in the church and society. Its national headquarters provides resources to help local ministries achieve these goals. Among its publications are the quarterly magazine *Open Hands*, the book *And God Loves Each One*, as well as other pamphlets, studies, and videos.

## Sex Information and Education Council of the United States (SIECUS)
130 W. 42nd St., Suite 2500, New York, NY 10036-7901
(212) 819-9770 • fax: (212) 819-9776

SIECUS is an organization of educators, physicians, social workers, and others who support the individual's right to acquire knowledge about sexuality and who encourage responsible sexual behavior. The council promotes comprehensive sex education for all children that includes AIDS education, teaching about homosexuality, and instruction about contraceptives and sexually transmitted diseases. Its publications include fact sheets, annotated bibliographies by topic, the booklet *Talk About Sex*, and the bimonthly *SIECUS Report*.

## Universal Fellowship of Metropolitan Community Churches (UFMCC)
8704 Santa Monica Blvd., 2nd Fl., West Hollywood, CA 90069
(310) 360-8640 • fax: (310) 360-8680
e-mail: UfmccHqc.aol.com • website: www.ufmcc.com

UFMCC works to confront poverty, sexism, racism, and homophobia through Christian social action. Composed of more than three hundred congregations, the fellowship accepts gays, lesbians, and bisexuals and works to incorporate them into the Christian church. UFMCC publications include the quarterly newsletter *Journey*, the brochures *Homosexuality: Not a Sin, Not a Sickness* and *Homosexuality: The Bible as Your Friend*, and the pamphlet *Homosexuality and the Conservative Christian*.

# Bibliography

**Books**

| | |
|---|---|
| Bruce Bagemihl | *Biological Exuberance: Animal Homosexuality and Natural Diversity*. New York: St. Martin's Press, 1999. |
| Robert M. Baird and Stuart E. Rosenbaum, eds. | *Same-Sex Marriage: The Moral and Legal Debate*. Amherst, NY: Prometheus Books, 1997. |
| Byrne Fone | *Homophobia: A History*. New York: Metropolitan Books, 2000. |
| Mary B. Harris | *School Experiences of Gay and Lesbian Youth*. New York: Harrington Park Press, 1997. |
| Keith Hartman | *Congregations in Conflict: The Battle over Homosexuality*. New Brunswick, NJ: Rutgers University Press, 1997. |
| John Harvey | *The Truth About Homosexuality: The Cry of the Faithful*. San Francisco: Ignatius Press, 1998. |
| Gregory M. Herek, Jared B. Jobe, and Ralph Carney | *Out in Force: Sexual Orientation and the Military*. Chicago: University of Chicago Press, 1996. |
| Didi Herman | *The Antigay Agenda: Orthodox Vision and the Christian Right*. Chicago: University of Chicago Press, 1997. |
| Noelle Howey and Ellen Samuels, eds. | *Out of the Ordinary: Essays on Growing Up with Gay, Lesbian, and Transgender Parents*. New York: St. Martin's Press, 2000. |
| Martin Kantor | *Homophobia: Description, Development, and Dynamics of Gay Bashing*. Westport, CT: Praeger, 1998. |
| Timothy F. Murphy | *Gay Science: The Ethics of Sexual Orientation Research*. New York: Columbia University Press, 1997. |
| Gabriel Rotello | *Sexual Ecology: AIDS and the Destiny of Gay Men*. New York: Penguin, 1998. |
| Jeffrey Satinover | *Homosexuality and the Politics of Truth*. Grand Rapids, MI: Baker Books, 1996. |
| Thomas E. Schmidt | *Straight and Narrow? Compassion and Clarity in the Homosexuality Debate*. Farmington, PA: Plough Books, 1998. |

# Bibliography

| Lacey M. Sloan and Nora Gustavsson, eds. | *Violence and Social Injustice Against Lesbian, Gay and Bisexual People*. New York: Haworth Press, 1998. |
| --- | --- |
| Charles W. Socarides | *Homosexuality: A Freedom Too Far*. Phoenix: Adam Margrave Books, 1995. |
| Edward Stein | *The Mismeasure of Desire: The Science, Theory, and Ethics of Sexual Orientation*. New York: Oxford University Press, 1999. |
| John R.W. Stott | *Same-Sex Partnerships: A Christian Perspective*. Grand Rapids, MI: Fleming H. Revell, 1998. |
| Mark Philip Strasser | *Legally Wed: Same-Sex Marriage and the Constitution*. Ithaca, NY: Cornell University Press, 1997. |
| Andrew Sullivan | *Same-Sex Marriage: Pro and Con: A Reader*. New York: Vintage Books, 1997. |
| Andrew Sullivan | *Virtually Normal: An Argument About Homosexuality*. New York: Knopf, 1995. |
| Edward Taussig | *501 Great Things About Being Gay*. Kansas City, MO: Andrews & McMeel, 1998. |

## Periodicals

| Mark Anderson | "Hope for Homosexuals," *New American*, September 28, 1998. |
| --- | --- |
| Paul Baumann | "My Son the Boy Scout," *Commonweal*, October 12, 2001. |
| Robert O. Blanchard | "The 'Hate Slate' Myth," *Reason*, May 1, 1999. |
| Linda Bowles | "No Child Is Born to Be Homosexual," *Conservative Chronicle*, May 30, 2001. |
| David Orgon Coolidge | "What the Vermont Court Has Wrought," *Weekly Standard*, January 17, 2000. |
| Randy Dotinga | "Holy Matrimony," *Advocate*, April 14, 1998. |
| Peggy Drexler | "Do Boys Need Daddies? The Moral Development of Sons of Lesbians," *In the Family*, Autumn 2000. |
| Robert Gahl Jr. | "Toward Effective Pastoral Care of Homosexual Persons," *Origins*, July 29, 1999. |
| John Gallagher | "Are We Really Asking for Special Rights?" *Advocate*, April 14, 1998. |
| David Gelernter | "Gay Rights and Wrongs," *Wall Street Journal*, August 13, 1998. |
| Jeffrey G. Gibson | "Lesbian and Gay Prospective: Adoptive Parents: The Legal Battle," *Human Rights*, Spring 1999. |
| Laurie Goodstein | "The Architect of the 'Gay Conversion' Campaign," *New York Times*, August 13, 1998. |

| Human Rights Watch | "Human Rights Watch World Report 2001: Lesbian and Gay Rights," 2001. www.hrc.org. |
| --- | --- |
| Toby Johnson | "The Evolution of Gay Consciousness," *Genre*, April 2000. |
| Simon LeVay | "A Difference in Hypothalamic Structure Between Heterosexual and Homosexual Men," *Science*, August 30, 1991. |
| Charles Moskos | "Don't Knock 'Don't Ask, Don't Tell,'" *Wall Street Journal*, December 16, 1999. |
| Carmen Pate | "Gay Adoption," Concerned Women for America, 1998, www.cwfa.org. |
| Mark E. Pietrzyk | "Pathology of the Ex-Gay Movement," *Gay & Lesbian Review*, Summer 2000. |
| Robert Pillard | "The Genetic Theory of Sexual Orientation," *Harvard Gay & Lesbian Review*, Winter 1997. |
| Stephen W. Potts | "Boy Scouts Need a Big Tent," *San Diego North County Times*, June 21, 1998. |
| Justin Raimondo | "Making Progress Backwards," *Free Inquiry*, Summer 2001. |
| Gabriel Rotello | "Gay and Lesbian Rights," *Social Policy*, Spring 1998. |
| Carl Rowan | "Why Rush to Hate Crimes Laws?" *Liberal Opinion Week*, October 26, 1998. |
| Gary Sanders | "Normal Families: Research on Gay and Lesbian Parenting," *In the Family*, January 1998. |
| Edward Stein | "Gay Rights Cannot Be Hatched in the Lab," *Harvard Gay & Lesbian Review*, Fall 1999. |
| Thomas Storck | "Is Opposition to Homosexual Activity 'Irrational'?" *New Oxford Review*, May 1997. |
| Andrew Sullivan | "Undone by 'Don't Ask, Don't Tell,'" *New York Times*, April 9, 1998. |
| Urvashi Vaid | "Seeking Common Ground," *Ms.*, September/October 1997. |
| Ralph Wedgewood | "What Are We Fighting For?" *Harvard Gay & Lesbian Review*, Fall 1997. |
| Alan Wolfe | "Can Gay-Rights Groups Handle Success?" *Wall Street Journal*, June 13, 2000. |

# Index

# Index

# Index